The Crossing, Vol. 1

Winston Churchill

ESPRIOS DIGITAL PUBLISHING

The Crossing

BY

WINSTON CHURCHILL

Author of
"Richard Carvel," "The Crisis,"
"The Celebrity," etc., etc.

New York
THE MACMILLAN COMPANY
LONDON: MACMILLAN & CO., LTD.
1904
All rights reserved

Copyright,
BY WINSTON CHURCHILL.

Copyright,
BY P. F. COLLIER & SON.

Copyright,
BY THE MACMILLAN COMPANY

Set up, electrotyped, and published, May, 1904

Norwood Press
J. S. Cushing & Co. — Berwick & Smith Co.
Norwood, Mass., U. S. A

CONTENTS

    Book I. The Borderland

I.   The Blue Wall

II.   Wars and Rumors of Wars

III.   Charlestown

IV.   Temple Bow

V.   Cram's Hell

VI.   Man proposes, but God disposes

VII.   In Sight of the Blue Wall once more

VIII.   The Nollichucky Trace

IX.   On the Wilderness Trail

X.   Harrodstown

XI.   Fragmentary

XII.   The Campaign begins

XIII.   Kaskaskia

XIV.   How the Kaskaskians were made Citizens

XV.   Days of Trial

XVI.   Davy goes to Cahokia

XVII.	The Sacrifice
XVIII.	"An' ye had been where I had been"
XIX.	The Hair Buyer trapped
XX.	The Campaign ends

The Crossing, Vol. 1

BOOK I. THE BORDERLAND

CHAPTER I

THE BLUE WALL

I WAS born under the Blue Ridge, and under that side which is blue in the evening light, in a wild land of game and forest and rushing waters. There, on the borders of a creek that runs into the Yadkin River, in a cabin that was chinked with red mud, I came into the world a subject of King George the Third, in that part of his realm known as the province of North Carolina.

The cabin reeked of corn-pone and bacon, and the odor of pelts. It had two shakedowns, on one of which I slept under a bearskin. A rough stone chimney was reared outside, and the fireplace was as long as my father was tall. There was a crane in it, and a bake kettle; and over it great buckhorns held my father's rifle when it was not in use. On other horns hung jerked bear's meat and venison hams, and gourds for drinking cups, and bags of seed, and my father's best hunting shirt; also, in a neglected corner, several articles of woman's attire from pegs. These once belonged to my mother. Among them was a gown of silk, of a fine, faded pattern, over which I was wont to speculate. The women at the Cross-Roads, twelve miles away, were dressed in coarse butternut wool and huge sunbonnets. But when I questioned my father on these matters he would give me no answers.

My father was—how shall I say what he was? To this day I can only surmise many things of him. He was a Scotchman born, and I know now that he had a slight Scotch accent. At the time of which I write, my early childhood, he was a frontiersman and hunter. I can see him now, with his hunting shirt and leggings and moccasins; his powder horn, engraved with wondrous scenes; his bullet pouch and tomahawk and hunting knife. He was a tall, lean man with a strange, sad face. And he talked little save when he drank too many "horns," as they were called in that country. These lapses of my father's were a perpetual source of wonder to me,—and, I must say, of delight. They occurred only when a passing traveller who hit his fancy chanced that way, or, what was almost as rare, a neighbor. Many a winter night I have lain awake under the skins, listening to a flow of language that held me spellbound, though I understood scarce a word of it.

"Virtuous and vicious every man must be,
Few in the extreme, but all in a degree."

The chance neighbor or traveller was no less struck with wonder. And many the time have I heard the query, at the Cross-Roads and elsewhere, "Whar Alec Trimble got his larnin'?"

The truth is, my father was an object of suspicion to the frontiersmen. Even as a child I knew this, and resented it. He had brought me up in solitude, and I was old for my age, learned in some things far beyond my years, and ignorant of others I should have known. I loved the man passionately. In the long winter evenings, when the howl of wolves and "painters" rose as the wind lulled, he taught me to read from the Bible and the "Pilgrim's Progress." I can see his long, slim fingers on the page. They seemed but ill fitted for the life he led.

The love of rhythmic language was somehow born into me, and many's the time I have held watch in the cabin day and night while my father was away on his hunts, spelling out the verses that have since become part of my life.

As I grew older I went with him into the mountains, often on his back; and spent the nights in open camp with my little moccasins drying at the blaze. So I learned to skin a bear, and fleece off the fat for oil with my hunting knife; and cure a deerskin and follow a trail. At seven I even shot the long rifle, with a rest. I learned to endure cold and hunger and fatigue and to walk in silence over the mountains, my father never saying a word for days at a spell. And often, when he opened his mouth, it would be to recite a verse of Pope's in a way that moved me strangely. For a poem is not a poem unless it be well spoken.

In the hot days of summer, over against the dark forest the bright green of our little patch of Indian corn rippled in the wind. And towards night I would often sit watching the deep blue of the mountain wall and dream of the mysteries of the land that lay beyond. And by chance, one evening as I sat thus, my father reading in the twilight, a man stood before us. So silently had he come up the path leading from the brook that we had not heard him. Presently my father looked up from his book, but did not rise. As for me, I had been staring for some time in astonishment, for he was a better-looking man than I had ever seen. He wore a deerskin hunting shirt dyed black, but, in place of a coonskin cap with the tail hanging down, a hat. His long rifle rested on the ground, and he held a roan horse by the bridle.

"Howdy, neighbor?" said he.

I recall a fear that my father would not fancy him. In such cases he would give a stranger food, and leave him to himself. My father's whims were past understanding. But he got up.

"Good evening," said he.

The visitor looked a little surprised, as I had seen many do, at my father's accent.

"Neighbor," said he, "kin you keep me over night?"

"Come in," said my father.

We sat down to our supper of corn and beans and venison, of all of which our guest ate sparingly. He, too, was a silent man, and scarcely a word was spoken during the meal. Several times he looked at me with such a kindly expression in his blue eyes, a trace of a smile around his broad mouth, that I wished he might stay with us always. But once, when my father said something about Indians, the eyes grew hard as flint. It was then I remarked, with a boy's wonder, that despite his dark hair he had yellow eyebrows.

After supper the two men sat on the log step, while I set about the task of skinning the deer my father had shot that day. Presently I felt a heavy hand on my shoulder.

"What's your name, lad?" he said.

I told him Davy.

The Crossing, Vol. 1

"Davy, I'll larn ye a trick worth a little time," said he, whipping out a knife. In a trice the red carcass hung between the forked stakes, while I stood with my mouth open. He turned to me and laughed gently.

"Some day you'll cross the mountains and skin twenty of an evening," he said. "Ye'll make a woodsman sure. You've got the eye, and the hand."

This little piece of praise from him made me hot all over.

"Game rare?" said he to my father.

"None sae good, now," said my father.

"I reckon not. My cabin's on Beaver Creek some forty mile above, and game's going there, too."

"Settlements," said my father. But presently, after a few whiffs of his pipe, he added, "I hear fine things of this land across the mountains, that the Indians call the Dark and Bluidy Ground."

"And well named," said the stranger.

"But a brave country," said my father, "and all tramped down with game. I hear that Daniel Boone and others have gone into it and come back with marvellous tales. They tell me Boone was there alone three months. He's saething of a man. D'ye ken him?"

The ruddy face of the stranger grew ruddier still.

"My name's Boone," he said.

"What!" cried my father, "it wouldn't be Daniel?"

"You've guessed it, I reckon."

My father rose without a word, went into the cabin, and immediately reappeared with a flask and a couple of gourds, one of which he handed to our visitor.

"Tell me aboot it," said he.

That was the fairy tale of my childhood. Far into the night I lay on the dewy grass listening to Mr. Boone's talk. It did not at first flow in a steady stream, for he was not a garrulous man, but my father's questions presently fired his enthusiasm. I recall but little of it, being so small a lad, but I crept closer and closer until I could touch this superior being who had been beyond the Wall. Marco Polo was no greater wonder to the Venetians than Boone to me.

He spoke of leaving wife and children, and setting out for the Unknown with other woodsmen. He told how, crossing over our blue western wall into a valley beyond, they found a "Warrior's Path" through a gap across another range, and so down into the fairest of promised lands. And as he talked he lost himself in the tale of it, and the very quality of his voice changed. He told of a land of wooded hill and pleasant vale, of clear water running over limestone down to the great river beyond, the Ohio—a land of glades, the fields of which were pied with flowers of wondrous beauty, where roamed the buffalo in countless thousands, where elk and deer abounded, and turkeys and feathered game, and bear in the tall brakes of cane. And, simply, he told how, when the others had left him, he stayed for three months roaming the hills alone with Nature herself.

"But did you no' meet the Indians?" asked my father.

"I seed one fishing on a log once," said our visitor, laughing, "but he fell into the water. I reckon he was drowned."

My father nodded comprehendingly,—even admiringly.

"And again!" said he.

"Wal," said Mr. Boone, "we fell in with a war party of Shawnees going back to their lands north of the great river. The critters took away all we had. It was hard," he added reflectively; "I had staked my fortune on the venter, and we'd got enough skins to make us rich. But, neighbor, there is land enough for you and me, as black and rich as Canaan."

"'The Lord is my shepherd,'" said my father, lapsing into verse. "'The Lord is my shepherd. I shall not want. He leadeth me into green pastures, and beside still waters.'"

For a time they were silent, each wrapped in his own thought, while the crickets chirped and the frogs sang. From the distant forest came the mournful hoot of an owl.

"And you are going back?" asked my father, presently.

"Aye, that I am. There are many families on the Yadkin below going, too. And you, neighbor, you might come with us. Davy is the boy that would thrive in that country."

My father did not answer. It was late indeed when we lay down to rest, and the night I spent between waking and dreaming of the wonderland beyond the mountains, hoping against hope that my father would go. The sun was just flooding the slopes when our guest arose to leave, and my father bade him God-speed with a heartiness that was rare to him. But, to my bitter regret, neither spoke of my father's going. Being a man of understanding, Mr. Boone knew it were little use to press. He patted me on the head.

"You're a wise lad, Davy," said he. "I hope we shall meet again."

He mounted his roan and rode away down the slope, waving his hand to us. And it was with a heavy heart that I went to feed our white mare, whinnying for food in the lean-to.

CHAPTER II

Wars and Rumors of Wars

AND so our life went on the same, but yet not the same. For I had the Land of Promise to dream of, and as I went about my tasks I conjured up in my mind pictures of its beauty. You will forgive a backwoods boy,—self-centred, for lack of wider interest, and with a little imagination. Bear hunting with my father, and an occasional trip on the white mare twelve miles to the Cross-Roads for salt and other necessaries, were the only diversions to break the routine of my days. But at the Cross-Roads, too, they were talking of Kaintuckee. For so the Land was called, the Dark and Bloody Ground.

The next year came a war on the Frontier, waged by Lord Dunmore, Governor of Virginia. Of this likewise I heard at the Cross-Roads, though few from our part seemed to have gone to it. And I heard there, for rumors spread over mountains, that men blazing in the new land were in danger, and that my hero, Boone, was gone out to save them. But in the autumn came tidings of a great battle far to the north, and of the Indians suing for peace.

The next year came more tidings of a sort I did not understand. I remember once bringing back from the Cross-Roads a crumpled newspaper, which my father read again and again, and then folded up and put in his pocket. He said nothing to me of these things. But the next time I went to the Cross-Roads, the woman asked me:—

"Is your Pa for the Congress?"

"What's that?" said I.

"I reckon he ain't," said the woman, tartly. I recall her dimly, a slattern creature in a loose gown and bare feet, wife of the storekeeper and wagoner, with a swarm of urchins about her. They were all very natural to me thus. And I remember a battle with one of these urchins in the briers, an affair which did not add to the love of their family for ours. There was no money in that country, and the store took our pelts in exchange for what we needed from civilization. Once a month would I load these pelts on the white mare, and make the journey by the path down the creek. At times I met other settlers there, some of them not long from Ireland, with the brogue still in their mouths. And again, I saw the wagoner with his great canvas-covered wagon standing at the door, ready to start for the town sixty miles away. 'Twas he brought the news of this latest war.

One day I was surprised to see the wagoner riding up the path to our cabin, crying out for my father, for he was a violent man. And a violent scene followed. They remained for a long time within the house, and when they came out the wagoner's face was red with rage. My father, too, was angry, but no more talkative than usual.

"Ye say ye'll not help the Congress?" shouted the wagoner.

"I'll not," said my father.

"Ye'll live to rue this day, Alec Trimble," cried the man. "Ye may think ye're too fine for the likes of us, but there's them in the settlement that knows about ye."

With that he flung himself on his horse, and rode away. But the next time I went to the Cross-Roads the woman drove me away with curses, and called me an aristocrat. Wearily I tramped back the dozen miles up the creek, beside the mare, carrying my pelts with me; stumbling on the stones, and scratched by the dry briers. For it was autumn, the woods all red and yellow against the green of the pines. I sat down beside the old beaver dam to gather courage to tell my father. But he only smiled bitterly when he heard it. Nor would he tell me what the word *aristocrat* meant.

That winter we spent without bacon, and our salt gave out at Christmas. It was at this season, if I remember rightly, that we had another visitor. He arrived about nightfall one gray day, his horse jaded and cut, and he was dressed all in wool, with a great coat wrapped about him, and high boots. This made me stare at him. When my father drew back the bolt of the door he, too, stared and fell back a step.

"Come in," said he.

"D'ye ken me, Alec?" said the man.

He was a tall, spare man like my father, a Scotchman, but his hair was in a cue.

"Come in, Duncan," said my father, quietly. "Davy, run out for wood."

Loath as I was to go, I obeyed. As I came back dragging a log behind me I heard them in argument, and in their talk there was much about the Congress, and a woman named Flora Macdonald, and a British fleet sailing southward.

"We'll have two thousand Highlanders and more to meet the fleet. And ye'll sit at hame, in this hovel ye've made yeresel" (and he glanced about disdainfully) "and no help the King?" He brought his fist down on the pine boards.

"Ye did no help the King greatly at Culloden, Duncan," said my father, dryly.

Our visitor did not answer at once.

"The Yankee Rebels 'll no help the House of Stuart," said he, presently. "And Hanover's coom to stay. Are ye, too, a Rebel, Alec Ritchie?"

I remember wondering why he said *Ritchie*.

"I'll no take a hand in this fight," answered my father.

And that was the end of it. The man left with scant ceremony, I guiding him down the creek to the main trail. He did not open his mouth until I parted with him.

"Puir Davy," said he, and rode away in the night, for the moon shone through the clouds.

I remember these things, I suppose, because I had nothing else to think about. And the names stuck in my memory, intensified by later events, until I began to write a diary.

And now I come to my travels. As the spring drew on I had had a feeling that we could not live thus forever, with no market for our pelts. And one day my father said to me abruptly: —

"Davy, we'll be travelling."

"Where?" I asked.

"Ye'll ken soon enough," said he. "We'll go at crack o' day."

We went away in the wild dawn, leaving the cabin desolate. We loaded the white mare with the pelts, and my father wore a woollen suit like that of our Scotch visitor, which I had never seen before. He had clubbed his hair. But, strangest of all, he carried in a small parcel the silk gown that had been my mother's. We had scant other baggage.

We crossed the Yadkin at a ford, and climbing the hills to the south of it we went down over stony traces, down and down, through rain and sun; stopping at rude cabins or taverns, until we came into the valley of another river. This I know now was the Catawba. My memories of that ride are as misty as the spring weather in the mountains. But presently the country began to open up into broad fields, some of these abandoned to pines. And at last, splashing through the stiff red clay that was up to the mare's fetlocks, we came to a place called Charlotte Town. What a day that was for me! And how I gaped at the houses there, finer than any I had ever dreamed of! That was my first sight of a town. And how I listened open-mouthed to the gentlemen at the tavern! One I recall had a fighting head with a lock awry, and a negro servant to wait on him, and was the principal spokesman. He, too, was talking of war. The Cherokees had risen on the western border. He was telling of the massacre of a settlement, in no mild language.

"Sirs," he cried, "the British have stirred the redskins to this. Will you sit here while women and children are scalped, and those devils" (he called them worse names) "Stuart and Cameron go unpunished?"

My father got up from the corner where he sat, and stood beside the man.

"I ken Alec Cameron," said he.

The man looked at him with amazement.

"Ay?" said he, "I shouldn't think you'd own it. Damn him," he cried, "if we catch him we'll skin him alive."

"I ken Cameron," my father repeated, "and I'll gang with you to skin him alive."

The man seized his hand and wrung it.

"But first I must be in Charlestown," said my father.

The next morning we sold our pelts. And though the mare was tired, we pushed southward, I behind the saddle. I had much to think about, wondering what was to become of me while my father went to skin Cameron. I had not the least doubt that he would do it. The world is a storybook to a lad of nine, and the thought of Charlestown filled me with a delight unspeakable. Perchance he would leave me in Charlestown.

At nightfall we came into a settlement called the Waxhaws. And there being no tavern there, and the mare being very jaded and the roads heavy, we cast about for a place to sleep. The sunlight slanting over the pine forest glistened on the pools in the wet fields. And it so chanced that splashing across these, swinging a milk-pail over his head, shouting at the top of his voice, was a red-headed lad of my own age. My father hailed him, and he came running towards us, still shouting, and vaulted the rails. He stood before us, eying me with a most mischievous look in his blue eyes, and dabbling in the red mud with his toes. I remember I thought him a queer-looking boy. He was lanky, and he had a very long face under his tousled hair.

My father asked him where he could spend the night.

"Wal," said the boy, "I reckon Uncle Crawford might take you in. And again he mightn't."

He ran ahead, still swinging the pail. And we, following, came at length to a comfortable-looking farmhouse. As we stopped at the doorway a stout, motherly woman filled it. She held her knitting in her hand.

"You Andy!" she cried, "have you fetched the milk?"

Andy tried to look repentant.

"I declare I'll tan you," said the lady. "Git out this instant. What rascality have you been in?"

The Crossing, Vol. 1

"I fetched home visitors, Ma," said Andy.

"Visitors!" cried the lady. "What 'll your Uncle Crawford say?" And she looked at us smiling, but with no great hostility.

"Pardon me, Madam," said my father, "if we seem to intrude. But my mare is tired, and we have nowhere to stay."

Uncle Crawford did take us in. He was a man of substance in that country, — a north of Ireland man by birth, if I remember right.

I went to bed with the red-headed boy, whose name was Andy Jackson. I remember that his mother came into our little room under the eaves and made Andy say his prayers, and me after him. But when she was gone out, Andy stumped his toe getting into bed in the dark and swore with a brilliancy and vehemence that astonished me.

It was some hours before we went to sleep, he plying me with questions about my life, which seemed to interest him greatly, and I returning in kind.

"My Pa's dead," said Andy. "He came from a part of Ireland where they are all weavers. We're kinder poor relations here. Aunt Crawford's sick, and Ma keeps house. But Uncle Crawford's good, an' lets me go to Charlotte Town with him sometimes."

I recall that he also boasted some about his big brothers, who were away just then.

Andy was up betimes in the morning, to see us start. But we didn't start, because Mr. Crawford insisted that the white mare should have a half day's rest. Andy, being hustled off unwillingly to the "Old Field" school, made me go with him. He was a very headstrong boy.

I was very anxious to see a school. This one was only a log house in a poor, piny place, with a rabble of boys and girls romping at the door. But when they saw us they stopped. Andy jumped into the air, let out a war-whoop, and flung himself into the midst, scattering them right and left, and knocking one boy over and over. "I'm Billy Buck!" he cried. "I'm a hull regiment o' Rangers. Let th' Cherokees mind me!"

"Way for Sandy Andy!" cried the boys. "Where'd you get the new boy, Sandy?"

"His name's Davy," said Andy, "and his Pa's goin' to fight the Cherokees. He kin lick tarnation out'n any o' you."

Meanwhile I held back, never having been thrown with so many of my own kind.

"He's shot painters and b'ars," said Andy. "An' skinned 'em. Kin you lick him, Smally? I reckon not."

Now I had not come to the school for fighting. So I held back. Fortunately for me, Smally held back also. But he tried skilful tactics.

"He kin throw you, Sandy."

Andy faced me in an instant.

"Kin you?" said he.

There was nothing to do but try, and in a few seconds we were rolling on the ground, to the huge delight of Smally and the others, Andy shouting all the while and swearing. We rolled and rolled and rolled in the mud, until we both lost our breath, and even Andy stopped swearing, for want of it. After a while the boys were silent, and the thing became grim earnest. At length, by some accident rather than my own strength, both his shoulders touched the ground. I released him. But he was on his feet in an instant and at me again like a wildcat.

"Andy won't stay throwed," shouted a boy. And before I knew it he had my shoulders down in a puddle. Then I went for him, and affairs were growing more serious than a wrestle, when Smally, fancying himself safe, and no doubt having a grudge, shouted out: —

"Tell him he slobbers, Davy."

Andy *did* slobber. But that was the end of me, and the beginning of Smally. Andy left me instantly, not without an intimation that he would come back, and proceeded to cover Smally with red clay and blood. However, in the midst of this turmoil the schoolmaster arrived, haled both into the schoolhouse, held court, and flogged

Andrew with considerable gusto. He pronounced these words afterwards, with great solemnity:—

"Andrew Jackson, if I catch ye fightin' once more, I'll be afther givin' ye lave to lave the school."

I parted from Andy at noon with real regret. He was the first boy with whom I had ever had any intimacy. And I admired him: chiefly, I fear, for his fluent use of profanity and his fighting qualities. He was a merry lad, with a wondrous quick temper but a good heart. And he seemed sorry to say good-by. He filled my pockets with June apples—unripe, by the way—and told me to remember him when I got *till* Charlestown.

I remembered him much longer than that, and usually with a shock of surprise.

CHAPTER III

CHARLESTOWN

DOWN and down we went, crossing great rivers by ford and ferry, until the hills flattened themselves and the country became a long stretch of level, broken by the forests only; and I saw many things I had not thought were on the earth. Once in a while I caught glimpses of great red houses, with stately pillars, among the trees. They put me in mind of the palaces in Bunyan, their windows all golden in the morning sun; and as we jogged ahead, I pondered on the delights within them. I saw gangs of negroes plodding to work along the road, an overseer riding behind them with his gun on his back; and there were whole cotton fields in these domains blazing in primrose flower,—a new plant here, so my father said. He was willing to talk on such subjects. But on others, and especially our errand to Charlestown, he would say nothing. And I knew better than to press him.

One day, as we were crossing a dike between rice swamps spread with delicate green, I saw the white tops of wagons flashing in the sun at the far end of it. We caught up with them, the wagoners cracking their whips and swearing at the straining horses. And lo! in front of the wagons was an army,—at least my boyish mind magnified it to such. Men clad in homespun, perspiring and spattered with mud, were straggling along the road by fours, laughing and joking together. The officers rode, and many of these had blue coats and buff waistcoats,—some the worse for wear. My father was pushing the white mare into the ditch to ride by, when one hailed him.

"Hullo, my man," said he, "are you a friend to Congress?"

"I'm off to Charlestown to leave the lad," said my father, "and then to fight the Cherokees."

"Good," said the other. And then, "Where are you from?"

"Upper Yadkin," answered my father. "And you?"

The officer, who was a young man, looked surprised. But then he laughed pleasantly.

"We're North Carolina troops, going to join Lee in Charlestown," said he. "The British are sending a fleet and regiments against it."

"Oh, aye," said my father, and would have passed on. But he was made to go before the Colonel, who plied him with many questions. Then he gave us a paper and dismissed us.

We pursued our journey through the heat that shimmered up from the road, pausing now and again in the shade of a wayside tree. At times I thought I could bear the sun no longer. But towards four o'clock of that day a great bank of yellow cloud rolled up, darkening the earth save for a queer saffron light that stained everything, and made our very faces yellow. And then a wind burst out of the east with a high mournful note, as from a great flute afar, filling the air with leaves and branches of trees. But it bore, too, a savor that was new to me,—a salt savor, deep and fresh, that I drew down into my lungs. And I knew that we were near the ocean. Then came the rain, in great billows, as though the ocean itself were upon us.

The next day we crossed a ferry on the Ashley River, and rode down the sand of Charlestown neck. And my most vivid remembrance is of the great trunks towering half a hundred feet in the air, with a tassel of leaves at the top, which my father said were palmettos. Something lay heavy on his mind. For I had grown to know his moods by a sort of silent understanding. And when the roofs and spires of the town shone over the foliage in the afternoon sun, I felt him give a great sigh that was like a sob.

And how shall I describe the splendor of that city? The sandy streets, and the gardens of flower and shade, heavy with the plant odors; and the great houses with their galleries and porticos set in the midst of the gardens, that I remember staring at wistfully. But before long we came to a barricade fixed across the street, and then to another. And presently, in an open space near a large building, was a company of soldiers at drill.

It did not strike me as strange then that my father asked his way of no man, but went to a little ordinary in a humbler part of the town. After a modest meal in a corner of the public room, we went out for a stroll. Then, from the wharves, I saw the bay dotted with islands, their white sand sparkling in the evening light, and fringed with strange trees, and beyond, of a deepening blue, the ocean. And nearer,—greatest of all delights to me,—riding on the swell was a fleet of ships. My father gazed at them long and silently, his palm over his eyes.

"Men-o'-war from the old country, lad," he said after a while. "They're a brave sight."

"And why are they here?" I asked.

"They've come to fight," said he, "and take the town again for the King."

It was twilight when we turned to go, and then I saw that many of the warehouses along the wharves were heaps of ruins. My father said this was that the town might be the better defended.

We bent our way towards one of the sandy streets where the great houses were. And to my surprise we turned in at a gate, and up a path leading to the high steps of one of these. Under the high portico the door was open, but the house within was dark. My father paused, and the hand he held to mine trembled. Then he stepped across the threshold, and raising the big polished knocker that hung on the panel, let it drop. The sound reverberated through the house, and then stillness. And then, from within, a shuffling sound, and an old negro came to the door. For an instant he stood staring through the dusk, and broke into a cry.

"Marse Alec!" he said.

"Is your master at home?" said my father.

Without another word he led us through a deep hall, and out into a gallery above the trees of a back garden, where a gentleman sat smoking a long pipe. The old negro stopped in front of him.

"Marse John," said he, his voice shaking, "heah's Marse Alec done come back."

The gentleman got to his feet with a start. His pipe fell to the floor, and the ashes scattered on the boards and lay glowing there.

"Alec!" he cried, peering into my father's face, "Alec! You're not dead."

"John," said my father, "can we talk here?"

"Good God!" said the gentleman, "you're just the same. To think of it—to think of it! Breed, a light in the drawing-room."

There was no word spoken while the negro was gone, and the time seemed very long. But at length he returned, a silver candlestick in each hand.

"Careful," cried the gentleman, petulantly, "you'll drop them."

He led the way into the house, and through the hall to a massive door of mahogany with a silver door-knob. The grandeur of the place awed me, and well it might. Boylike, I was absorbed in this. Our little mountain cabin would almost have gone into this one room. The candles threw their flickering rays upward until they danced on the high ceiling. Marvel of marvels, in the oval left clear by the heavy, rounded cornice was a picture.

The negro set down the candles on the marble top of a table. But the air of the room was heavy and close, and the gentleman went to a window and flung it open. It came down instantly with a crash, so that the panes rattled again.

"Curse these Rebels," he shouted, "they've taken our window weights to make bullets."

Calling to the negro to pry open the window with a walking-stick, he threw himself into a big, upholstered chair. 'Twas then I remarked the splendor of his clothes, which were silk. And he wore a waistcoat all sewed with flowers. With a boy's intuition, I began to dislike him intensely.

"Damn the Rebels!" he began. "They've driven his Lordship away. I hope his Majesty will hang every mother's son of 'em. All pleasure of life is gone, and they've folly enough to think they can resist the fleet. And the worst of it is," cried he, "the worst of it is, I'm forced to smirk to them, and give good gold to their government." Seeing that my father did not answer, he asked: "Have you joined the Highlanders? You were always for fighting."

"I'm to be at Cherokee Ford on the twentieth," said my father. "We're to scalp the redskins and Cameron, though 'tis not known."

"Cameron!" shrieked the gentleman. "But that's the other side, man! Against his Majesty?"

"One side or t'other," said my father, "'tis all one against Alec Cameron."

The gentleman looked at my father with something like terror in his eyes.

"You'll never forgive Cameron," he said.

"I'll no forgive anybody who does me a wrong," said my father.

"And where have you been all these years, Alec?" he asked presently. "Since you went off with—"

"I've been in the mountains, leading a pure life," said my father. "And we'll speak of nothing, if you please, that's gone by."

"And what will you have me do?" said the gentleman, helplessly.

"Little enough," said my father. "Keep the lad till I come again. He's quiet. He'll no trouble you greatly. Davy, this is Mr. Temple. You're to stay with him till I come again."

"Come here, lad," said the gentleman, and he peered into my face. "You'll not resemble your mother."

"He'll resemble no one," said my father, shortly. "Good-by, Davy. Keep this till I come again." And he gave me the parcel made of my mother's gown. Then he lifted me in his strong arms and kissed me, and strode out of the house. We listened in silence as he went down the steps, and until his footsteps died away on the path. Then the gentleman rose and pulled a cord hastily. The negro came in.

"Put the lad to bed, Breed," said he.

"Whah, suh?"

"Oh, anywhere," said the master. He turned to me. "I'll be better able to talk to you in the morning, David," said he.

I followed the old servant up the great stairs, gulping down a sob that would rise, and clutching my mother's gown tight under my arm. Had my father left me alone in our cabin for a fortnight, I should not have minded. But here, in this strange house, amid such strange surroundings, I was heartbroken. The old negro was very kind. He led me into a little bedroom, and placing the candle on a polished dresser, he regarded me with sympathy.

"So you're Miss Lizbeth's boy," said he. "An' she dade. An' Marse Alec rough an' hard es though he been bo'n in de woods. Honey, ol' Breed 'll tek care ob you. I'll git you one o' dem night rails Marse Nick has, and some ob his'n close in de mawnin'."

These things I remember, and likewise sobbing myself to sleep in the four-poster. Often since I have wished that I had questioned Breed of many things on which I had no curiosity then, for he was my chief companion in the weeks that followed. He awoke me bright and early the next day.

"Heah's some close o' Marse Nick's you kin wear, honey," he said.

"Who is Master Nick?" I asked.

Breed slapped his thigh.

"Marse Nick Temple, Marsa's son. He's 'bout you size, but he ain' no mo' laik you den a jack rabbit's laik an' owl. Dey ain' none laik Marse Nick fo' gittin' into trouble — and gittin' out agin."

"Where is he now?" I asked.

"He at Temple Bow, on de Ashley Ribber. Dat's de Marsa's barony."

"His what?"

"De place whah he lib at, in de country."

"And why isn't the master there?"

I remember that Breed gave a wink, and led me out of the window onto a gallery above the one where we had found the master the night before. He pointed across the dense foliage of the garden to a strip of water gleaming in the morning sun beyond.

"See dat boat?" said the negro. "Sometime de Marse he tek ar ride in dat boat at night. Sometime gentlemen comes heah in a pow'ful hurry to git away, out'n de harbor whah de English is at."

By that time I was dressed, and marvellously uncomfortable in Master Nick's clothes. But as I was going out of the door, Breed hailed me.

"Marse Dave,"—it was the first time I had been called that,—"Marse Dave, you ain't gwineter tell?"

"Tell what?" I asked.

"Bout'n de boat, and Marsa agwine away nights."

"No," said I, indignantly.

"I knowed you wahn't," said Breed. "You don' look as if you'd tell anything."

We found the master pacing the lower gallery. At first he barely glanced at me, and nodded. After a while he stopped, and began to put to me many questions about my life: when and how I had lived. And to some of my answers he exclaimed, "Good God!" That was all. He was a handsome man, with hands like a woman's, well set off by the lace at his sleeves. He had fine-cut features, and the white linen he wore was most becoming.

"David," said he, at length, and I noted that he lowered his voice, "David, you seem a discreet lad. Pay attention to what I tell you. And mark! if you disobey me, you will be well whipped. You have this house and garden to play in, but you are by no means to go out at the front of the house. And whatever you may see or hear, you are to tell no one. Do you understand?"

"Yes, sir," I said.

"For the rest," said he, "Breed will give you food, and look out for your welfare."

And so he dismissed me. They were lonely days after that for a boy used to activity, and only the damp garden paths and lawns to run on. The creek at the back of the garden was stagnant and marshy when the water fell, and overhung by leafy boughs. On each side of the garden was a high brick wall. And though I was often tempted to climb it, I felt that disobedience was disloyalty to my father. Then there was the great house, dark and lonely in its magnificence, over which I roamed until I knew every corner of it.

I was most interested of all in the pictures of men and women in quaint, old-time costumes, and I used during the great heat of the day to sit in the drawing-room and study these, and wonder who they were and when they lived. Another amusement I had was to climb into the deep windows and peer through the blinds across the front garden into the street. Sometimes men stopped and talked loudly there, and again a rattle of drums would send me running to see the soldiers. I recall that I had a poor enough notion of what the fighting was all about. And no wonder. But I remember chiefly my insatiable longing to escape from this prison, as the great house soon became for me. And I yearned with a yearning I cannot express for our cabin in the hills and the old life there.

I caught glimpses of the master on occasions only, and then I avoided him; for I knew he had no wish to see me. Sometimes he would be seated in the gallery, tapping his foot on the floor, and sometimes pacing the garden walks with his hands opening and shutting. And one night I awoke with a start, and lay for a while listening until I heard something like a splash, and the scraping of the bottom-boards of a boat. Irresistibly I jumped out of bed, and running to the gallery rail I saw two dark figures moving among the leaves below. The next morning I came suddenly on a strange gentleman in the gallery. He wore a flowered dressing-gown like the one I had seen on the master, and he had a jolly, round face. I stopped and stared.

"Who the devil are you?" said he, but not unkindly.

"My name is David Trimble," said I, "and I come from the mountains."

He laughed.

"Mr. David Trimble-from-the-mountains, who the devil am I?"

"I don't know, sir," and I started to go away, not wishing to disturb him.

"Avast!" he cried. "Stand fast. See that you remember that."

"I'm not here of my free will, sir, but because my father wishes it. And I'll betray nothing."

Then he stared at me.

"How old did you say you were?" he demanded.

"I didn't say," said I.

"And you are of Scotch descent?" said he.

"I didn't say so, sir."

"You're a rum one," said he, laughing again, and he disappeared into the house.

That day, when Breed brought me my dinner on my gallery, he did not speak of a visitor. You may be sure I did not mention the circumstance. But Breed always told me the outside news.

"Dey's gittin' ready fo' a big fight, Marse Dave," said he. "Mister Moultrie in the fo't in de bay, an' Marse Gen'l Lee tryin' for to boss him. Dey's Rebels. An' Marse Admiral Parker an' de King's reg'ments fixin' fo' to tek de fo't, an' den Charlesto'n. Dey say Mister Moultrie ain't got no mo' chance dan a treed 'possum."

"Why, Breed?" I asked. I had heard my father talk of England's power and might, and Mister Moultrie seemed to me a very brave man in his little fort.

"Why!" exclaimed the old negro. "You ain't neber read no hist'ry books. I knows some of de gentlemen wid Mister Moultrie. Dey ain't no soldiers. Some is fine gentlemen, to be suah, but it's jist foolishness to fight dat fleet an' army. Marse Gen'l Lee hisself, he done sesso. I heerd him."

"And he's on Mister Moultrie's side?" I asked.

"Sholy," said Breed. "He's de Rebel gen'l."

"Then he's a knave and a coward!" I cried with a boy's indignation. "Where did you hear him say that?" I demanded, incredulous of some of Breed's talk.

"Right heah in dis house," he answered, and quickly clapped his hand to his mouth, and showed the whites of his eyes. "You ain't agwineter tell dat, Marse Dave?"

"Of course not," said I. And then: "I wish I could see Mister Moultrie in his fort, and the fleet."

"Why, honey, so you kin," said Breed.

The good-natured negro dropped his work and led the way upstairs, I following expectant, to the attic. A rickety ladder rose to a kind of tower (cupola, I suppose it would be called), whence the bay spread out before me like a picture, the white islands edged with the whiter lacing of the waves. There, indeed, was the fleet, but far away, like toy ships on the water, and the bit of a fort perched on the sandy edge of an island. I spent most of that day there, watching anxiously for some movement. But none came.

That night I was again awakened. And running into the gallery, I heard quick footsteps in the garden. Then there was a lantern's flash, a smothered oath, and all was dark again. But in the flash I had seen distinctly three figures. One was Breed, and he held the lantern; another was the master; and the third, a stout one muffled in a cloak, I made no doubt was my jolly friend. I lay long awake, with a boy's curiosity, until presently the dawn broke, and I arose and dressed, and began to wander about the house. No Breed was sweeping the gallery, nor was there any sign of the master. The house was as still as a tomb, and the echoes of my footsteps rolled through the halls and chambers. At last, prompted by curiosity and fear, I sought the kitchen, where I had often sat with Breed as he cooked the master's dinner. This was at the bottom and end of the house. The great fire there was cold, and the pots and pans hung neatly on their hooks, untouched that day. I was running through the wet garden, glad to be out in the light, when a sound stopped me.

It was a dull roar from the direction of the bay. Almost instantly came another, and another, and then several broke together. And I knew that the battle had begun. Forgetting for the moment my loneliness, I ran into the house and up the stairs two at a time, and up the ladder into the cupola, where I flung open the casement and leaned out.

There was the battle indeed,—a sight so vivid to me after all these years that I can call it again before me when I will. The toy men-o'-war, with sails set, ranging in front of the fort. They looked at my distance to be pressed against it. White puffs, like cotton balls, would dart one after another from a ship's side, melt into a cloud, float over her spars, and hide her from my view. And then presently the roar would reach me, and answering puffs along the line of the fort. And I could see the mortar shells go up and up, leaving a scorched trail behind, curve in a great circle, and fall upon the little garrison. Mister Moultrie became a real person to me then, a vivid picture in my boyish mind—a hero beyond all other heroes.

As the sun got up in the heavens and the wind fell, the cupola became a bake-oven. But I scarcely felt the heat. My whole soul was out in the bay, pent up with the men in the fort. How long could they hold out? Why were they not all killed by the shot that fell like hail among them? Yet puff after puff sprang from their guns, and the sound of it was like a storm coming nearer in the heat. But at noon it seemed to me as though some of the ships were sailing. It was true. Slowly they drew away from the others, and presently I thought they had stopped again. Surely two of them were stuck together, then three were fast on a shoal. Boats, like black bugs in the water, came and went between them and the others. After a long time the two that were together got apart and away. But the third stayed there, immovable, helpless.

Throughout the afternoon the fight kept on, the little black boats coming and going. I saw a mast totter and fall on one of the ships. I saw the flag shot away from the fort, and reappear again. But now the puffs came from her walls slowly and more slowly, so that my heart sank with the setting sun. And presently it grew too dark to see aught save the red flashes. Slowly, reluctantly, the noise died down until at last a great silence reigned, broken only now and again by voices in the streets below me. It was not until then that I realized that I had been all day without food—that I was alone in the dark of a great house.

I had never known fear in the woods at night. But now I trembled as I felt my way down the ladder, and groped and stumbled through the black attic for the stairs. Every noise I made seemed louder an hundred fold than the battle had been, and when I barked my shins, the pain was sharper than a knife. Below, on the big stairway, the echo of my footsteps sounded again from the empty rooms, so that I was taken with a panic and fled downward, sliding and falling, until I reached the hall. Frantically as I tried, I could not unfasten the bolts on the front door. And so, running into the drawing-room, I pried open the window, and sat me down in the embrasure to think, and to try to quiet the thumpings of my heart.

By degrees I succeeded. The still air of the night and the heavy, damp odors of the foliage helped me. And I tried to think what was right for me to do. I had promised the master not to leave the place, and that promise seemed in pledge to my father. Surely the master would come back—or Breed. They would not leave me here alone without food much longer. Although I was young, I was brought up to responsibility. And I inherited a conscience that has since given me much trouble.

From these thoughts, trying enough for a starved lad, I fell to thinking of my father on the frontier fighting the Cherokees. And so I dozed away to dream of him. I remember that he was skinning Cameron,—I had often pictured it,—and Cameron yelling, when I was awakened with a shock by a great noise.

I listened with my heart in my throat. The noise seemed to come from the hall,—a prodigious pounding. Presently it stopped, and a man's voice cried out:—

"Ho there, within!"

My first impulse was to answer. But fear kept me still.

"Batter down the door," some one shouted.

There was a sound of shuffling in the portico, and the same voice:—

"Now then, all together, lads!"

Then came a straining and splitting of wood, and with a crash the door gave way. A lantern's rays shot through the hall.

"The house is as dark as a tomb," said a voice.

"And as empty, I reckon," said another. "John Temple and his spy have got away."

"We'll have a search," answered the first voice.

They stood for a moment in the drawing-room door, peering, and then they entered. There were five of them. Two looked to be gentlemen, and three were of rougher appearance. They carried lanterns.

"That window's open," said one of the gentlemen. "They must have been here to-day. Hello, what's this?" He started back in surprise.

I slid down from the window-seat, and stood facing them, not knowing what else to do. They, too, seemed equally confounded.

"It must be Temple's son," said one, at last. "I had thought the family at Temple Bow. What's your name, my lad?"

"David Trimble, sir," said I.

"And what are you doing here?" he asked more sternly.

"I was left in Mr. Temple's care by my father."

"Oho!" he cried. "And where is your father?"

"He's gone to fight the Cherokees," I answered soberly. "To skin a man named Cameron."

At that they were silent for an instant, and then the two broke into a laugh.

"Egad, Lowndes," said the gentleman, "here is a fine mystery. Do you think the boy is lying?"

The other gentleman scratched his forehead.

"I'll have you know I don't lie, sir," I said, ready to cry.

"No," said the other gentleman. "A backwoodsman named Trimble went to Rutledge with credentials from North Carolina, and has gone off to Cherokee Ford to join McCall."

"Bless my soul!" exclaimed the first gentleman. He came up and laid his hand on my shoulder, and said:—

"Where is Mr. Temple?"

"That I don't know, sir."

"When did he go away?"

I did not answer at once.

"That I can't tell you, sir."

"Was there any one with him?"

"That I can't tell you, sir."

"The devil you can't!" he cried, taking his hand away. "And why not?"

I shook my head, sorely beset.

"Come, Mathews," cried the gentleman called Lowndes. "We'll search first, and attend to the lad after."

And so they began going through the house, prying into every cupboard and sweeping under every bed. They even climbed to the attic; and noting the open casement in the cupola, Mr. Lowndes said:—

"Some one has been here to-day."

"It was I, sir," I said. "I have been here all day."

"And what doing, pray?" he demanded.

"Watching the battle. And oh, sir," I cried, "can you tell me whether Mister Moultrie beat the British?"

"He did so," cried Mr. Lowndes. "He did, and soundly."

He stared at me. I must have looked my pleasure.

"Why, David," says he, "you are a patriot, too."

"I am a Rebel, sir," I cried hotly.

Both gentlemen laughed again, and the men with them.

"The lad is a character," said Mr. Lowndes.

We made our way down into the garden, which they searched last. At the creek's side the boat was gone, and there were footsteps in the mud.

"The bird has flown, Lowndes," said Mr. Mathews.

"And good riddance for the Committee," answered that gentleman, heartily. "He got to the fleet in fine season to get a round shot in the middle. David," said he, solemnly, "remember it never pays to try to be two things at once."

"I'll warrant he stayed below water," said Mr. Mathews. "But what shall we do with the lad?"

"I'll take him to my house for the night," said Mr. Lowndes, "and in the morning we'll talk to him. I reckon he should be sent to Temple Bow. He is connected in some way with the Temples."

"God help him if he goes there," said Mr. Mathews, under his breath. But I heard him.

They locked up the house, and left one of the men to guard it, while I went with Mr. Lowndes to his residence. I remember that people were gathered in the streets as we passed, making merry, and that they greeted Mr. Lowndes with respect and good cheer. His house, too, was set in a garden and quite as fine as Mr. Temple's. It was ablaze with candles, and I caught glimpses of fine gentlemen and ladies in the rooms. But he hurried me through the hall, and into a little chamber at the rear where a writing-desk was set. He turned and faced me.

"You must be tired, David," he said.

I nodded.

"And hungry? Boys are always hungry."

"Yes, sir."

"You had no dinner?"

"No, sir," I answered, off my guard.

"Mercy!" he said. "It is a long time since breakfast."

"I had no breakfast, sir."

"Good God!" he said, and pulled the velvet handle of a cord. A negro came.

"Is the supper for the guests ready?"

"Yes, Marsa."

"Then bring as much as you can carry here," said the gentleman. "And ask Mrs. Lowndes if I may speak with her."

Mrs. Lowndes came first. And such a fine lady she was that she frightened me, this being my first experience with ladies. But when Mr. Lowndes told her my story, she ran to me impulsively and put her arms about me.

"Poor lad!" she said. "What a shame!"

I think that the tears came then, but it was small wonder. There were tears in her eyes, too.

Such a supper as I had I shall never forget. And she sat beside me for long, neglecting her guests, and talking of my life. Suddenly she turned to her husband, calling him by name.

"He is Alec Ritchie's son," she said, "and Alec has gone against Cameron."

Mr. Lowndes did not answer, but nodded.

"And must he go to Temple Bow?"

"My dear," said Mr. Lowndes, "I fear it is our duty to send him there."

CHAPTER IV

TEMPLE BOW

IN the morning I started for Temple Bow on horseback behind one of Mr. Lowndes' negroes. Good Mrs. Lowndes had kissed me at parting, and tucked into my pocket a parcel of sweetmeats. There had been a few grave gentlemen to see me, and to their questions I had replied what I could. But tell them of Mr. Temple I would not, save that he himself had told me nothing. And Mr. Lowndes had presently put an end to their talk.

"The lad knows nothing, gentlemen," he had said, which was true.

"David," said he, when he bade me farewell, "I see that your father has brought you up to fear God. Remember that all you see in this life is not to be imitated."

And so I went off behind his negro. He was a merry lad, and despite the great heat of the journey and my misgivings about Temple Bow, he made me laugh. I was sad at crossing the ferry over the Ashley, through thinking of my father, but I reflected that it could not be long now ere I saw him again. In the middle of the day we stopped at a tavern. And at length, in the abundant shade of evening, we came to a pair of great ornamental gates set between brick pillars capped with white balls, and turned into a drive. And presently, winding through the trees, we were in sight of a long, brick mansion trimmed with white, and a velvet lawn before it all flecked with shadows. In front of the portico was a saddled horse, craning his long neck at two panting hounds stretched on the ground. A negro boy in blue clutched the bridle. On the horse-block a gentleman in white reclined. He wore shiny boots, and he held his hat in his hand, and he was gazing up at a lady who stood on the steps above him.

The lady I remember as well—Lord forbid that I should forget her. And her laugh as I heard it that evening is ringing now in my ears. And yet it was not a laugh. Musical it was, yet there seemed no pleasure in it: rather irony, and a great weariness of the amusements of this world: and a note, too, from a vanity never ruffled. It stopped abruptly as the negro pulled up his horse before her, and she stared at us haughtily.

"What's this?" she said.

"Pardon, Mistis," said the negro, "I'se got a letter from Marse Lowndes."

"Mr. Lowndes should instruct his niggers," she said. "There is a servants' drive." The man was turning his horse when she cried: "Hold! Let's have it."

He dismounted and gave her the letter, and I jumped to the ground, watching her as she broke the seal, taking her in, as a boy will, from the flowing skirt and tight-laced stays of her salmon silk to her high and powdered hair. She must have been about thirty. Her face was beautiful, but had no particle of expression in it, and was dotted here and there with little black patches of plaster. While she was reading, a sober gentleman in black silk breeches and severe coat came out of the house and stood beside her.

"Heigho, parson," said the gentleman on the horse-block, without moving, "are you to preach against loo or lansquenet to-morrow?"

"Would it make any difference to you, Mr. Riddle?"

Before he could answer there came a great clatter behind them, and a boy of my own age appeared. With a leap he landed sprawling on the indolent gentleman's shoulders, nearly upsetting him.

"You young rascal!" exclaimed the gentleman, pitching him on the drive almost at my feet; then he fell back again to a position where he could look up at the lady.

"Harry Riddle," cried the boy, "I'll ride steeplechases and beat you some day."

"Hush, Nick," cried the lady, petulantly, "I'll have no nerves left me." She turned to the letter again, holding it very near to her eyes, and made a wry face of impatience. Then she held the sheet out to Mr. Riddle.

"A pretty piece of news," she said languidly. "Read it, Harry."

The gentleman seized her hand instead. The lady glanced at the clergyman, whose back was turned, and shook her head.

"How tiresome you are!" she said.

"What's happened?" asked Mr. Riddle, letting go as the parson looked around.

"Oh, they've had a battle," said the lady, "and Moultrie and his Rebels have beat off the King's fleet."

"The devil they have!" exclaimed Mr. Riddle, while the parson started forwards. "Anything more?"

"Yes, a little." She hesitated. "That husband of mine has fled Charlestown. They think he went to the fleet." And she shot a meaning look at Mr. Riddle, who in turn flushed red. I was watching them.

"What!" cried the clergyman, "John Temple has run away?"

"Why not," said Mr. Riddle. "One can't live between wind and water long. And Charlestown's—uncomfortable in summer."

At that the clergyman cast one look at them—such a look as I shall never forget—and went into the house.

"Mamma," said the boy, "where has father gone? Has he run away?"

"Yes. Don't bother me, Nick."

"I don't believe it," cried Nick, his high voice shaking. "I'd—I'd disown him."

At that Mr. Riddle burst into a hearty laugh.

"Come, Nick," said he, "it isn't so bad as that. Your father's for his Majesty, like the rest of us. He's merely gone over to fight for him." And he looked at the lady and laughed again. But I liked the boy.

As for the lady, she curled her lip. "Mr. Riddle, don't be foolish," she said. "If we are to play, send your horse to the stables." Suddenly her eye lighted on me. "One more brat," she sighed. "Nick, take him to the nursery, or the stable. And both of you keep out of my sight."

Nick strode up to me.

"Don't mind her. She's always saying, 'Keep out of my sight.'" His voice trembled. He took me by the sleeve and began pulling me around the house and into a little summer bower that stood there; for he had a masterful manner.

"What's your name?" he demanded.

"David Trimble," I said.

"Have you seen my father in town?"

The intense earnestness of the question surprised an answer out of me.

"Yes."

"Where?" he demanded.

"In his house. My father left me with your father."

"Tell me about it."

I related as much as I dared, leaving out Mr. Temple's double dealing; which, in truth, I did not understand. But the boy was relentless.

"Why," said he, "my father was a friend of Mr. Lowndes and Mr. Mathews. I have seen them here drinking with him. And in town. And he ran away?"

"I do not know where he went," said I, which was the truth.

He said nothing, but hid his face in his arms over the rail of the bower. At length he looked up at me fiercely.

"If you ever tell this, I will kill you," he cried. "Do you hear?"

That made me angry.

"Yes, I hear," I said. "But I am not afraid of you."

He was at me in an instant, knocking me to the floor, so that the breath went out of me, and was pounding me vigorously ere I recovered from the shock and astonishment of it and began to defend myself. He was taller than I, and wiry, but not so rugged. Yet there was a look about him that was far beyond his strength. A look that meant, *never say die*. Curiously, even as I fought desperately I compared him with that other lad I had known, Andy Jackson. And this one, though not so powerful, frightened me the more in his relentlessness.

Perhaps we should have been fighting still had not some one pulled us apart, and when my vision cleared I saw Nick, struggling and kicking, held tightly in the hands of the clergyman. And it was all that gentleman could do to hold him. I am sure it was quite five minutes before he forced the lad, exhausted, on to the seat. And then there was a defiance about his nostrils that showed he was undefeated. The clergyman, still holding him with one hand, took out his handkerchief with the other and wiped his brow.

I expected a scolding and a sermon. To my amazement the clergyman said quietly:—

"Now what was the trouble, David?"

"I'll not be the one to tell it, sir," I said, and trembled at my temerity.

The parson looked at me queerly.

"Then you are in the right of it," he said. "It is as I thought; I'll not expect Nicholas to tell me."

"I will tell you, sir," said Nicholas. "He was in the house with my father when—when he ran away. And I said that if he ever spoke of it to any one, I would kill him."

For a while the clergyman was silent, gazing with a strange tenderness at the lad, whose face was averted.

"And you, David?" he said presently.

"I—I never mean to tell, sir. But I was not to be frightened."

"Quite right, my lad," said the clergyman, so kindly that it sent a strange thrill through me. Nicholas looked up quickly.

"You won't tell?" he said.

"No," I said.

"You can let me go now, Mr. Mason," said he. Mr. Mason did. And he came over and sat beside me, but said nothing more.

After a while Mr. Mason cleared his throat.

"Nicholas," said he, "when you grow older you will understand these matters better. Your father went away to join the side he believes in, the side we all believe in—the King's side."

"Did he ever pretend to like the other side?" asked Nick, quickly.

"When you grow older you will know his motives," answered the clergyman, gently. "Until then; you must trust him."

"You never pretended," cried Nick.

"Thank God I never was forced to do so," said the clergyman, fervently.

It is wonderful that the conditions of our existence may wholly change without a seeming strangeness. After many years only vivid snatches of what I saw and heard and did at Temple Bow come back to me. I understood but little the meaning of the seigniorial life there. My chief wonder now is that its golden surface was not more troubled by the winds then brewing. It was a new life to me, one that I had not dreamed of.

After that first falling out, Nick and I became inseparable. Far slower than he in my likes and dislikes, he soon became a passion with me. Even as a boy, he did everything with a grace unsurpassed; the dash and daring of his pranks took one's breath; his generosity to those he loved was prodigal. Nor did he ever miss a chance to score those under his displeasure. At times he was reckless beyond words to describe, and again he would fall sober for a day. He could be cruel and tender in the same hour; abandoned and freezing in his dignity. He had an old negro mammy whose worship for him and his possessions was idolatry. I can hear her now calling and calling, "Marse Nick, honey, yo' supper's done got cole," as she searched patiently among the magnolias. And suddenly there would be a shout, and Mammy's turban go flying from her woolly head, or Mammy herself would be dragged down from behind and sat upon.

We had our supper, Nick and I, at twilight, in the children's dining room. A little white room, unevenly panelled, the silver candlesticks and yellow flames fantastically reflected in the mirrors between the deep windows, and the moths and June-bugs tilting at the lights. We sat at a little mahogany table eating porridge and cream from round blue bowls, with Mammy to wait on us. Sometimes there floated in upon us the hum of revelry from the great drawing-room where Madame had her company. Often the good Mr. Mason would come in to us (he cared little for the parties), and talk to us of our day's doings. Nick had his lessons from the clergyman in the winter time.

Mr. Mason took occasion once to question me on what I knew. Some of my answers, in especial those relating to my knowledge of the Bible, surprised him. Others made him sad.

"David," said he, "you are an earnest lad, with a head to learn, and you will. When your father comes, I shall talk with him." He paused—"I knew him," said he, "I knew him ere you were born. A just man, and upright, but with a great sorrow. We must never be hasty in our judgments. But you will never be hasty, David," he added, smiling at me. "You are a good companion for Nicholas."

Nicholas and I slept in the same bedroom, at a corner of the long house, and far removed from his mother. She would not be disturbed by the noise he made in the mornings. I remember that he had cut in the solid shutters of that room, folded into the embrasures, "*Nicholas Temple, His Mark,*" and a long, flat sword. The first night in that room we slept but little, near the whole of it being occupied with tales of my adventures and of my life in the mountains. Over and over again I must tell him of the "painters" and wildcats, of deer and bear and wolf. Nor was he ever satisfied. And at length I came to speak of that land where I had often lived in fancy—the land beyond the mountains of which Daniel Boone had told. Of its forest and glade, its countless herds of elk and buffalo, its salt-licks and Indians, until we fell asleep from sheer exhaustion.

"I will go there," he cried in the morning, as he hurried into his clothes; "I will go to that land as sure as my name is Nick Temple. And you shall go with me, David."

"Perchance I shall go before you," I answered, though I had small hopes of persuading my father.

He would often make his exit by the window, climbing down into the garden by the protruding bricks at the corner of the house; or sometimes go shouting down the long halls and through the gallery to the great stairway, a smothered oath from behind the closed bedroom doors proclaiming that he had waked a guest. And many days we spent in the wood, playing at hunting game—a poor enough amusement for me, and one that Nick soon tired of. They were thick, wet woods, unlike our woods of the mountains; and more than once we had excitement enough with the snakes that lay there.

I believe that in a week's time Nick was as conversant with my life as I myself. For he made me tell of it again and again, and of Kentucky. And always as he listened his eyes would glow and his breast heave with excitement.

"Do you think your father will take you there, David, when he comes for you?"

I hoped so, but was doubtful.

"I'll run away with you," he declared. "There is no one here who cares for me save Mr. Mason and Mammy."

And I believe he meant it. He saw but little of his mother, and nearly always something unpleasant was coupled with his views. Sometimes we ran across her in the garden paths walking with a gallant,—oftenest Mr. Riddle. It was a beautiful garden, with hedge-bordered walks and flowers wondrously massed in color, a high brick wall surrounding it. Frequently Mrs. Temple and Mr. Riddle would play at cards there of an afternoon, and when that musical, unbelieving laugh of hers came floating over the wall, Nick would say:—

"Mamma is winning."

Once we heard high words between the two, and running into the garden found the cards scattered on the grass, and the couple gone.

Of all Nick's escapades,—and he was continually in and out of them,—I recall only a few of the more serious. As I have said, he was a wild lad, sobered by none of the things which had gone to make my life, and what he took into his head to do he generally did,—or, if balked, flew into such a rage as to make one believe he could not live. Life was always war with him, or some semblance of a struggle. Of his many wild doings I recall well the time when—fired by my tales of hunting—he went out to attack the young bull in the paddock with a bow and arrow. It made small difference to the bull that the arrow was too blunt to enter his hide. With a bellow that frightened the idle negroes at the slave quarters, he started for Master Nick. I, who had been taught by my father never to run any unnecessary risk, had taken the precaution to provide as large a stone as I could comfortably throw, and took station on the fence. As the furious animal came charging, with his head lowered, I struck him by a good fortune between the eyes, and Nicholas got over. We were standing on the far side, watching him pawing the broken bow, when, in the crowd of frightened negroes, we discovered the parson beside us.

"David," said he, patting me with a shaking hand, "I perceive that you have a cool head. Our young friend here has a hot one. Dr. Johnson may not care for Scotch blood, and yet I think a wee bit of it is not to be despised."

I wondered whether Dr. Johnson was staying in the house, too.

How many slaves there were at Temple Bow I know not, but we used to see them coming home at night in droves, the overseers riding beside them with whips and guns. One day a huge Congo chief, not long from Africa, nearly killed an overseer, and escaped to the swamp. As the day fell, we heard the baying of the bloodhounds hot upon his trail. More ominous still, a sound like a rising wind came from the direction of the quarters. Into our little dining-room burst Mrs. Temple herself, slamming the door behind her. Mr. Mason, who was sitting with us, rose to calm her.

"The Rebels!" she cried. "The Rebels have taught them this, with their accursed notions of liberty and equality. We shall all be murdered by the blacks because of the Rebels. Oh, hell-fire is too good for them. Have the house barred and a watch set to-night. What shall we do?"

"I pray you compose yourself, Madame," said the clergyman. "We can send for the militia."

"The militia!" she shrieked; "the Rebel militia! They would murder us as soon as the niggers."

"They are respectable men," answered Mr. Mason, "and were at Fanning Hall to-day patrolling."

"I would rather be killed by whites than blacks," said the lady. "But who is to go for the militia?"

"I will ride for them," said Mr. Mason. It was a dark, lowering night, and spitting rain.

"And leave me defenceless!" she cried. "You do not stir, sir."

"It is a pity," said Mr. Mason—he was goaded to it, I suppose—"'tis a pity Mr. Riddle did not come to-night."

She shot at him a withering look, for even in her fear she would brook no liberties. Nick spoke up:—

"I will go," said he; "I can get through the woods to Fanning Hall—"

"And I will go with him," I said.

"Let the brats go," she said, and cut short Mr. Mason's expostulations. She drew Nick to her and kissed him. He wriggled away, and without more ado we climbed out of the dining-room windows into the night. Running across the lawn, we left the lights of the great house twinkling behind us in the rain. We had to pass the long line of cabins at the quarters. Three overseers with lanterns stood guard there; the cabins were dark, the wretches within silent and cowed. Thence we felt with our feet for the path across the fields, stumbled over a sty, and took our way through the black woods. I was at home here, and Nick was not to be frightened. At intervals the mournful bay of a bloodhound came to us from a distance.

"Suppose we should meet the Congo chief," said Nick, suddenly.

The idea had occurred to me.

"She needn't have been so frightened," said he, in scornful remembrance of his mother's actions.

We pressed on. Nick knew the path as only a boy can. Half an hour passed. It grew brighter. The rain ceased, and a new moon shot out between the leaves. I seized his arm.

"What's that?" I whispered.

"A deer."

But I, cradled in woodcraft, had heard plainly a man creeping through the underbrush beside us. Fear of the Congo chief and pity for the wretch tore at my heart. Suddenly there loomed in front of us, on the path, a great, naked man. We stood with useless limbs, staring at him.

Then, from the trees over our heads, came a chittering and a chattering such as I had never heard. The big man before us dropped to the earth, his head bowed, muttering. As for me, my fright increased. The chattering stopped, and Nick stepped forward and laid his hand on the negro's bare shoulder.

"We needn't be afraid of him now, Davy," he said. "I learned that trick from a Portuguese overseer we had last year."

"You did it!" I exclaimed, my astonishment overcoming my fear.

"It's the way the monkeys chatter in the Canaries," he said. "Manuel had a tame one, and I heard it talk. Once before I tried it on the chief, and he fell down. He thinks I'm a god."

It must have been a weird scene to see the great negro following two boys in the moonlight. Indeed, he came after us like a dog. At length we were in sight of the lights of Fanning Hall. The militia was there. We were challenged by the guard, and caused sufficient amazement when we appeared in the hall before the master, who was a bachelor of fifty.

"'Sblood, Nick Temple!" he cried, "what are you doing here with that big Congo for a dog? The sight of him frightens me."

The negro, indeed, was a sight to frighten one. The black mud of the swamps was caked on him, and his flesh was torn by brambles.

"He ran away," said Nick; "and I am taking him home."

"You—you are taking him home!" sputtered Mr. Fanning.

"Do you want to see him act?" said Nick. And without waiting for a reply he filled the hall with a dozen monkeys. Mr. Fanning leaped back into a doorway, but the chief prostrated himself on the floor. "Now do you believe I can take him home?" said Nick.

"'Swounds!" said Mr. Fanning, when he had his breath. "You beat the devil, Nicholas Temple. The next time you come to call I pray you leave your travelling show at home."

"Mamma sent me for the militia," said Nick.

"She did!" said Mr. Fanning, looking grim. "An insurrection is a bad thing, but there was no danger for two lads in the woods, I suppose."

"There's no danger anyway," said Nick. "The niggers are all scared to death."

Mr. Fanning burst out into a loud laugh, stopped suddenly, sat down, and took Nick on his knee. It was an incongruous scene. Mr. Fanning almost cried.

"Bless your soul," he said, "but you are a lad. Would to God I had you instead of—"

He paused abruptly.

"I must go home," said Nick; "she will be worried."

"*She* will be worried!" cried Mr. Fanning, in a burst of anger. Then he said: "You shall have the militia. You shall have the militia." He rang a bell and sent his steward for the captain, a gawky country farmer, who gave a gasp when he came upon the scene in the hall.

"And mind," said Nick to the captain, "you are to keep your men away from him, or he will kill one of them."

The captain grinned at him curiously.

"I reckon I won't have to tell them to keep away," said he.

Mr. Fanning started us off for the walk with pockets filled with sweetmeats, which we nibbled on the way back. We made a queer procession, Nick and I striding ahead to show the path, followed by the now servile chief, and after him the captain and his twenty men in single file. It was midnight when we saw the lights of Temple Bow through the trees. One of the tired overseers met us near the kitchen. When he perceived the Congo his face lighted up with rage, and he instinctively reached for his whip. But the chief stood before him, immovable, with arms folded, and a look on his face that meant danger.

"He will kill you, Emory," said Nick; "he will kill you if you touch him."

Emory dropped his hand, limply.

"He will go to work in the morning," said Nick; "but mind you, not a lash."

"Very good, Master Nick," said the man; "but who's to get him in his cabin?"

"I will," said Nick. He beckoned to the Congo, who followed him over to quarters and went in at his door without a protest.

The next morning Mrs. Temple looked out of her window and saw the militiamen on the lawn.

"Pooh!" she said, "are those butternuts the soldiers that Nick went to fetch?"

CHAPTER V

Cram's Hell

AFTER that my admiration for Nick Temple increased greatly, whether excited by his courage and presence of mind, or his ability to imitate men and women and creatures, I know not. One of our amusements, I recall, was to go to the Congo's cabin to see him fall on his face, until Mr. Mason put a stop to it. The clergyman let us know that we were encouraging idolatry, and he himself took the chief in hand.

Another incident comes to me from those bygone days. The fear of negro insurrections at the neighboring plantations being temporarily lulled, the gentry began to pluck up courage for their usual amusements. There were to be races at some place a distance away, and Nick was determined to go. Had he not determined that I should go, all would have been well. The evening before he came upon his mother in the garden. Strange to say, she was in a gracious mood and alone.

"Come and kiss me, Nick," she said. "Now, what do you want?"

"I want to go to the races," he said.

"You have your pony. You can follow the coach."

"David is to ride the pony," said Nick, generously. "May I go in the coach?"

"No," she said, "there is no room for you."

Nicholas flared up. "Harry Riddle is going in the coach. I don't see why you can't take me sometimes. You like him better than me."

The lady flushed very red.

"How dare you, Nick!" she cried angrily. "What has Mr. Mason been putting into your head?"

"Nothing," said Nick, quite as angrily. "Any one can see that you like Harry. And I *will* ride in the coach."

"You'll not," said his mother.

I had heard nothing of this. The next morning he led out his pony from the stables for me to ride, and insisted. And, supposing he was to go in the coach, I put foot in the stirrup. The little beast would scarce stand still for me to mount.

"You'll not need the whip with her," said Nick, and led her around by the side of the house, in view of the portico, and stood there at her bridle. Presently, with a great noise and clatter of hoofs, the coach rounded the drive, the powdered negro coachman pulling up the four horses with much ceremony at the door. It was a wondrous great vehicle, the bright colors of its body flashing in the morning light. I had examined it more than once, and with awe, in the coach-house. It had glass windows and a lion on a blue shield on the door, and within it was all salmon silk, save the painted design on the ceiling. Great leather straps held up this house on wheels, to take the jolts of the road. And behind it was a platform. That morning two young negroes with flowing blue coats stood on it. They leaped to the ground when the coach stopped, and stood each side of the door, waiting for my lady to enter.

She came down the steps, laughing, with Mr. Riddle, who was in his riding clothes, for he was to race that day. He handed her in, and got in after her. The coachman cracked his whip, the coach creaked off down the drive, I in the trees one side waiting for them to pass, and wondering what Nick was to do. He had let go my bridle, folded his whip in his hand, and with a shout of "Come on, Davy," he ran for the coach, which was going slowly, caught hold of the footman's platform, and pulled himself up.

What possessed the footman I know not. Perchance fear of his mistress was greater than fear of his young master; but he took the lad by the shoulders—gently, to be sure—and pushed him into the road, where he fell and rolled over. I guessed what would happen. Picking himself up, Nick was at the man like a hurricane, seizing him swiftly by the leg. The negro fell upon the platform, clutching wildly, where he lay in a sheer fright, shrieking for mercy, his cries rivalled by those of the lady within. The coachman frantically pulled his horses to a stand, the other footman jumped off, and Mr. Harry Riddle came flying out of the coach door, to behold Nicholas beating the negro with his riding-whip.

"You young devil," cried Mr. Riddle, angrily, striding forward, "what are you doing?"

"Keep off, Harry," said Nicholas. "I am teaching this nigger that he is not to lay hands on his betters." With that he gave the boy one more cut, and turned from him contemptuously.

"What is it, Harry?" came in a shrill voice from within the coach.

"It's Nick's pranks," said Mr. Riddle, grinning in spite of his anger; "he's ruined one of your footmen. You little scoundrel," cried Mr. Riddle, advancing again, "you've frightened your mother nearly to a swoon."

"Serves her right," said Nick.

"What!" cried Mr. Riddle. "Come down from there instantly."

Nick raised his whip. It was not that that stopped Mr. Riddle, but a sign about the lad's nostrils.

"Harry Riddle," said the boy, "if it weren't for you, I'd be riding in this coach to-day with my mother. I don't want to ride with her, but I will go to the races. If you try to take me down, I'll do my best to kill you," and he lifted the loaded end of the whip.

Mrs. Temple's beautiful face had by this time been thrust out of the door.

"For the love of heaven, Harry, let him come in with us. We're late enough as it is."

Mr. Riddle turned on his heel. He tried to glare at Nick, but he broke into a laugh instead.

"Come down, Satan," says he. "God help the woman you love and the man you fight."

And so Nicholas jumped down, and into the coach. The footman picked himself up, more scared than injured, and the vehicle took its lumbering way for the race-course, I following.

I have seen many courses since, but none to equal that in the gorgeous dress of those who watched. There had been many, many more in former years, so I heard people say. This was the only sign that a war was in progress,—the scanty number of gentry present,—

for all save the indifferent were gone to Charlestown or elsewhere. I recall it dimly, as a blaze of color passing: merrymaking, jesting, feasting,—a rare contrast, I thought, to the sight I had beheld in Charlestown Bay but a while before. Yet so runs the world,—strife at one man's home, and peace and contentment at his neighbor's; sorrow here, and rejoicing not a league away.

Master Nicholas played one prank that evening that was near to costing dear. My lady Temple made up a party for Temple Bow at the course, two other coaches to come and some gentlemen riding. As Nick and I were running through the paddock we came suddenly upon Mr. Harry Riddle and a stout, swarthy gentleman standing together. The stout gentleman was counting out big gold pieces in his hand and giving them to Mr. Riddle.

"Lucky dog!" said the stout gentleman; "you'll ride back with her, and you've won all I've got." And he dug Mr. Riddle in the ribs.

"You'll have it again when we play to-night, Darnley," answered Mr. Riddle, crossly. "And as for the seat in the coach, you are welcome to it. That firebrand of a lad is on the front seat."

"D—n the lad," said the stout gentleman. "I'll take it, and you can ride my horse. He'll—he'll carry you, I reckon." His voice had a way of cracking into a mellow laugh.

At that Mr. Riddle went off in a towering bad humor, and afterwards I heard him cursing the stout gentleman's black groom as he mounted his great horse. And then he cursed the horse as it reared and plunged, while the stout gentleman stood at the coach door, cackling at his discomfiture. The gentleman did ride home with Mrs. Temple, Nick going into another coach. I afterwards discovered that the gentleman had bribed him with a guinea. And Mr. Riddle more than once came near running down my pony on his big charger, and he swore at me roundly, too.

That night there was a gay supper party in the big dining room at Temple Bow. Nick and I looked on from the gallery window. It was a pretty sight. The long mahogany board reflecting the yellow flames of the candles, and spread with bright silver and shining dishes loaded with dainties, the gentlemen and ladies in brilliant dress, the hurrying servants,—all were of a new and strange world to me. And presently, after the ladies were gone, the gentlemen tossed off their wine and roared over their jokes, and followed into the drawing-room. This I noticed, that only Mr. Harry Riddle sat silent and morose, and that he had drunk more than the others.

"Come, Davy," said Nick to me, "let's go and watch them again."

"But how?" I asked, for the drawing-room windows were up some distance from the ground, and there was no gallery on that side.

"I'll show you," said he, running into the garden. After searching awhile in the dark, he found a ladder the gardener had left against a tree; after much straining, we carried the ladder to the house and set it up under one of the windows of the drawing-room. Then we both clambered cautiously to the top and looked in.

The company were at cards, silent, save for a low remark now and again. The little tables were ranged along by the windows, and it chanced that Mr. Harry Riddle sat so close to us that we could touch him. On his right sat Mr. Darnley, the stout gentleman, and in the other seats two ladies. Between Mr. Riddle and Mr. Darnley was a pile of silver and gold pieces. There was not room for two of us in comfort at the top of the ladder, so I gave place to Nick, and sat on a lower rung. Presently I saw him raise himself, reach in, and duck quickly.

"Feel that," he whispered to me, chuckling and holding out his hand.

It was full of money.

"But that's stealing, Nick," I said, frightened.

"Of course I'll give it back," he whispered indignantly.

Instantly there came loud words and the scraping of chairs within the room, and a woman's scream. I heard Mr. Riddle's voice say thickly, amid the silence that followed:—

"Mr. Darnley, you're a d—d thief, sir."

"You shall answer for this, when you are sober, sir," said Mr. Darnley.

Then there came more scraping of chairs, all the company talking excitedly at once. Nick and I scrambled to the ground, and we did the very worst thing we could possibly have done,—we took the ladder away.

There was little sleep for me that night. I had first of all besought Nick to go up into the drawing-room and give the money back. But some strange obstinacy in him resisted.

"'Twill serve Harry well for what he did to-day," said he.

My next thought was to find Mr. Mason, but he was gone up the river to visit a sick parishioner. I had seen enough of the world to know that gentlemen fought for less than what had occurred in the drawing-room that evening. And though I had neither love nor admiration for Mr. Riddle, and though the stout gentleman was no friend of mine, I cared not to see either of them killed for a prank. But Nick would not listen to me, and went to sleep in the midst of my urgings.

"Davy," said he, pinching me, "do you know what you are?"

"No," said I.

"You're a granny," he said. And that was the last word I could get out of him. But I lay awake a long time, thinking. Breed had whiled away for me one hot morning in Charlestown with an account of the gentry and their doings, many of which he related in an awed whisper that I could not understand. They were wild doings indeed to me. But strangest of all seemed the duels, conducted with a decorum and ceremony as rigorous as the law.

"Did you ever see a duel, Breed?" I had asked.

"Yessah," said Breed, dramatically, rolling the whites of his eyes.

"Where?"

"Whah? Down on de riveh bank at Temple Bow in de ea'ly mo'nin'! Dey mos' commonly fights at de dawn."

Breed had also told me where he was in hiding at the time, and that was what troubled me. Try as I would, I could not remember. It had sounded like *Clam Shell*. That I recalled, and how Breed had looked out at the sword-play through the cracks of the closed shutters, agonized between fear of ghosts within and the drama without. At the first faint light that came into our window I awakened Nick.

"Listen," I said; "do you know a place called *Clam Shell*?"

He turned over, but I punched him persistently until he sat up.

"What the deuce ails you, Davy?" he asked, rubbing his eyes. "Have you nightmare?"

"Do you know a place called *Clam Shell*, down on the river bank, Nick?"

"Why," he replied, "you must be thinking of Cram's Hell."

"What's that?" I asked.

"It's a house that used to belong to Cram, who was an overseer. The niggers hated him, and he was killed in bed by a big black nigger chief from Africa. The niggers won't go near the place. They say it's haunted."

"Get up," said I; "we're going there now."

Nick sprang out of bed and began to get into his clothes.

"Is it a game?" he asked.

"Yes." He was always ready for a game.

We climbed out of the window, and made our way in the mist through the long, wet grass, Nick leading. He took a path through a dark forest swamp, over logs that spanned the stagnant waters, and at length, just as the mist was growing pearly in the light, we came out at a tumble-down house that stood in an open glade by the river's bank.

"What's to do now?" said Nick.

"We must get into the house," I answered. But I confess I didn't care for the looks of it.

Nick stared at me.

"Very good, Davy," he said; "I'll follow where you go."

It was a Saturday morning. Why I recall this I do not know. It has no special significance.

I tried the door. With a groan and a shriek it gave way, disclosing the blackness inside. We started back involuntarily. I looked at Nick, and Nick at me. He was very pale, and so must I have been. But such was the respect we each held for the other's courage that neither dared flinch. And so I walked in, although it seemed as if my shirt was made of needle points and my hair stood on end. The crackings of the old floor were to me like the shots in Charlestown Bay. Our hearts beating wildly, we made our way into a farther room. It was like walking into the beyond.

"Is there a window here?" I asked Nick, my voice sounding like a shout.

"Yes, ahead of us."

Groping for it, I suddenly received a shock that set me reeling. Human nature could stand no more. We both turned tail and ran out of the house as fast as we could, and stood in the wet grass, panting. Then shame came.

"Let's open the window first," I suggested. So we walked around the house and pried the solid shutter from its fastenings. Then, gathering our courage, we went in again at the door. In the dim light let into the farther room we saw a four-poster bed, old and cheap, with ragged curtains. It was this that I had struck in my groping.

"The chief killed Cram there," said Nick, in an awed voice, "in that bed. What do you want to do here, Davy?"

"Wait," I said, though I had as little mind to wait as ever in my life. "Stand here by the window."

We waited there. The mist rose. The sun peeped over the bank of dense green forest and spread rainbow colors on the still waters of the river. Now and again a fish broke, or a great bird swooped down and slit the surface. A far-off snatch of melody came to our ears,— the slaves were going to work. Nothing more. And little by little grave misgivings gnawed at my soul of the wisdom of coming to this place. Doubtless there were many other spots.

"Davy," said Nick, at last, "I'm sorry I took that money. What are we here for?"

The Crossing, Vol. 1

"Hush!" I whispered; "do you hear anything?"

I did, and distinctly. For I had been brought up in the forest.

"I hear voices," he said presently, "coming this way."

They were very clear to me by then. Emerging from the forest path were five gentlemen. The leader, more plainly dressed than the others, carried a leather case. Behind him was the stout figure of Mr. Darnley, his face solemn; and last of all came Mr. Harry Riddle, very pale, but cutting the tops of the long grass with a switch. Nick seized my arm.

"They are going to fight," said he.

"Yes," I replied, "and we are here to stop them, now."

"No, not now," he said, holding me still. "We'll have some more fun out of this yet."

"Fun?" I echoed.

"Yes," he said excitedly. "Leave it to me. I shan't let them fight."

And that instant we changed generals, David giving place to Nicholas.

Mr. Riddle retired with one gentleman to a side of the little patch of grass, and Mr. Darnley and a friend to another. The fifth gentleman took a position halfway between the two, and, opening the leather case, laid it down on the grass, where its contents glistened.

"That's Dr. Ball," whispered Nick. And his voice shook with excitement.

Mr. Riddle stripped off his coat and waistcoat and ruffles, and his sword-belt, and Mr. Darnley did the same. Both gentlemen drew their swords and advanced to the middle of the lawn, and stood opposite one another, with flowing linen shirts open at the throat, and bared heads. They were indeed a contrast. Mr. Riddle, tall and white, with closed lips, glared at his opponent. Mr. Darnley cut a merrier figure,—rotund and flushed, with fat calves and short arms, though his countenance was sober enough. All at once the two were circling their swords in the air, and then Nick had flung open the shutter and leaped through the window, and was running and shouting towards the astonished gentlemen, all of whom wheeled to face him. He jingled as he ran.

"What in the devil's name now?" cried Mr. Riddle, angrily. "Here's this imp again."

Nicholas stopped in front of him, and, thrusting his hand in his breeches pocket, fished out a handful of gold and silver, which he held out to the confounded Mr. Riddle.

"Harry," said he, "here's something of yours I found last night."

"You found?" echoed Mr. Riddle, in a strange voice, amidst a dead silence. "You found where?"

"On the table beside you."

"And where the deuce were you?" Mr. Riddle demanded.

"In the window behind you," said Nick, calmly.

This piece of information, to Mr. Riddle's plain discomfiture, was greeted with a roar of laughter, Mr. Darnley himself laughing loudest. Nor were these gentlemen satisfied with that. They crowded around Mr. Riddle and slapped him on the back, Mr. Darnley joining in with the rest. And presently Mr. Riddle flung away his sword, and laughed, too, giving his hand to Mr. Darnley.

At length Mr. Darnley turned to Nick, who had stood all this while behind them, unmoved.

"My friend," said he, seriously, "such is your regard for human life, you will probably one day be a pirate or an outlaw. This time we've had a laugh. The next time somebody will be weeping. I wish I were your father."

"I wish you were," said Nick.

This took Mr. Darnley's breath. He glanced at the other gentlemen, who returned his look significantly. He laid his hand kindly on the lad's head.

"Nick," said he, "I wish to God I were your father."

After that they all went home, very merry, to breakfast, Nick and I coming after them. Nick was silent until we reached the house.

"Davy," said he, then, "how old are you?"

"Ten," I answered. "How old did you believe me?"

"Eighty," said he.

The next day, being Sunday, we all gathered in the little church to hear Mr. Mason preach. Nick and I sat in the high box pew of the family with Mrs. Temple, who paid not the least attention to the sermon. As for me, the rhythm of it held me in fascination. Mr. Mason had written it out and that afternoon read over this part of it to Nick. The quotation I recall, having since read it many times, and the gist of it was in this wise:—

"And he said unto him, 'What thou wilt have thou wilt have, despite the sin of it. Blessed are the stolid, and thrice cursed he who hath imagination,—for that imagination shall devour him. And in thy life a sin shall be presented unto thee with a great longing. God, who is in heaven, gird thee for that struggle, my son, for it will surely come. That it may be said of you, 'Behold, I have refined thee, but not with silver, I have chosen thee in the furnace of affliction.' Seven days shalt thou wrestle with thy soul; seven nights shall evil haunt thee, and how thou shalt come forth from that struggle no man may know.'"

CHAPTER VI

Man proposes, but God disposes

A WEEK passed, and another Sunday came,—a Sunday so still and hot and moist that steam seemed to rise from the heavy trees,—an idle day for master and servant alike. A hush was in the air, and a presage of we knew not what. It weighed upon my spirits, and even Nick's, and we wandered restlessly under the trees, seeking for distraction.

About two o'clock a black line came on the horizon, and slowly crept higher until it broke into giant, fantastic shapes. Mutterings arose, but the sun shone hot as ever.

"We're to have a hurricane," said Nick. "I wish we might have it and be done with it."

At five the sun went under. I remember that Madame was lolling listless in the garden, daintily arrayed in fine linen, trying to talk to Mr. Mason, when a sound startled us. It was the sound of swift hoof beats on the soft drive.

Mrs. Temple got up, an unusual thing. Perchance she was expecting a message from some of the gentlemen; or else she may well have been tired of Mr. Mason. Nick and I were before her, and, running through the house, arrived at the portico in time to see a negro ride up on a horse covered with lather.

It was the same negro who had fetched me hither from Mr. Lowndes. And when I saw him my heart stood still lest he had brought news of my father.

"What's to do, boy?" cried Nicholas to him.

The boy held in his hand a letter with a great red seal.

"Fo' Mistis Temple," he said, and, looking at me queerly, he took off his cap as he jumped from the horse. Mistress Temple herself having arrived, he handed her the letter. She took it, and broke the seal carelessly.

"Oh," she said, "it's only from Mr. Lowndes. I wonder what he wishes now."

Every moment of her reading was for me an agony, and she read slowly. The last words she spoke aloud:—

"'If you do not wish the lad, send him to me, as Kate is very fond of him.' So Kate is very fond of him," she repeated. And handing the letter to Mr. Mason, she added, "Tell him, Parson."

The words burned into my soul and seared it. And to this day I tremble with anger as I think of them. The scene comes before me: the sky, the darkened portico, and Nicholas running after his mother crying: "Oh, mamma, how could you! How could you!"

Mr. Mason bent over me in compassion, and smoothed my hair.

"David," said he, in a thick voice, "you are a brave boy, David. You will need all your courage now, my son. May God keep your nature sweet!"

He led me gently into the arbor and told me how, under Captain Baskin, the detachment had been ambushed by the Cherokees; and how my father, with Ensign Calhoun and another, had been killed, fighting bravely. The rest of the company had cut their way through and reached the settlements after terrible hardships.

I was left an orphan.

I shall not dwell here on the bitterness of those moments. We have all known sorrows in our lives,—great sorrows. The clergyman was a wise man, and did not strive to comfort me with words. But he sat there under the leaves with his arm about me until a blinding bolt split the blackness of the sky and the thunder rent our ears, and a Caribbean storm broke over Temple Bow with all the fury of the tropics. Then he led me through the drenching rain into the house, nor heeded the wet himself on his Sunday coat.

A great anger stayed me in my sorrow. I would no longer tarry under Mrs. Temple's roof, though the world without were a sea or a desert. The one resolution to escape rose stronger and stronger within me, and I determined neither to eat nor sleep until I had got away. The thought of leaving Nick was heavy indeed; and when he ran to me in the dark hall and threw his arms around me, it needed all my strength to keep from crying aloud.

"Davy," he said passionately, "Davy, you mustn't mind what she says. She never means anything she says—she never cares for anything save her pleasure. You and I will stay here until we are old enough to run away to Kentucky. Davy! Answer me, Davy!"

I could not, try as I would. There were no words that would come with honesty. But I pulled him down on the mahogany settle near the door which led into the back gallery, and there we sat huddled together in silence, while the storm raged furiously outside and the draughts banged the great doors of the house. In the lightning flashes I saw Nick's face, and it haunted me afterwards through many years of wandering. On it was written a sorrow for me greater than my own sorrow. For God had given to this lad every human passion and compassion.

The storm rolled away with the night, and Mammy came through the hall with a candle.

"Whah is you, Marse Nick? Whah is you, honey? You' suppah's ready."

And so we went into our little dining room, but I would not eat. The good old negress brushed her eyes with her apron as she pressed a cake upon me she had made herself, for she had grown fond of me. And presently we went away silently to bed.

It was a long, long time before Nick's breathing told me that he was asleep. He held me tightly clutched to him, and I know that he feared I would leave him. The thought of going broke my heart, but I never once wavered in my resolve, and I lay staring into the darkness, pondering what to do. I thought of good Mr. Lowndes and his wife, and I decided to go to Charlestown. Some of my boyish motives come back to me now: I should be near Nick; and even at that age,—having lived a life of self-reliance,—I thought of gaining an education and of rising to a place of trust. Yes, I would go to Mr. Lowndes, and ask him to let me work for him and so earn my education.

With a heavy spirit I crept out of bed, slowly disengaging Nick's arm lest he should wake. He turned over and sighed in his sleep. Carefully I dressed myself, and after I was dressed I could not refrain from slipping to the bedside to bend over him once again,—for he was the only one in my life with whom I had found true companionship. Then I climbed carefully out of the window, and so down the corner of the house to the ground.

It was starlight, and a waning moon hung in the sky. I made my way through the drive between the black shadows of the forest, and came at length to the big gates at the entrance, locked for the night. A strange thought of their futility struck me as I climbed the rail fence beside them, and pushed on into the main road, the mud sucking under my shoes as I went. As I try now to cast my memory back I can recall no fear, only a vast sense of loneliness, and the very song of it seemed to be sung in never ending refrain by the insects of the night. I had been alone in the mountains before. I have crossed great strips of wilderness since, but always there was love to go back to. Then I was leaving the only being in the world that remained to me.

I must have walked two hours or more before I came to the mire of a cross-road, and there I stood in a quandary of doubt as to which side led to Charlestown.

As I lingered a light began to tremble in the heavens. A cock crew in the distance. I sat down on a fallen log to rest. But presently, as the light grew, I heard shouts which drew nearer and deeper and brought me to my feet in an uncertainty of expectation. Next came the rattling of chains, the scramble of hoofs in the mire, and here was a wagon with a big canvas cover. Beside the straining horses was a great, burly man with a red beard, cracking his long whip, and calling to the horses in a strange tongue. He stopped still beside his panting animals when he saw me, his high boots sunk in the mud.

"Gut morning, poy," he said, wiping his red face with his sleeve; "what you do here?"

"I am going to Charlestown," I answered.

"Ach!" he cried, "dot is pad. Mein poy, he run avay. You are ein gut poy, I know. I vill pay ein gut price to help me vit mein wagon—*ja*."

"Where are you going?" I demanded, with a sudden wavering.

"Up country—pack country. You know der Proad River—yes?"

No, I did not. But a longing came upon me for the old backwoods life, with its freedom and self-reliance, and a hatred for this steaming country of heat and violent storms, and artificiality and pomp. And I had a desire, even at that age, to make my own way in the world.

"What will you give me?" I asked.

At that he put his finger to his nose.

"Thruppence py the day."

I shook my head. He looked at me queerly.

"How old you pe,—twelve, yes?"

Now I had no notion of telling him. So I said: "Is this the Charlestown road?"

"Fourpence!" he cried, "dot is riches."

"I will go for sixpence," I answered.

"Mein Gott!" he cried, "sixpence. Dot is robbery." But seeing me obdurate, he added: "I vill give it, because ein poy I must have. Vat is your name,—Tavid? You are ein sharp poy, Tavid."

And so I went with him.

In writing a biography, the relative value of days and years should hold. There are days which count in space for years, and years for days. I spent the time on the whole happily with this Dutchman, whose name was Hans Köppel. He talked merrily save when he spoke of the war against England, and then contemptuously, for he was a bitter English partisan. And in contrast to this he would dwell for hours on a king he called Friedrich der Grosse, and a war he waged that was a war; and how this mighty king had fought a mighty queen at Rossbach and Leuthen in his own country,—battles that were battles.

"And you were there, Hans?" I asked him once.

"*Ja*," he said, "but I did not stay."

"You ran away?"

"*Ja*," Hans would answer, laughing, "run avay. I love peace, Tavid. Dot is vy I come here, and now," bitterly, "and now ve haf var again once."

I would say nothing; but I must have looked my disapproval, for he went on to explain that in Saxe-Gotha, where he was born, men were made to fight whether they would or no; and they were stolen from their wives at night by soldiers of the great king, or lured away by fair promises.

Travelling with incredible slowness, in due time we came to a county called Orangeburg, where all were Dutchmen like Hans, and very few spoke English. And they all thought like Hans, and loved peace, and hated the Congress. On Sundays, as we lay over at the taverns, these would be filled with a rollicking crowd of fiddlers and dancers, quaintly dressed, the women bringing their children and babies. At such times Hans would be drunk, and I would have to feed the tired horses and mount watch over the cargo. I had many adventures, but none worth the telling here. And at length we came to Hans's farm, in a prettily rolling country on the Broad River. Hans's wife spoke no English at all, nor did the brood of children running about the house. I had small fancy for staying in such a place, and so Hans paid me two crowns for my three weeks' service; I think, with real regret, for labor was scarce in those parts, and though I was young, I knew how to work. And I could at least have guided his plough in the furrow and cared for his cattle.

It was the first money I had earned in my life, and a prouder day than many I have had since.

For the convenience of travellers passing that way, Hans kept a tavern,—if it could have been dignified by such a name. It was in truth merely a log house with shakedowns, and stood across the rude road from his log farmhouse. And he gave me leave to sleep there and to work for my board until I cared to leave. It so chanced that on the second day after my arrival a pack-train came along, guided by a nettlesome old man and a strong, black-haired lass of sixteen or thereabouts. The old man, whose name was Ripley, wore a nut-brown hunting shirt trimmed with red cotton; and he had no sooner slipped the packs from his horses than he began to rail at Hans, who stood looking on.

"You damned Dutchmen be all Tories, and worse," he cried; "you stay here and till your farms while our boys are off in the hill towns fighting Cherokees. I wish the devils had every one of your fat sculps. Polly Ann, water the nags."

Hans replied to this sally with great vigor, lapsing into Dutch. Polly Ann led the scrawny ponies to the trough, but her eyes snapped with merriment as she listened. She was a wonderfully comely lass, despite her loose cotton gown and poke-bonnet and the shoepacks on her feet. She had blue eyes, the whitest, strongest of teeth, and the rosiest of faces.

"Gran'pa hates a Dutchman wuss'n pizen," she said to me. "So do I. We've all been burned out and sculped up river—and they never give us so much as a man or a measure of corn."

I helped her feed the animals, and tether them, and loose their bells for the night, and carry the packs under cover.

"All the boys is gone to join Rutherford and lam the Indians," she continued, "so Gran'pa and I had to go to the settlements. There wahn't any one else. What's your name?" she demanded suddenly.

I told her.

She sat down on a log at the corner of the house, and pulled me down beside her.

"And whar be you from?"

I told her. It was impossible to look into her face and not tell her. She listened eagerly, now with compassion, and now showing her white teeth in amusement. And when I had done, much to my discomfiture, she seized me in her strong arms and kissed me.

"Poor Davy," she cried, "you ain't got a home. You shall come home with us."

Catching me by the hand, she ran like a deer across the road to where her grandfather was still quarrelling violently with Hans, and pulled him backward by the skirts of his hunting shirt. I looked for another and mightier explosion from the old backwoodsman, but to my astonishment he seemed to forget Hans's existence, and turned and smiled on her benevolently.

"Polly Ann," said he, "what be you about now?"

"Gran'pa," said she, "here's Davy Trimble, who's a good boy, and his pa is just killed by the Cherokees along with Baskin, and he wants work and a home, and he's comin' along with us."

"All right, David," answered Mr. Ripley, mildly, "ef Polly Ann says so, you kin come. Whar was you raised?"

I told him on the upper Yadkin.

"You don't tell me," said he. "Did ye ever know Dan'l Boone?"

"I did, indeed, sir," I answered, my face lighting up. "Can you tell me where he is now?"

"He's gone to Kaintuckee, them new settlements, fer good. And ef I wasn't eighty years old, I'd go thar, too."

"I reckon I'll go thar when I'm married," said Polly Ann, and blushed redder than ever. Drawing me to her, she said, "I'll take you, too, Davy."

"When you marry that wuthless Tom McChesney," said her grandfather, testily.

"He's not wuthless," said Polly, hotly. "He's the best man in Rutherford's army. He'll git more sculps then any of 'em,—you see."

"Tavy is ein gut poy," Hans put in, for he had recovered his composure. "I wish much he stay mit me."

As for me, Polly Ann never consulted me on the subject—nor had she need to. I would have followed her to kingdom come, and at the thought of reaching the mountains my heart leaped with joy. We all slept in the one flea-infested, windowless room of the "tavern" that night; and before dawn I was up and untethered the horses, and Polly Ann and I together lifted the two bushels of alum salt on one of the beasts and the ploughshare on the other. By daylight we had left Hans and his farm forever.

I can see the lass now, as she strode along the trace by the flowing river, through sunlight and shadow, straight and supple and strong. Sometimes she sang like a bird, and the forest rang. Sometimes she would make fun of her grandfather or of me; and again she would be silent for an hour at a time, staring ahead, and then I knew she was thinking of that Tom McChesney. She would wake from those reveries with a laugh, and give me a push to send me rolling down a bank.

"What's the matter, Davy? You look as solemn as a wood-owl. What a little wiseacre you be!"

Once I retorted, "You were thinking of that Tom McChesney."

"Ay, that she was, I'll warrant," snapped her grandfather.

Polly Ann replied, with a merry peal of laughter, "You are both jealous of Tom—both of you. But, Davy, when you see him you'll love him as much as I do."

"I'll not," I said sturdily.

"He's a man to look upon—"

"He's a rip-roarer," old man Ripley put in. "Ye're daft about him."

"That I am," said Polly, flushing and subsiding; "but he'll not know it."

As we rose into the more rugged country we passed more than one charred cabin that told its silent story of Indian massacre. Only on the scattered hill farms women and boys and old men were working in the fields, all save the scalawags having gone to join Rutherford. There were plenty of these around the taverns to make eyes at Polly Ann and open love to her, had she allowed them; but she treated them in return to such scathing tirades that they were glad to desist—all but one. He must have been an escaped redemptioner, for he wore jauntily a swanskin three-cornered hat and stained breeches of a fine cloth. He was a bold, vain fellow.

"My beauty," says he, as we sat at supper, "silver and Wedgwood better become you than pewter and a trencher."

"And I reckon a rope would sit better on your neck than a ruff," retorted Polly Ann, while the company shouted with laughter. But he was not the kind to become discomfited.

"I'd give a guinea to see you in silk. But I vow your hair looks better as it is."

"Not so yours," said she, like lightning; "'twould look better to me hanging on the belt of one of them red devils."

In the morning, when he would have lifted the pack of alum salt, Polly Ann gave him a push that sent him sprawling. But she did it in such good nature withal that the fellow mistook her. He scrambled to his feet, flung his arm about her waist, and kissed her. Whereupon I hit him with a sapling, and he staggered and let her go.

"You imp of hell!" he cried, rubbing the bump. He made a vicious dash at me that boded no good, but I slipped behind the hominy block; and Polly Ann, who was like a panther on her feet, dashed at him and gave him a buffet in the cheek that sent him reeling again.

After that we were more devoted friends than ever.

We travelled slowly, day by day, until I saw the mountains lift blue against the western sky, and the sight of them was like home once more. I loved them; and though I thought with sadness of my father, I was on the whole happier with Polly Ann than I had been in the lonely cabin on the Yadkin. Her spirits flagged a little as she drew near home, but old Mr. Ripley's rose.

"There's Burr's," he would say, "and O'Hara's and Williamson's," marking the cabins set amongst the stump-dotted corn-fields. "And thar," sweeping his hand at a blackened heap of logs lying on the stones, "thar's whar Nell Tyler and her baby was sculped."

"Poor Nell," said Polly Ann, the tears coming into her eyes as she turned away.

"And Jim Tyler was killed gittin' to the fort. He can't say I didn't warn him."

"I reckon he'll never say nuthin', now," said Polly Ann.

It was in truth a dismal sight,—the shapeless timbers, the corn, planted with such care, choked with weeds, and the poor utensils of the little family scattered and broken before the door-sill. These same Indians had killed my father; and there surged up in my breast that hatred of the painted race felt by every backwoods boy in my time.

Towards the end of the day the trace led into a beautiful green valley, and in the middle of it was a stream shining in the afternoon sun. Then Polly Ann fell entirely silent. And presently, as the shadows grew purple, we came to a cabin set under some spreading trees on a knoll where a woman sat spinning at the door, three children playing at her feet. She stared at us so earnestly that I looked at Polly Ann, and saw her redden and pale. The children were the first to come shouting at us, and then the woman dropped her wool and ran down the slope straight into Polly Ann's arms. Mr. Ripley halted the horses with a grunt.

The two women drew off and looked into each other's faces. Then Polly Ann dropped her eyes.

"Have ye—?" she said, and stopped.

"No, Polly Ann, not one word sence Tom and his Pa went. What do folks say in the settlements?"

Polly Ann turned up her nose.

"They don't know nuthin' in the settlements," she replied.

"I wrote to Tom and told him you was gone," said the older woman. "I knowed he'd wanter hear."

And she looked meaningly at Polly Ann, who said nothing. The children had been pulling at the girl's skirts, and suddenly she made a dash at them. They scattered, screaming with delight, and she after them.

"Howdy, Mr. Ripley?" said the woman, smiling a little.

"Howdy, Mis' McChesney?" said the old man, shortly.

So this was the mother of Tom, of whom I had heard so much. She was, in truth, a motherly-looking person, her fleshy face creased with strong character.

"Who hev ye brought with ye?" she asked, glancing at me.

"A lad Polly Ann took a shine to in the settlements," said the old man. "Polly Ann! Polly Ann!" he cried sharply, "we'll hev to be gittin' home." And then, as though an afterthought (which it really was not), he added, "How be ye for salt, Mis' McChesney?"

"So-so," said she.

"Wal, I reckon a little might come handy," said he. And to the girl who stood panting beside him, "Polly, give Mis' McChesney some salt."

Polly Ann did, and generously,—the salt they had carried with so much labor threescore and ten miles from the settlements. Then we took our departure, the girl turning for one last look at Tom's mother, and at the cabin where he had dwelt. We were all silent the rest of the way, climbing the slender trail through the forest over the gap into the next valley. For I was jealous of Tom. I am not ashamed to own it now.

In the smoky haze that rises just before night lets her curtain fall, we descended the farther slope, and came to Mr. Ripley's cabin.

CHAPTER VII

IN SIGHT OF THE BLUE WALL ONCE MORE

POLLY ANN lived alone with her grandfather, her father and mother having been killed by Indians some years before. There was that bond between us, had we needed one. Her father had built the cabin, a large one with a loft and a ladder climbing to it, and a sleeping room and a kitchen. The cabin stood on a terrace that nature had levelled, looking across a swift and shallow stream towards the mountains. There was the truck patch, with its yellow squashes and melons, and cabbages and beans, where Polly Ann and I worked through the hot mornings; and the corn patch, with the great stumps of the primeval trees standing in it. All around us the silent forest threw its encircling arms, spreading up the slopes, higher and higher, to crown the crests with the little pines and hemlocks and balsam fir.

There had been no meat save bacon since the McChesneys had left, for of late game had become scarce, and old Mr. Ripley was too feeble to go on the long hunts. So one day, when Polly Ann was gone across the ridge, I took down the long rifle from the buckhorns over the hearth, and the hunting knife and powder-horn and pouch beside it, and trudged up the slope to a game trail I discovered. All day I waited, until the forest light grew gray, when a buck came and stood over the water, raising his head and stamping from time to time. I took aim in the notch of a sapling, brought him down, cleaned and skinned and dragged him into the water, and triumphantly hauled one of his hams down the trail. Polly Ann gave a cry of joy when she saw me.

"Davy," she exclaimed, "little Davy, I reckoned you was gone away from us. Gran'pa, here is Davy back, and he has shot a deer."

"You don't say?" replied Mr. Ripley, surveying me and my booty with a grim smile.

"How could you, Gran'pa?" said Polly Ann, reproachfully.

"Wal," said Mr. Ripley, "the gun was gone, an' Davy. I reckon he ain't sich a little rascal after all."

Polly Ann and I went up the next day, and brought the rest of the buck merrily homeward. After that I became the hunter of the family; but oftener than not I returned tired and empty-handed, and ravenously hungry. Indeed, our chief game was rattlesnakes, which we killed by the dozens in the corn and truck patches.

As Polly Ann and I went about our daily chores, we would talk of Tom McChesney. Often she would sit idle at the hand-mill, a light in her eyes that I would have given kingdoms for. One ever memorable morning, early in the crisp autumn, a grizzled man strode up the trail, and Polly Ann dropped the ear of corn she was husking and stood still, her bosom heaving. It was Mr. McChesney, Tom's father—alone.

"No, Polly Ann," he cried, "there ain't nuthin' happened. We've laid out the hill towns. But the Virginny men wanted a guide, and Tom volunteered, and so he ain't come back with Rutherford's boys."

Polly Ann seized him by the shoulders, and looked him in the face.

"Be you tellin' the truth, Warner McChesney?" she said in a hard voice.

"As God hears me," said Warner McChesney, solemnly. "He sent ye this."

He drew from the bosom of his hunting shirt a soiled piece of birch bark, scrawled over with rude writing. Polly seized it, and flew into the house.

The hickories turned a flaunting yellow, the oaks a copper-red, the leaves crackled on the Catawba vines, and still Tom McChesney did not come. The Cherokees were homeless and houseless and subdued,—their hill towns burned, their corn destroyed, their squaws and children wanderers. One by one the men of the Grape Vine settlement returned to save what they might of their crops, and plough for the next year—Burrs, O'Haras, Williamsons, and Winns. Yes, Tom had gone to guide the Virginia boys. All had tales to tell of his prowess, and how he had saved Rutherford's men from ambush at the risk of his life. To all of which Polly Ann listened with conscious pride, and replied with sallies.

"I reckon I don't care if he never comes back," she would cry. "If he likes the Virginny boys more than me, there be others here I fancy more than him."

Whereupon the informant, if he were not bound in matrimony, would begin to make eyes at Polly Ann. Or, if he were bolder, and went at the wooing in the more demonstrative fashion of the backwoods—Polly Ann had a way of hitting him behind the ear with most surprising effect.

One windy morning when the leaves were kiting over the valley we were getting ready for pounding hominy, when a figure appeared on the trail. Steadying the hood of her sunbonnet with her hand, the girl gazed long and earnestly, and a lump came into my throat at the thought that the comer might be Tom McChesney. Polly Ann sat down at the block again in disgust.

"It's only Chauncey Dike," she said.

"Who's Chauncey Dike?" I asked.

"He reckons he's a buck," was all that Polly Ann vouchsafed.

Chauncey drew near with a strut. He had very long black hair, a new coonskin cap with a long tassel, and a new blue-fringed hunting shirt. What first caught my eye was a couple of withered Indian scalps that hung by their long locks from his girdle. Chauncey Dike was certainly handsome.

"Wal, Polly Ann, are ye tired of hanging out fer Tom?" he cried, when a dozen paces away.

"I wouldn't be if you was the only one left ter choose," Polly Ann retorted.

Chauncey Dike stopped in his tracks and haw-hawed with laughter. But I could see that he was not very much pleased.

"Wal," said he, "I 'low ye won't see Tom very soon. He's gone to Kaintuckee."

"Has he?" said Polly Ann, with brave indifference.

"He met a gal on the trail—a blazin' fine gal," said Chauncey Dike. "She was goin' to Kaintuckee. And Tom—he 'lowed he'd go 'long."

Polly Ann laughed, and fingered the withered pieces of skin at Chauncey's girdle.

"Did Tom give you them sculps?" she asked innocently.

Chauncey drew up stiffly.

"Who? Tom McChesney? I reckon he ain't got none to give. This here's from a big brave at Noewee, whar the Virginny boys was surprised." And he held up the one with the longest tuft. "He'd liked to tomahawked me out'n the briers, but I throwed him fust."

"Shucks," said Polly Ann, pounding the corn, "I reckon you found him dead."

But that night, as we sat before the fading red of the backlog, the old man dozing in his chair, Polly Ann put her hand on mine.

"Davy," she said softly, "do you reckon he's gone to Kaintuckee?"

How could I tell?

The days passed. The wind grew colder, and one subdued dawn we awoke to find that the pines had fantastic white arms, and the stream ran black between white banks. All that day, and for many days after, the snow added silently to the thickness of its blanket, and winter was upon us. It was a long winter and a rare one. Polly Ann sat by the little window of the cabin, spinning the flax into linsey-woolsey. And she made a hunting shirt for her grandfather, and another little one for me which she fitted with careful fingers. But as she spun, her wheel made the only music—for Polly Ann sang no more. Once I came on her as she was thrusting the tattered piece of birch bark into her gown, but she never spoke to me more of Tom McChesney. When, from time to time, the snow melted on the hillsides, I sometimes surprised a deer there and shot him with the heavy rifle. And so the months wore on till spring.

The buds reddened and popped, and the briers grew pink and white. Through the lengthening days we toiled in the truck patch, but always as I bent to my work Polly Ann's face saddened me—it had once been so bright, and it should have been so at this season. Old Mr. Ripley grew querulous and savage and hard to please. In the evening, when my work was done, I often lay on the banks of the stream staring at the high ridge (its ragged edges the setting sun burned a molten gold), and the thought grew on me that I might make my way over the mountains into that land beyond, and find Tom for Polly Ann. I even climbed the watershed to the east as far as the O'Hara farm, to sound that big Irishman about the trail. For he had once gone to Kentucky, to come back with his scalp and little besides. O'Hara, with his brogue, gave me such a terrifying notion of the horrors of the Wilderness Trail that I threw up all thought of following it alone, and so I resolved to wait until I heard of some settlers going over it. But none went from the Grape Vine settlement that spring.

War was a-waging in Kentucky. The great Indian nations were making a frantic effort to drive from their hunting grounds the little bands of settlers there, and these were in sore straits.

So I waited, and gave Polly Ann no hint of my intention.

Sometimes she herself would slip away across the notch to see Mrs. McChesney and the children. She never took me with her on these journeys, but nearly always when she came back at nightfall her eyes would be red, and I knew the two women had been weeping together. There came a certain hot Sunday in July when she went on this errand, and Grandpa Ripley having gone to spend the day at old man Winn's, I was left alone. I remember I sat on the squared log of the door-step, wondering whether, if I were to make my way to Salisbury, I could fall in with a party going across the mountains into Kentucky. And wondering, likewise, what Polly Ann would do without me. I was cleaning the long rifle,—a labor I loved,—when suddenly I looked up, startled to see a man standing in front of me. How he got there I know not. I stared at him. He was a young man, very spare and very burned, with bright red hair and blue eyes that had a kind of laughter in them, and yet were sober. His buckskin hunting shirt was old and stained and frayed by the briers, and his leggins and moccasins were wet from fording the stream. He leaned his chin on the muzzle of his gun.

"Folks live here, sonny?" said he.

I nodded.

"Whar be they?"

"Out," said I.

"Comin' back?" he asked.

"To-night," said I, and began to rub the lock.

"Be they good folks?" said he.

"Yes," I answered.

"Wal," said he, making a move to pass me, "I reckon I'll slip in and take what I've a mind to, and move on."

Now I liked the man's looks very much, but I did not know what he would do. So I got in his way and clutched the gun. It was loaded, but not primed, and I emptied a little powder from the flask in the pan. At that he grinned.

"You're a good boy, sonny," he said. "Do you reckon you could hit me if you shot?"

"Yes," I said. But I knew I could scarcely hold the gun out straight without a rest.

"And do you reckon I could hit you fust?" he asked.

At that I laughed, and he laughed.

"What's your name?"

I told him.

"Who do you love best in all the world?" said he.

It was a queer question. But I told him Polly Ann Ripley.

"Oh!" said he, after a pause. "And what's *she* like?"

"She's beautiful," I said; "she's been very kind to me. She took me home with her from the settlements when I had no place to go. She's good."

"And a sharp tongue, I reckon," said he.

"When people need it," I answered.

"Oh!" said he. And presently, "She's very merry, I'll warrant."

"She used to be, but that's gone by," I said.

The Crossing, Vol. 1

"Gone by!" said he, his voice falling, "is she sick?"

"No," said I, "she's not sick, she's sad."

"Sad?" said he. It was then I noticed that he had a cut across his temple, red and barely healed. "Do you reckon your Polly Ann would give me a little mite to eat?"

This time I jumped up, ran into the house, and got down some cornpone and a leg of turkey. For that was the rule of the border. He took them in great bites, but slowly, and he picked the bones clean.

"I had breakfast yesterday morning," said he, "about forty mile from here."

"And nothing since?" said I, in astonishment.

"Fresh air and water and exercise," said he, and sat down on the grass. He was silent for a long while, and so was I. For a notion had struck me, though I hardly dared to give it voice.

"Are you going away?" I asked at last.

He laughed.

"Why?" said he.

"If you were going to Kaintuckee—" I began, and faltered. For he stared at me very hard.

"Kaintuckee!" he said. "There's a country! But it's full of blood and Injun varmints now. Would you leave Polly Ann and go to Kaintuckee?"

"Are you going?" I said.

"I reckon I am," he said, "as soon as I kin."

"Will you take me?" I asked, breathless. "I—I won't be in your way, and I can walk—and—shoot game."

At that he bent back his head and laughed, which made me redden with anger. Then he turned and looked at me more soberly.

"You're a queer little piece," said he. "Why do you want to go thar?"

"I want to find Tom McChesney for Polly Ann," I said.

He turned away his face.

"A good-for-nothing scamp," said he.

"I have long thought so," I said.

He laughed again. It was a laugh that made me want to join him, had I not been irritated.

"And he's a scamp, you say. And why?"

"Else he would be coming back to Polly Ann."

"Mayhap he couldn't," said the stranger.

"Chauncey Dike said he went off with another girl, into Kaintuckee."

"And what did Polly Ann say to that?" the stranger demanded.

"She asked Chauncey if Tom McChesney gave him the scalps he had on his belt."

At that he laughed in good earnest, and slapped his breech-clouts repeatedly. All at once he stopped, and stared up the ridge.

"Is that Polly Ann?" said he.

I looked, and far up the trail was a speck.

"I reckon it is," I answered, and wondered at his eyesight. "She travels over to see Tom McChesney's Ma once in a while."

He looked at me queerly.

"I reckon I'll go here and sit down, Davy," said he, "so's not to be in the way." And he walked around the corner of the house.

Polly Ann sauntered down the trail slowly, as was her wont after such an occasion. And the man behind the house twice whispered with extreme caution, "How near is she?" before she came up the path.

"Have you been lonesome, Davy?" she said.

"No," said I, "I've had a visitor."

"It's not Chauncey Dike again?" she said. "He doesn't dare show his face here."

"No, it wasn't Chauncey. This man would like to have seen you, Polly Ann. He—" here I braced myself,—"he knew Tom McChesney. He called him a good-for-nothing scamp."

"He did—did he!" said Polly Ann, very low. "I reckon it was good for him I wasn't here."

I grinned.

"What are you laughing at, you little monkey," said Polly Ann, crossly. "'Pon my soul, sometimes I reckon you are a witch."

"Polly Ann," I said, "did I ever do anything but good to you?"

She made a dive at me, and before I could escape caught me in her strong young arms and hugged me.

"You're the best friend I have, little Davy," she cried.

"I reckon that's so," said the stranger, who had risen and was standing at the corner.

Polly Ann looked at him like a frightened doe. And as she stared, uncertain whether to stay or fly, the color surged into her cheeks and mounted to her fair forehead.

"Tom!" she faltered.

"I've come back, Polly Ann," said he. But his voice was not so clear as a while ago.

Then Polly Ann surprised me.

"What made you come back?" said she, as though she didn't care a minkskin. Whereat Mr. McChesney shifted his feet.

"I reckon it was to fetch you, Polly Ann."

"I like that!" cried she. "He's come to fetch me, Davy." That was the first time in months her laugh had sounded natural. "I heerd you fetched one gal acrost the mountains, and now you want to fetch another."

"Polly Ann," says he, "there was a time when you knew a truthful man from a liar."

"That time's past," retorted she; "I reckon all men are liars. What are ye tom-foolin' about here for, Tom McChesney, when yere Ma's breakin' her heart? I wonder ye come back at all."

"Polly Ann," says he, very serious, "I ain't a boaster. But when I think what I come through to git here, I wonder that I come back at all. The folks shut up at Harrod's said it was sure death ter cross the mountains now. I've walked two hundred miles, and fed seven times, and my sculp's as near hangin' on a Red Stick's belt as I ever want it to be."

"Tom McChesney," said Polly Ann, with her hands on her hips and her sunbonnet tilted, "that's the longest speech you ever made in your life."

I declare I lost my temper with Polly Ann then, nor did I blame Tom McChesney for turning on his heel and walking away. But he had gone no distance at all before Polly Ann, with three springs, was at his shoulder.

"Tom!" she said very gently.

He hesitated, stopped, thumped the stock of his gun on the ground, and wheeled. He looked at her doubtingly, and her eyes fell to the ground.

"Tom McChesney," said she, "you're a born fool with wimmen."

"Thank God for that," said he, his eyes devouring her.

"Ay," said she. And then, "You want me to go to Kaintuckee with you?"

"That's what I come for," he stammered, his assurance all run away again.

"I'll go," she answered, so gently that her words were all but blown away by the summer wind. He laid his rifle against a stump at the edge of the corn-field, but she bounded clear of him. Then she stood, panting, her eyes sparkling.

"I'll go," she said, raising her finger, "I'll go for one thing."

"What's that?" he demanded.

"That you'll take Davy along with us."

This time Tom had her, struggling like a wild thing in his arms, and kissing her black hair madly. As for me, I might have been in the next settlement for all they cared. And then Polly Ann, as red as a holly berry, broke away from him and ran to me, caught me up, and hid her face in my shoulder. Tom McChesney stood looking at us, grinning, and that day I ceased to hate him.

"There's no devil ef I don't take him, Polly Ann," said he. "Why, he was a-goin' to Kaintuckee ter find me for you."

"What?" said she, raising her head.

"That's what he told me afore he knew who I was. He wanted to know ef I'd fetch him thar."

"Little Davy!" cried Polly Ann.

The last I saw of them that day they were going off up the trace towards his mother's, Polly Ann keeping ahead of him and just out of his reach. And I was very, very happy. For Tom McChesney had come back at last, and Polly Ann was herself once more.

As long as I live I shall never forget Polly Ann's wedding.

She was all for delay, and such a bunch of coquetry as I have never seen. She raised one objection after another; but Tom was a firm man, and his late experiences in the wilderness had made him impatient of trifling. He had promised the Kentucky settlers, fighting for their lives in their blockhouses, that he would come back again. And a resolute man who was a good shot was sorely missed in the country in those days.

It was not the thousand dangers and hardships of the journey across the Wilderness Trail that frightened Polly Ann. Not she. Nor would she listen to Tom when he implored her to let him return alone, to come back for her when the redskins had got over the first furies of their hatred. As for me, the thought of going with them into that promised land was like wine. Wondering what the place was like, I could not sleep of nights.

"Ain't you afeerd to go, Davy?" said Tom to me.

"You promised Polly Ann to take me," said I, indignantly.

"Davy," said he, "you ain't over handsome. 'Twouldn't improve yere looks to be bald. They hev a way of takin' yere ha'r. Better stay behind with Gran'pa Ripley till I kin fetch ye both."

"Tom," said Polly Ann, "you kin just go back alone if you don't take Davy."

So one of the Winn boys agreed to come over to stay with old Mr. Ripley until quieter times.

The preparations for the wedding went on apace that week. I had not thought that the Grape Vine settlement held so many people. And they came from other settlements, too, for news spread quickly in that country, despite the distances. Tom McChesney was plainly a favorite with the men who had marched with Rutherford. All the week they came, loaded with offerings, turkeys and venison and pork and bear meat—greatest delicacy of all—until the cool spring was filled for the feast. From thirty miles down the Broad, a gaunt Baptist preacher on a fat white pony arrived the night before. He had been sent for to tie the knot.

Polly Ann's wedding-day dawned bright and fair, and long before the sun glistened on the corn tassels we were up and clearing out the big room. The fiddlers came first—a merry lot. And then the guests from afar began to arrive. Some of them had travelled half the night. The bridegroom's friends were assembling at the McChesney place. At last, when the sun was over the stream, rose such Indian war-whoops and shots from the ridge trail as made me think the redskins were upon us. The shouts and hurrahs grew louder and louder, the quickening thud of horses' hoofs was heard in the woods, and there burst into sight of the assembly by the truck patch two wild figures on crazed horses charging down the path towards the house. We scattered to right and left. On they came, leaping logs and brush and ditches, until one of them pulled up, yelling madly, at the very door, the foam-flecked sides of his horse moving with quick heaves.

It was Chauncey Dike, and he had won the race for the bottle of "Black Betty,"—Chauncey Dike, his long, black hair shining with bear's oil. Amid the cheers of the bride's friends he leaped from his saddle, mounted a stump and, flapping his arms, crowed in victory. Before he had done the vanguard of the groom's friends were upon us, pell-mell, all in the finest of backwoods regalia,—new hunting shirts, trimmed with bits of color, and all armed to the teeth—scalping knife, tomahawk, and all. Nor had Chauncey Dike forgotten the scalp of the brave who leaped at him out of the briers at Neowee.

Polly Ann was radiant in a white linen gown, woven and sewed by her own hands. It was not such a gown as Mrs. Temple, Nick's mother, would have worn, and yet she was to me an hundred times more beautiful than that lady in all her silks. Peeping out from under it were the little blue-beaded moccasins which Tom himself had brought across the mountains in the bosom of his hunting shirt. Polly Ann was radiant, and yet at times so rapturously shy that when the preacher announced himself ready to tie the knot she ran into the house and hid in the cupboard—for Polly Ann was a child of nature. Thence, coloring like a wild rose, she was dragged by a boisterous bevy of girls in linsey-woolsey to the spreading maple of the forest that stood on the high bank over the stream. The assembly fell solemn, and not a sound was heard save the breathing of Nature in the heyday of her time. And though I was happy, the sobs rose in my throat. There stood Polly Ann, as white now as the bleached linen she wore, and Tom McChesney, tall and spare and broad, as strong a figure of a man as ever I laid eyes on. God had truly made that couple for wedlock in His leafy temple.

The deep-toned words of the preacher in prayer broke the stillness. They were made man and wife. And then began a day of merriment, of unrestraint, such as the backwoods alone knows. The feast was spread out in the long grass under the trees—sides of venison, bear meat, corn-pone fresh baked by Mrs. McChesney and Polly Ann herself, and all the vegetables in the patch. There was no stint, either, of maple beer and rum and "Black Betty," and toasts to the bride and groom amidst gusts of laughter "that they might populate Kaintuckee." And Polly Ann would have it that I should sit by her side under the maple.

The fiddlers played, and there were foot races and shooting matches. Ay, and wrestling matches in the severe manner of the backwoods between the young bucks, more than one of which might have ended seriously were it not for the high humor of the crowd. Tom McChesney himself was in most of them, a hot favorite. By a trick he had learned in the Indian country he threw Chauncey Dike (no mean adversary) so hard that the backwoods dandy lay for a moment in sleep. Contrary to the custom of many, Tom was not in the habit of crowing on such occasions, nor did he even smile as he helped Chauncey to his feet. But Polly Ann knew, and I knew, that he was thinking of what Chauncey had said to her.

So the long summer afternoon wore away into twilight, and the sun fell behind the blue ridges we were to cross. Pine knots were lighted in the big room, the fiddlers set to again, and then came jigs and three and four handed reels that made the puncheons rattle,—chicken-flutter and cut-the-buckle,—and Polly Ann was the leader now, the young men flinging the girls from fireplace to window in the reels, and back again; and when, panting and perspiring, the lass was too tired to stand longer, she dropped into the hospitable lap of the nearest buck who was perched on the bench along the wall awaiting his chance. For so it went in the backwoods in those days, and long after, and no harm in it that ever I could see.

Well, suddenly, as if by concert, the music stopped, and a shout of laughter rang under the beams as Polly Ann flew out of the door with the girls after her, as swift of foot as she. They dragged her, a struggling captive, to the bride-chamber which made the other end of the house, and when they emerged, blushing and giggling and subdued, the fun began with Tom McChesney. He gave the young men a pretty fight indeed, and long before they had him conquered the elder guests had made their escape through door and window.

All night the reels and jigs went on, and the feasting and drinking too. In the fine rain that came at dawn to hide the crests, the company rode wearily homeward through the notches.

CHAPTER VIII

THE NOLLICHUCKY TRACE

Some to endure, and many to quail,
Some to conquer, and many to fail,
Toiling over the Wilderness Trail.

As long as I live I shall never forget the morning we started on our journey across the Blue Wall. Before the sun chased away the filmy veil of mist from the brooks in the valley, the McChesneys, father, mother, and children, were gathered to see us depart. And as they helped us to tighten the packsaddles Tom himself had made from chosen tree-forks, they did not cease lamenting that we were going to certain death. Our scrawny horses splashed across the stream, and we turned to see a gaunt and lonely figure standing apart against the sun, stern and sorrowful. We waved our hands, and set our faces towards Kaintuckee.

Tom walked ahead, rifle on shoulder, then Polly Ann; and lastly I drove the two shaggy ponies, the instruments of husbandry we had been able to gather awry on their packs,—a scythe, a spade, and a hoe. I triumphantly carried the axe.

It was not long before we were in the wilderness, shut in by mountain crags, and presently Polly Ann forgot her sorrows in the perils of the trace. Choked by briers and grapevines, blocked by sliding stones and earth, it rose and rose through the heat and burden of the day until it lost itself in the open heights. As the sun was wearing down to the western ridges the mischievous sorrel mare turned her pack on a sapling, and one of the precious bags burst. In an instant we were on our knees gathering the golden meal in our hands. Polly Ann baked journeycakes on a hot stone from what we saved under the shiny ivy leaves, and scarce had I spancelled the horses ere Tom returned with a fat turkey he had shot.

"Was there ever sech a wedding journey!" said Polly Ann, as we sat about the fire, for the mountain air was chill. "And Tom and Davy as grave as parsons. Ye'd guess one of you was Rutherford himself, and the other Mr. Boone."

No wonder he was grave. I little realized then the task he had set himself, to pilot a woman and a lad into a country haunted by frenzied savages, when single men feared to go this season. But now he smiled, and patted Polly Ann's brown hand.

"It's one of yer own choosing, lass," said he.

"Of my own choosing!" cried she. "Come, Davy, we'll go back to Grandpa."

Tom grinned.

"I reckon the redskins won't bother us till we git by the Nollichucky and Watauga settlements," he said.

"The redskins!" said Polly Ann, indignant; "I reckon if one of 'em did git me he'd kiss me once in a while."

Whereupon Tom, looking more sheepish still, tried to kiss her, and failed ignominiously, for she vanished into the dark woods.

"If a redskin got you here," said Tom, when she had slipped back, "he'd fetch you to Nick-a-jack Cave."

"What's that?" she demanded.

"Where all the red and white and yellow scalawags over the mountains is gathered," he answered. And he told of a deep gorge between towering mountains where a great river cried angrily, of a black cave out of which a black stream ran, where a man could paddle a dugout for miles into the rock. The river was the Tennessee, and the place the resort of the Chickamauga bandits, pirates of the mountains, outcasts of all nations. And Dragging Canoe was their chief.

It was on the whole a merry journey, the first part of it, if a rough one. Often Polly Ann would draw me to her and whisper: "We'll hold out, Davy. He'll never know." When the truth was that the big fellow was going at half his pace on our account. He told us there was no fear of redskins here, yet, when the scream of a painter or the hoot of an owl stirred me from my exhausted slumber, I caught sight of him with his back to a tree, staring into the forest, his rifle at his side. The day was dawning.

"Turn about's fair," I expostulated.

"Ye'll need yere sleep, Davy," said he, "or ye'll never grow any bigger."

"I thought Kaintuckee was to the west," I said, "and you're making north." For I had observed him day after day. We had left the trails. Sometimes he climbed tree, and again he sent me to the upper branches, whence I surveyed a sea of tree-tops waving in the wind, and looked onward to where a green velvet hollow lay nestling on the western side of a saddle-backed ridge.

"North!" said Tom to Polly Ann, laughing. "The little devil will beat me at woodcraft soon. Ay, north, Davy. I'm hunting for the Nollichucky Trace that leads to the Watauga settlement."

It was wonderful to me how he chose his way through the mountains. Once in a while we caught sight of a yellow blaze in a tree, made by himself scarce a month gone, when he came southward alone to fetch Polly Ann. Again, the tired roan shied back from the bleached bones of a traveller, picked clean by wolves. At sundown, when we loosed our exhausted horses to graze on the wet grass by the streams, Tom would go off to look for a deer or turkey, and often not come back to us until long after darkness had fallen.

"Davy'll take care of you, Polly Ann," he would say as he left us.

And she would smile at him bravely and say, "I reckon I kin look out for Davy awhile yet."

But when he was gone, and the crooning stillness set in, broken only by the many sounds of the night, we would sit huddled together by the fire. It was dread for him she felt, not for herself. And in both our minds rose red images of hideous foes skulking behind his brave form as he trod the forest floor. Polly Ann was not the woman to whimper.

And yet I have but dim recollections of this journey. It was no hardship to a lad brought up in woodcraft. Fear of the Indians, like a dog shivering with the cold, was a deadened pain on the border.

Strangely enough it was I who chanced upon the Nollichucky Trace, which follows the meanderings of that river northward through the great Smoky Mountains. It was made long ago by the Southern Indians as they threaded their way to the Hunting Lands of Kaintuckee, and shared now by Indian traders. The path was redolent with odors, and bright with mountain shrubs and flowers,—the pink laurel bush, the shining rhododendron, and the grape and plum and wild crab. The clear notes of the mountain birds were in our ears by day, and the music of the water falling over the ledges, mingled with that of the leaves rustling in the wind, lulled us to sleep at night. High above us, as we descended, the gap, from naked crag to timber-covered ridge, was spanned by the eagle's flight. And virgin valleys, where future generations were to be born, spread out and narrowed again,—valleys with a deep carpet of cane and grass, where the deer and elk and bear fed unmolested.

It was perchance the next evening that my eyes fell upon a sight which is one of the wonders of my boyish memories. The trail slipped to the edge of a precipice, and at our feet the valley widened. Planted amidst giant trees, on a shining green lawn that ran down to the racing Nollichucky was the strangest house it has ever been my lot to see—of no shape, of huge size, and built of logs, one wing hitched to another by "dog alleys" (as we called them); and from its wide stone chimneys the pearly smoke rose upward in the still air through the poplar branches. Beyond it a setting sun gilded the corn-fields, and horses and cattle dotted the pastures. We stood for a while staring at this oasis in the wilderness, and to my boyish fancy it was a fitting introduction to a delectable land.

"Glory be to heaven!" exclaimed Polly Ann.

"It's Nollichucky Jack's house," said Tom.

"And who may he be?" said she.

"Who may he be!" cried Tom; "Captain John Sevier, king of the border, and I reckon the best man to sweep out redskins in the Watauga settlements."

"Do you know him?" said she.

"I was chose as one of his scouts when we fired the Cherokee hill towns last summer," said Tom, with pride. "Thar was blood and thunder for ye! We went down the Great War-path which lies below us, and when we was through there wasn't a corn-shuck or a wigwam or a war post left. We didn't harm the squaws nor the children, but there warn't no prisoners took. When Nollichucky Jack strikes I reckon it's more like a thunderbolt nor anything else."

"Do you think he's at home, Tom?" I asked, fearful that I should not see this celebrated person.

"We'll soon l'arn," said he, as we descended. "I heerd he was agoin' to punish them Chickamauga robbers by Nick-a-jack."

Just then we heard a prodigious barking, and a dozen hounds came charging down the path at our horses' legs, the roan shying into the truck patch. A man's voice, deep, clear, compelling, was heard calling:—

"Vi! Flora! Ripper!"

I saw him coming from the porch of the house, a tall slim figure in a hunting shirt—that fitted to perfection—and cavalry boots. His face, his carriage, his quick movement and stride filled my notion of a hero, and my instinct told me he was a gentleman born.

"Why, bless my soul, it's Tom McChesney!" he cried, ten paces away, while Tom grinned with pleasure at the recognition. "But what have you here?"

"A wife," said Tom, standing on one foot.

Captain Sevier fixed his dark blue eyes on Polly Ann with approbation, and he bowed to her very gracefully.

"Where are you going, Ma'am, may I ask?" he said.

"To Kaintuckee," said Polly Ann.

"To Kaintuckee!" cried Captain Sevier, turning to Tom. "Egad, then, you've no right to a wife,—and to such a wife," and he glanced again at Polly Ann. "Why, McChesney, you never struck me as a rash man. Have you lost your senses, to take a woman into Kentucky this year?"

"So the forts be still in trouble?" said Tom.

"Trouble?" cried Mr. Sevier, with a quick fling of his whip at an unruly hound, "Harrodstown, Boonesboro, Logan's Fort at St. Asaph's,—they don't dare stick their noses outside the stockades. The Indians have swarmed into Kentucky like red ants, I tell you. Ten days ago, when I was in the Holston settlements, Major Ben Logan came in. His fort had been shut up since May, they were out of powder and lead, and somebody had to come. How did he come? As the wolf lopes, nay, as the crow flies over crag and ford, Cumberland, Clinch, and all, forty miles a day for five days, and never saw a trace—for the war parties were watching the Wilderness Road." And he swung again towards Polly Ann. "You'll not go to Kaintuckee, ma'am; you'll stay here with us until the redskins are beaten off there. He may go if he likes."

"I reckon we didn't come this far to give out, Captain Sevier," said she.

"You don't look to be the kind to give out, Mrs. McChesney," said he. "And yet it may not be a matter of giving out," he added more soberly. This mixture of heartiness and gravity seemed to sit well on him. "Surely you have been enterprising, Tom. Where in the name of the Continental Congress did you get the lad?"

"I married him along with Polly Ann," said Tom. "That was the bargain, and I reckon he was worth it."

"I'd take a dozen to get her," declared Mr. Sevier, while Polly Ann blushed. "Well, well, supper's waiting us, and cider and applejack, for we don't get a wedding party every day. Some gentlemen are here whose word may have more weight and whose attractions may be greater than mine."

He whistled to a negro lad, who took our horses, and led us through the court-yard and the house to the lawn at the far side of it. A rude table was set there under a great tree, and around it three gentlemen were talking. My memory of all of them is more vivid than it might be were their names not household words in the Western country. Captain Sevier startled them.

"My friends," said he, "if you have despatches for Kaintuckee, I pray you get them ready over night."

They looked up at him, one sternly, the other two gravely.

"What the devil do you mean, Sevier?" said the stern one.

"That my friend, Tom McChesney, is going there with his wife, unless we can stop him," said Sevier.

"Stop him!" thundered the stern gentleman, kicking back his chair and straightening up to what seemed to me a colossal height. I stared at him, boylike. He had long, iron-gray hair and a creased, fleshy face and sunken eyes. He looked as if he might stop anybody as he turned upon Tom. "Who the devil is this Tom McChesney?" he demanded.

Sevier laughed.

"The best scout I ever laid eyes on," said he. "A deadly man with a Deckard, an unerring man at choosing a wife" (and he bowed to the reddening Polly Ann), "and a fool to run the risk of losing her."

"Tut, tut," said the iron gentleman, who was the famous Captain Evan Shelby of King's Meadows, "he'll leave her here in our settlements while he helps us fight Dragging Canoe and his Chickamauga pirates."

"If he leaves me," said Polly Ann, her eyes flashing, "that's an end to the bargain. He'll never find me more."

Captain Sevier laughed again.

"There's spirit for you," he cried, slapping his whip against his boot.

At this another gentleman stood up, a younger counterpart of the first, only he towered higher and his shoulders were broader. He had a big-featured face, and pleasant eyes—that twinkled now—sunken in, with fleshy creases at the corners.

"Tom McChesney," said he, "don't mind my father. If any man besides Logan can get inside the forts, you can. Do you remember me?"

"I reckon I do, Mr. Isaac Shelby," said Tom, putting a big hand into Mr. Shelby's bigger one. "I reckon I won't soon forget how you stepped out of ranks and tuk command when the boys was runnin', and turned the tide."

He looked like the man to step out of ranks and take command.

"Pish!" said Mr. Isaac Shelby, blushing like a girl; "where would I have been if you and Moore and Findley and the rest hadn't stood 'em off till we turned round?"

By this time the third gentleman had drawn my attention. Not by anything he said, for he remained silent, sitting with his dark brown head bent forward, quietly gazing at the scene from under his brows. The instant he spoke they turned towards him. He was perhaps forty, and broad-shouldered, not so tall as Mr. Sevier.

"Why do you go to Kaintuckee, McChesney?" he asked.

"I give my word to Mr. Harrod and Mr. Clark to come back, Mr. Robertson," said Tom.

"And the wife? If you take her, you run a great risk of losing her."

"And if he leaves me," said Polly Ann, flinging her head, "he will lose me sure."

The others laughed, but Mr. Robertson merely smiled.

"Faith," cried Captain Sevier, "if those I met coming back helter-skelter over the Wilderness Trace had been of that stripe, they'd have more men in the forts now."

With that the Captain called for supper to be served where we sat. He was a widower, with lads somewhere near my own age, and I recall being shown about the place by them. And later, when the fireflies glowed and the Nollichucky sang in the darkness, we listened to the talk of the war of the year gone by. I needed not to be told that before me were the renowned leaders of the Watauga settlements. My hero worship cried it aloud within me. These captains dwelt on the border-land of mystery, conquered the wilderness, and drove before them its savage tribes by their might. When they spoke of the Cherokees and told how that same Stuart—the companion of Cameron—was urging them to war against our people, a fierce anger blazed within me. For the Cherokees had killed my father.

I remember the men,—scarcely what they said: Evan Shelby's words, like heavy blows on an anvil; Isaac Shelby's, none the less forceful; James Robertson compelling his listeners by some strange power. He was perchance the strongest man there, though none of us guessed, after ruling that region, that he was to repeat untold hardships to found and rear another settlement farther west. But best I loved to hear Captain Sevier, whose talk lacked not force, but had a daring, a humor, a lightness of touch, that seemed more in keeping with that world I had left behind me in Charlestown. Him I loved, and at length I solved the puzzle. To me he was Nick Temple grown to manhood.

I slept in the room with Captain Sevier's boys, and one window of it was of paper smeared with bear's grease, through which the sunlight came all bleared and yellow in the morning. I had a boy's interest in affairs, and I remember being told that the gentlemen were met here to discuss the treaty between themselves and the great Oconostota, chief of the Cherokees, and also to consider the policy of punishing once for all Dragging Canoe and his bandits at Chickamauga.

As we sat at breakfast under the trees, these gentlemen generously dropped their own business to counsel Tom, and I observed with pride that he had gained their regard during the last year's war. Shelby's threats and Robertson's warnings and Sevier's exhortations having no effect upon his determination to proceed to Kentucky, they began to advise him how to go, and he sat silent while they talked. And finally, when they asked him, he spoke of making through Carter's Valley for Cumberland Gap and the Wilderness Trail.

"Egad," cried Captain Sevier, "I have so many times found the boldest plan the safest that I have become a coward that way. What do you say to it, Mr. Robertson?"

Mr. Robertson leaned his square shoulders over the table.

"He may fall in with a party going over," he answered, without looking up.

Polly Ann looked at Tom as if to say that the whole Continental Army could not give her as much protection.

We left that hospitable place about nine o'clock, Mr. Robertson having written a letter to Colonel Daniel Boone,—shut up in the fort at Boonesboro,—should we be so fortunate as to reach Kaintuckee: and another to a young gentleman by the name of George Rogers Clark, apparently a leader there. Captain Sevier bowed over Polly Ann's hand as if she were a great lady, and wished her a happy honeymoon, and me he patted on the head and called a brave lad. And soon we had passed beyond the corn-field into the Wilderness again.

Our way was down the Nollichucky, past the great bend of it below Lick Creek, and so to the Great War-path, the trail by which countless parties of red marauders had travelled north and south. It led, indeed, northeast between the mountain ranges. Although we kept a watch by day and night, we saw no sign of Dragging Canoe or his men, and at length we forded the Holston and came to the scattered settlement in Carter's Valley.

I have since racked my brain to remember at whose cabin we stopped there. He was a rough backwoodsman with a wife and a horde of children. But I recall that a great rain came out of the mountains and down the valley. We were counting over the powder gourds in our packs, when there burst in at the door as wild a man as has ever been my lot to see. His brown beard was grown like a bramble patch, his eye had a violet light, and his hunting shirt was in tatters. He was thin to gauntness, ate ravenously of the food that was set before him, and throwing off his soaked moccasins, he spread his scalded feet to the blaze, and the steaming odor of drying leather filled the room.

"Whar be ye from?" asked Tom.

For answer the man bared his arm, then his shoulder, and two angry scars, long and red, revealed themselves, and around his wrists were deep gouges where he had been bound.

"They killed Sue," he cried, "sculped her afore my very eyes. And they chopped my boy outen the hickory withes and carried him to the Creek Nation. At a place where there was a standin' stone I broke loose from three of 'em and come here over the mountains, and I ain't had nothin', stranger, but berries and chainey brier-root for ten days. God damn 'em!" he cried, standing up and tottering with the pain in his feet, "if I can get a Deckard—"

"Will you go back?" said Tom.

"Go back!" he shouted, "I'll go back and fight 'em while I have blood in my body."

He fell into a bunk, but his sorrow haunted him even in his troubled sleep, and his moans awed us as we listened. The next day he told us his story with more calmness. It was horrible indeed, and might well have frightened a less courageous woman than Polly Ann. Imploring her not to go, he became wild again, and brought tears to her eyes when he spoke of his own wife. "They tomahawked her, ma'am, because she could not walk, and the baby beside her, and I standing by with my arms tied."

As long as I live I shall never forget that scene, and how Tom pleaded with Polly Ann to stay behind, but she would not listen to him.

"You're going, Tom?" she said.

"Yes," he answered, turning away, "I gave 'em my word."

"And your word to me?" said Polly Ann.

He did not answer.

We fixed on a Saturday to start, to give the horses time to rest, and in the hope that we might hear of some relief party going over the Gap. On Thursday Tom made a trip to the store in the valley, and came back with a Deckard rifle he had bought for the stranger, whose name was Weldon. There was no news from Kaintuckee, but the Carter's Valley settlers seemed to think that matters were better there. It was that same night, I believe, that two men arrived from Fort Chiswell. One, whose name was Cutcheon, was a little man with a short forehead and a bad eye, and he wore a weather-beaten blue coat of military cut. The second was a big, light-colored, fleshy man, and a loud talker. He wore a hunting shirt and leggings. They were both the worse for rum they had had on the road, the big man talking very loud and boastfully.

"Afeard to go to Kaintuckee!" said he. "I've met a parcel o' cowards on the road, turned back. There ain't nothin' to be afeard of, eh, stranger?" he added, to Tom, who paid no manner of attention to him. The small man scarce opened his mouth, but sat with his head bowed forward on his breast when he was not drinking. We passed a dismal, crowded night in the room with such companions. When they heard that we were to go over the mountains, nothing would satisfy the big man but to go with us.

"Come, stranger," said he to Tom, "two good rifles such as we is ain't to be throwed away."

"Why do you want to go over?" asked Tom. "Be ye a Tory?" he demanded suspiciously.

"Why do you go over?" retorted Riley, for that was his name. "I reckon I'm no more of a Tory than you."

"Whar did ye come from?" said Tom.

"Chiswell's mines, taking out lead for the army o' Congress. But there ain't excitement enough in it."

"And you?" said Tom, turning to Cutcheon and eying his military coat.

"I got tired of their damned discipline," the man answered surlily. He was a deserter.

"Look you," said Tom, sternly, "if you come, what I say is law."

Such was the sacrifice we were put to by our need of company. But in those days a man was a man, and scarce enough on the Wilderness Trail in that year of '77. So we started away from Carter's Valley on a bright Saturday morning, the grass glistening after a week's rain, the road sodden, and the smell of the summer earth heavy. Tom and Weldon walked ahead, driving the two horses, followed by Cutcheon, his head dropped between his shoulders. The big man, Riley, regaled Polly Ann.

"My pluck is," said he, "my pluck is to give a redskin no chance. Shoot 'em down like hogs. It takes a good un to stalk me, Ma'am. Up on the Kanawha I've had hand-to-hand fights with 'em, and made 'em cry quits."

"Law!" exclaimed Polly Ann, nudging me, "it was a lucky thing we run into you in the valley."

But presently we left the road and took a mountain trail,—as stiff a climb as we had yet had. Polly Ann went up it like a bird, talking all the while to Riley, who blew like a bellows. For once he was silent.

We spent two, perchance three, days climbing and descending and fording. At night Tom would suffer none to watch save Weldon and himself, not trusting Riley or Cutcheon. And the rascals were well content to sleep. At length we came to a cabin on a creek, the corn between the stumps around it choked with weeds, and no sign of smoke in the chimney. Behind it slanted up, in giant steps, a forest-clad hill of a thousand feet, and in front of it the stream was dammed and lined with cane.

"Who keeps house?" cried Tom, at the threshold.

He pushed back the door, fashioned in one great slab from a forest tree. His welcome was an angry whir, and a huge yellow rattler lay coiled within, his head reared to strike. Polly Ann leaned back.

"Mercy," she cried, "that's a bad sign."

But Tom killed the snake, and we made ready to use the cabin that night and the next day. For the horses were to be rested and meat was to be got, as we could not use our guns so freely on the far side of Cumberland Gap. In the morning, before he and Weldon left, Tom took me around the end of the cabin.

"Davy," said he, "I don't trust these rascals. Kin you shoot a pistol?"

I reckoned I could.

He had taken one out of the pack he had got from Captain Sevier and pushed it between the logs where the clay had fallen out. "If they try anything," said he, "shoot 'em. And don't be afeard of killing 'em." He patted me on the back, and went off up the slope with Weldon. Polly Ann and I stood watching them until they were out of sight.

About eleven o'clock Riley and Cutcheon moved off to the edge of a cane-brake near the water, and sat there for a while, talking in low tones. The horses were belled and spancelled near by, feeding on the cane and wild grass, and Polly Ann was cooking journey-cakes on a stone.

"What makes you so sober, Davy?" she said.

I didn't answer.

"Davy," she cried, "be happy while you're young. 'Tis a fine day, and Kaintuckee's over yonder." She picked up her skirts and sang:—

"First upon the heeltap,
Then upon the toe."

The men by the cane-brake turned and came towards us.

"Ye're happy to-day, Mis' McChesney," said Riley.

"Why shouldn't I be?" said Polly Ann; "we're all a-goin' to Kaintuckee."

"We're a-goin' back to Cyarter's Valley," said Riley, in his blustering way. "This here ain't as excitin' as I thought. I reckon there ain't no redskins nohow."

"What!" cried Polly Ann, in loud scorn, "ye're a-goin' to desert? There'll be redskins enough by and by, I'll warrant ye."

"How'd you like to come along of us," says Riley; "that ain't any place for wimmen, over yonder."

"Along of you!" cried Polly Ann, with flashing eyes. "Do you hear that, Davy?"

I did. Meanwhile the man Cutcheon was slowly walking towards her. It took scarce a second for me to make up my mind. I slipped around the corner of the house, seized the pistol, primed it with a trembling hand, and came back to behold Polly Ann, with flaming cheeks, facing them. They did not so much as glance at me. Riley held a little back of the two, being the coward. But Cutcheon stood ready, like a wolf.

I did not wait for him to spring, but, taking the best aim I could with my two hands, fired. With a curse that echoed in the crags, he threw up his arms and fell forward, writhing, on the turf.

"Run for the cabin, Polly Ann," I shouted, "and bar the door."

There was no need. For an instant Riley wavered, and then fled to the cane.

Polly Ann and I went to the man on the ground, and turned him over. His eyes slid upwards. There was a bloody froth on his lips.

"Davy!" cried she, awestricken, "Davy, ye've killed him!"

I grew dizzy and sick at the thought, but she caught me and held me to her. Presently we sat down on the door log, gazing at the corpse. Then I began to reflect, and took out my powder gourd and loaded the pistol.

"What are ye a-doing?" she said.

"In case the other one comes back," said I.

"Pooh," said Polly Ann, "*he'll* not come back." Which was true. I have never laid eyes on Riley to this day.

"I reckon we'd better fetch it out of the sun," said she, after a while. And so we dragged it under an oak, covered the face, and left it.

He was the first man I ever killed, and the business by no means came natural to me. And that day the journey-cakes which Polly Ann had made were untasted by us both. The afternoon dragged interminably. Try as we would, we could not get out of our minds the Thing that lay under the oak.

It was near sundown when Tom and Weldon appeared on the mountain side carrying a buck between them. Tom glanced from one to the other of us keenly. He was very quick to divine.

"Whar be they?" said he.

"Show him, Davy," said Polly Ann.

I took him over to the oak, and Polly Ann told him the story. He gave me one look, I remember, and there was more of gratitude in it than in a thousand words. Then he seized a piece of cold cake from the stone.

"Which trace did he take?" he demanded of me.

But Polly Ann hung on his shoulder.

"Tom, Tom!" she cried, "you beant goin' to leave us again. Tom, he'll die in the wilderness, and we must git to Kaintuckee."

The next vivid thing in my memory is the view of the last barrier Nature had reared between us and the delectable country. It stood like a lion at the gateway, and for some minutes we gazed at it in terror from Powell's Valley below. How many thousands have looked at it with sinking hearts! How many weaklings has its frown turned back! There seemed to be engraved upon it the dark history of the dark and bloody land beyond. Nothing in this life worth having is won for the asking; and the best is fought for, and bled for, and died for. Written, too, upon that towering wall of white rock, in the handwriting of God Himself, is the history of the indomitable Race to which we belong.

For fifty miles we travelled under it, towards the Gap, our eyes drawn to it by a resistless fascination. The sun went over it early in the day, as though glad to leave the place, and after that a dark scowl would settle there. At night we felt its presence, like a curse. Even Polly Ann was silent. And she had need to be now. When it was necessary, we talked in low tones, and the bell-clappers on the horses were not loosed at night. It was here, but four years gone, that Daniel Boone's family was attacked, and his son killed by the Indians.

We passed, from time to time, deserted cabins and camps, and some places that might once have been called settlements: Elk Garden, where the pioneers of the last four years had been wont to lay in a simple supply of seed corn and Irish potatoes; and the spot where Henderson and his company had camped on the way to establish Boonesboro two years before. And at last we struck the trace that mounted upward to the Gateway itself.

CHAPTER IX

ON THE WILDERNESS TRAIL

AND now we had our hands upon the latch, and God alone knew what was behind the gate. Toil, with a certainty, but our lives had known it. Death, perchance. But Death had been near to all of us, and his presence did not frighten. As we climbed towards the Gap, I recalled with strange aptness a quaint saying of my father's that Kaintuckee was the Garden of Eden, and that men were being justly punished with blood for their presumption.

As if to crown that judgment, the day was dark and lowering, with showers of rain from time to time. And when we spoke,—Polly Ann and I,—it was in whispers. The trace was very narrow, with Daniel Boone's blazes, two years old, upon the trees; but the way was not over steep. Cumberland Mountain was as silent and deserted as when the first man had known it.

Alas, for the vanity of human presage! We gained the top, and entered unmolested. No Eden suddenly dazzled our eye, no splendor burst upon it. Nothing told us, as we halted in our weariness, that we had reached the Promised Land. The mists weighed heavily on the evergreens of the slopes and hid the ridges, and we passed that night in cold discomfort. It was the first of many without a fire.

The next day brought us to the Cumberland, tawny and swollen from the rains, and here we had to stop to fell trees to make a raft on which to ferry over our packs. We bound the logs together with grapevines, and as we worked my imagination painted for me many a red face peering from the bushes on the farther shore. And when we got into the river and were caught and spun by the hurrying stream, I hearkened for a shot from the farther bank. While Polly Ann and I were scrambling to get the raft landed, Tom and Weldon swam over with the horses. And so we lay the second night dolefully in the rain. But not so much as a whimper escaped from Polly Ann. I have often told her since that the sorest trial she had was the guard she kept on her tongue,—a hardship indeed for one of Irish inheritance. Many a pull had she lightened for us by a flash of humor.

The next morning the sun relented, and the wine of his dawn was wine indeed to our flagging hopes. Going down to wash at the river's brink, I heard a movement in the cane, and stood frozen and staring until a great, bearded head, black as tar, was thrust out between the stalks and looked at me with blinking red eyes. The next step revealed the hump of the beast, and the next his tasselled tail lashing his dirty brown quarters. I did not tarry longer, but ran to tell Tom. He made bold to risk a shot and light a fire, and thus we had buffalo meat for some days after.

We were still in the mountains. The trail led down the river for a bit through the worst of canebrakes, and every now and again we stopped while Tom and Weldon scouted. Once the roan mare made a dash through the brake, and, though Polly Ann burst through one way to head her off and I another, we reached the bank of Richland Creek in time to see her nose and the top of her pack above the brown water. There was nothing for it but to swim after her, which I did, and caught her quietly feeding in the cane on the other side. By great good fortune the other horse bore the powder.

"Drat you, Nancy," said Polly Ann to the mare, as she handed me my clothes, "I'd sooner carry the pack myself than be bothered with you."

"Hush," said I, "the redskins will get us."

Polly Ann regarded me scornfully as I stood bedraggled before her.

"Redskins!" she cried. "Nonsense! I reckon it's all talk about redskins."

But we had scarce caught up ere we saw Tom standing rigid with his hand raised. Before him, on a mound bared of cane, were the charred remains of a fire. The sight of them transformed Weldon. His eyes glared again, even as when we had first seen him, curses escaped under his breath, and he would have darted into the cane had not Tom seized him sternly by the shoulder. As for me, my heart hammered against my ribs, and I grew sick with listening. It was at that instant that my admiration for Tom McChesney burst bounds, and that I got some real inkling of what woodcraft might be. Stepping silently between the tree trunks, his eyes bent on the leafy loam, he found a footprint here and another there, and suddenly he went into the cane with a sign to us to remain. It seemed an age before he returned. Then he began to rake the ashes, and, suddenly bending down, seized something in them,—the broken bowl of an Indian pipe.

"Shawnees!" he said; "I reckoned so." It was at length the beseeching in Polly Ann's eyes that he answered.

"A war party—tracks three days old. They took poplar."

To take poplar was our backwoods expression for embarking in a canoe, the dugouts being fashioned from the great poplar trees.

I did not reflect then, as I have since and often, how great was the knowledge and resource Tom practised that day. Our feeling for him (Polly Ann's and mine) fell little short of worship. In company ill at ease, in the forest he became silent and masterful—an unerring woodsman, capable of meeting the Indian on his own footing. And, strangest thought of all, he and many I could name who went into Kentucky, had escaped, by a kind of strange fate, being born in the north of Ireland. This was so of Andrew Jackson himself.

The rest of the day he led us in silence down the trace, his eye alert to penetrate every corner of the forest, his hand near the trigger of his long Deckard. I followed in boylike imitation, searching every thicket for alien form and color, and yearning for stature and responsibility. As for poor Weldon, he would stride for hours at a time with eyes fixed ahead, a wild figure,—ragged and fringed. And we knew that the soul within him was torn with thoughts of his dead wife and of his child in captivity. Again, when the trance left him, he was an addition to our little party not to be despised.

At dark Polly Ann and I carried the packs across a creek on a fallen tree, she taking one end and I the other. We camped there, where the loam was trampled and torn by countless herds of bison, and had only parched corn and the remains of a buffalo steak for supper, as the meal was mouldy from its wetting, and running low. When Weldon had gone a little distance up the creek to scout, Tom relented from the sternness which his vigilance imposed and came and sat down on a log beside Polly Ann and me.

"'Tis a hard journey, little girl," he said, patting her; "I reckon I done wrong to fetch you."

I can see him now, as the twilight settled down over the wilderness, his honest face red and freckled, but aglow with the tenderness it had hidden during the day, one big hand enfolding hers, and the other on my shoulder.

"Hark, Davy!" said Polly Ann, "he's fair tired of us already. Davy, take me back."

"Hush, Polly Ann," he answered, delighted at her raillery. "But I've a word to say to you. If we come on to the redskins, you and Davy make for the cane as hard as you kin kilter. Keep out of sight."

"As hard as we kin kilter!" exclaimed Polly Ann, indignantly. "I reckon not, Tom McChesney. Davy taught me to shoot long ago, afore you made up your mind to come back from Kaintuckee."

Tom chuckled. "So Davy taught you to shoot," he said, and checked himself. "He ain't such a bad one with a pistol,"—and he patted me,—"but I allow ye'd better hunt kiver just the same. And if they ketch ye, Polly Ann, just you go along and pretend to be happy, and tear off a snatch of your dress now and then, if you get a chance. It wouldn't take me but a little time to run into Harrodstown or Boone's Station from here, and fetch a party to follow ye."

Two days went by,—two days of strain in sunlight, and of watching and fitful sleep in darkness. But the Wilderness Trail was deserted. Here and there a lean-to—silent remnant of the year gone by—spoke of the little bands of emigrants which had once made their way so cheerfully to the new country. Again it was a child's doll, the rags of it beaten by the weather to a rusty hue. Every hour that we progressed seemed to justify the sagacity and boldness of Tom's plan, nor did it appear to have entered a painted skull that a white man would have the hardihood to try the trail this year. There were neither signs nor sounds save Nature's own, the hoot of the wood-owl, the distant bark of a mountain wolf, the whir of a partridge as she left her brood. At length we could stand no more the repression that silence and watching put upon us, and when a rotten bank gave way and flung Polly Ann and the sorrel mare into a creek, even Weldon smiled as we pulled her, bedraggled and laughing, from the muddy water. This was after we had ferried the Rockcastle River.

Our trace rose and fell over height and valley, until we knew that we were come to a wonderland at last. We stood one evening on a spur as the setting sun flooded the natural park below us with a crystal light and, striking a tall sycamore, turned its green to gold. We were now on the hills whence the water ran down to nourish the fat land, and I could scarce believe that the garden spot on which our eyes feasted could be the scene of the blood and suffering of which we had heard. Here at last was the fairyland of my childhood, the country beyond the Blue Wall.

We went down the river that led into it, with awe, as though we were trespassers against God Himself,—as though He had made it too beautiful and too fruitful for the toilers of this earth. And you who read this an hundred years hence may not believe the marvels of it to the pioneer, and in particular to one born and bred in the scanty, hard soil of the mountains. Nature had made it for her park,—ay, and scented it with her own perfumes. Giant trees, which had watched generations come and go, some of which mayhap had been saplings when the Norman came to England, grew in groves,— the gnarled and twisted oak, and that godsend to the settlers, the sugar-maple; the coffee tree with its drooping buds; the mulberry, the cherry, and the plum; the sassafras and the pawpaw; the poplar and the sycamore, slender maidens of the forest, garbed in daintier colors,—ay, and that resplendent brunette with the white flowers, the magnolia; and all underneath, in the green shade, enamelled banks which the birds themselves sought to rival.

At length, one afternoon, we came to the grove of wild apple trees so lovingly spoken of by emigrants as the Crab Orchard, and where formerly they had delighted to linger. The plain near by was flecked with the brown backs of feeding buffalo, but we dared not stop, and pressed on to find a camp in the forest. As we walked in the filtered sunlight we had a great fright, Polly Ann and I. Shrill, discordant cries suddenly burst from the branches above us, and a flock of strange, green birds flecked with red flew over our heads. Even Tom, intent upon the trail, turned and laughed at Polly Ann as she stood clutching me.

"Shucks," said he, "they're only paroquets."

We made our camp in a little dell where there was short green grass by the brookside and steep banks overgrown with brambles on either hand. Tom knew the place, and declared that we were within thirty miles of the station. A giant oak had blown down across the water, and, cutting out a few branches of this, we spread our blankets under it on the turf. Tethering our faithful beasts, and cutting a quantity of pea-vine for their night's food, we lay down to sleep, Tom taking the first watch.

I had the second, for Tom trusted me now, and glorying in that trust I was alert and vigilant. A shy moon peeped at me between the trees, and was fantastically reflected in the water. The creek rippled over the limestone, and an elk screamed in the forest far beyond. When at length I had called Weldon to take the third watch, I lay down with a sense of peace, soothed by the sweet odors of the night.

I awoke suddenly. I had been dreaming of Nick Temple and Temple Bow, and my father coming back to me there with a great gash in his shoulder like Weldon's. I lay for a moment dazed by the transition, staring through the gray light. Then I sat up, the soft stamping and snorting of the horses in my ears. The sorrel mare had her nose high, her tail twitching, but there was no other sound in the leafy wilderness. With a bound of returning sense I looked for Weldon. He had fallen asleep on the bank above, his body dropped across the trunk of the oak. I leaped on the trunk and made my way along it, stepping over him, until I reached and hid myself in the great roots of the tree on the bank above. The cold shiver of the dawn was in my body as I waited and listened. Should I wake Tom? The vast forest was silent, and yet in its shadowy depths my imagination drew moving forms. I hesitated.

The light grew: the boles of the trees came out, one by one, through the purple. The tangled mass down the creek took on a shade of green, and a faint breath came from the southward. The sorrel mare sniffed it, and stamped. Then silence again,—a long silence. Could it be that the cane moved in the thicket? Or had my eyes deceived me?

The Crossing, Vol. 1

I stared so hard that it seemed to rustle all over. Perhaps some deer were feeding there, for it was no unusual thing, when we rose in the morning, to hear the whistle of a startled doe near our camping ground. I was thoroughly frightened now,—and yet I had the speculative Scotch mind. The thicket was some one hundred and fifty yards above, and on the flooded lands at a bend. If there were Indians in it, they could not see the sleeping forms of our party under me because of a bend in the stream. They might have seen me, though I had kept very still in the twisted roots of the oak, and now I was cramped. If Indians were there, they could determine our position well enough by the occasional stamping and snorting of the horses. And this made my fear more probable, for I had heard that horses and cattle often warned pioneers of the presence of redskins.

Another thing: if they were a small party, they would probably seek to surprise us by coming out of the cane into the creek bed above the bend, and stalk down the creek. If a large band, they would surround and overpower us. I drew the conclusion that it must be a small party—if a party at all. And I would have given a shot in the arm to be able to see over the banks of the creek. Finally I decided to awake Tom.

It was no easy matter to get down to where he was without being seen by eyes in the cane. I clung to the under branches of the oak, finally reached the shelving bank, and slid down slowly. I touched him on the shoulder. He awoke with a start, and by instinct seized the rifle lying beside him.

"What is it, Davy?" he whispered.

I told what had happened and my surmise. He glanced then at the restless horses and nodded, pointing up at the sleeping figure of Weldon, in full s sight on the log. The Indians must have seen him.

Tom picked up the spare rifle.

"Davy," said he, "you stay here beside Polly Ann, behind the oak. You kin shoot with a rest; but don't shoot," said he, earnestly, "for God's sake don't shoot unless you're sure to kill."

I nodded. For a moment he looked at the face of Polly Ann, sleeping peacefully, and the fierce light faded from his eyes. He brushed her on the cheek and she awoke and smiled at him, trustfully, lovingly. He put his finger to his lips.

"Stay with Davy," he said. Turning to me, he added: "When you wake Weldon, wake him easy. So." He put his hand in mine, and gradually tightened it. "Wake him that way, and he won't jump."

Polly Ann asked no questions. She looked at Tom, and her soul was in her face. She seized the pistol from the blanket. Then we watched him creeping down the creek on his belly, close to the bank. Next we moved behind the fallen tree, and I put my hand in Weldon's. He woke with a sigh, started, but we drew him down behind the log. Presently he climbed cautiously up the bank and took station in the muddy roots of the tree. Then we waited, watching Tom with a prayer in our hearts. Those who have not felt it know not the fearfulness of waiting for an Indian attack.

At last Tom reached the bend in the bank, beside some red-bud bushes, and there he stayed. A level shaft of light shot through the forest. The birds, twittering, awoke. A great hawk soared high in the blue over our heads. An hour passed. I had sighted the rifle among the yellow leaves of the fallen oak an hundred times. But Polly Ann looked not once to the right or left. Her eyes and her prayers followed the form of her husband.

Then, like the cracking of a great drover's whip, a shot rang out in the stillness, and my hands tightened over the rifle-stock. A piece of bark struck me in the face, and a dead leaf fluttered to the ground. Almost instantly there was another shot, and a blue wisp of smoke rose from the red-bud bushes, where Tom was. The horses whinnied, there was a rustle in the cane, and silence. Weldon bent over.

"My God!" he whispered hoarsely, "he hit one. Tom hit one."

I felt Polly Ann's hand on my face.

"Davy dear," she said, "are ye hurt?"

"No," said I, dazed, and wondering why Weldon had not been shot long ago as he slumbered. I was burning to climb the bank and ask him whether he had seen the Indian fall.

Again there was silence,—a silence even more awful than before. The sun crept higher, the magic of his rays turning the creek from black to crystal, and the birds began to sing again. And still there was no sign of the treacherous enemy that lurked about us. Could Tom get back? I glanced at Polly Ann. The same question was written in her yearning eyes, staring at the spot where the gray of his hunting shirt showed through the bushes at the bend. Suddenly her hand tightened on mine. The hunting shirt was gone!

After that, in the intervals when my terror left me, I tried to speculate upon the plan of the savages. Their own numbers could not be great, and yet they must have known from our trace how few we were. Scanning the ground, I noted that the forest was fairly clean of undergrowth on both sides of us. Below, the stream ran straight, but there were growths of cane and briers. Looking up, I saw Weldon faced about. It was the obvious move.

But where had Tom gone?

Next my eye was caught by a little run fringed with bushes that curved around the cane near the bend. I traced its course, unconsciously, bit by bit, until it reached the edge of a bank not fifty feet away.

All at once my breath left me. Through the tangle of bramble stems at the mouth of the run, above naked brown shoulders there glared at me, hideously streaked with red, a face. Had my fancy lied? I stared again until my eyes were blurred, now tortured by doubt, now so completely convinced that my fingers almost released the trigger,—for I had thrown the sights into line over the tree. I know not to this day whether I shot from determination or nervousness. My shoulder bruised by the kick, the smoke like a veil before my face, it was some moments ere I knew that the air was full of whistling bullets; and then the gun was torn from my hands, and I saw Polly Ann ramming in a new charge.

"The pistol, Davy," she cried.

One torture was over, another on. Crack after crack sounded from the forest—from here and there and everywhere, it seemed—and with a song that like a hurtling insect ran the scale of notes, the bullets buried themselves in the trunk of our oak with a chug. Once in a while I heard Weldon's answering shot, but I remembered my promise to Tom not to waste powder unless I were sure. The agony was the breathing space we had while they crept nearer. Then we thought of Tom, and I dared not glance at Polly Ann for fear that the sight of her face would unnerve me.

Then a longing to kill seized me, a longing so strange and fierce that I could scarce be still. I know now that it comes in battle to all men, and with intensity to the hunted, and it explained to me more clearly what followed. I fairly prayed for the sight of a painted form, and time after time my fancy tricked me into the notion that I had one. And even as I searched the brambles at the top of the run a puff of smoke rose out of them, a bullet burying itself in the roots near Weldon, who fired in return. I say that I have some notion of what possessed the man, for he was crazed with passion at fighting the race which had so cruelly wronged him. Horror-struck, I saw him swing down from the bank, splash through the water with raised tomahawk, and gain the top of the run. In less time than it takes me to write these words he had dragged a hideous, naked warrior out of the brambles, and with an avalanche of crumbling earth they slid into the waters of the creek. Polly Ann and I stared transfixed at the fearful fight that followed, nor can I give any adequate description of it. Weldon had struck through the brambles, but the savage had taken the blow on his gun-barrel and broken the handle of the tomahawk, and it was man to man as they rolled in the shallow water, locked in a death embrace. Neither might reach for his knife, neither was able to hold the other down, Weldon's curses surcharged with hatred, the Indian straining silently save for a gasp or a guttural note, the white a bearded madman, the savage a devil with a glistening, paint-streaked body, his features now agonized as his muscles strained and cracked, now lighted with a diabolical joy. But the pent-up rage of months gave the white man strength.

Polly Ann and I were powerless for fear of shooting Weldon, and gazed absorbed at the fiendish scene with eyes not to be withdrawn. The tree-trunk shook. A long, bronze arm reached out from above, and a painted face glowered at us from the very roots where Weldon had lain. That moment I took to be my last, and in it I seemed to taste all eternity. I heard but faintly a noise beyond. It was the shock of the heavy Indian falling on Polly Ann and me as we cowered under the trunk, and even then there was an instant that we stood gazing at him as at a worm writhing in the clay. It was she who fired the pistol and made the great hole in his head, and so he twitched and died. After that a confusion of shots, war-whoops, a vision of two naked forms flying from tree to tree towards the cane, and then—God be praised—Tom's voice shouting:—

"Polly Ann! Polly Ann!"

Before she had reached the top of the bank Tom had her in his arms, and a dozen tall gray figures leaped the six feet into the stream and stopped. My own eyes turned with theirs to see the body of poor Weldon lying face downward in the water. But beyond it a tragedy awaited me. Defiant, immovable, save for the heaving of his naked chest, the savage who had killed him stood erect with folded arms facing us. The smoke cleared away from a gleaming rifle-barrel, and the brave staggered and fell and died as silent as he stood, his feathers making ripples in the stream. It was cold-blooded, if you like, but war in those days was to the death, and knew no mercy. The tall backwoodsman who had shot him waded across the stream, and in the twinkling of an eye seized the scalp-lock and ran it round with his knife, holding up the bleeding trophy with a shout. Staggering to my feet, I stretched myself, but I had been cramped so long that I tottered and would have fallen had not Tom's hand steadied me.

"Davy!" he cried. "Thank God, little Davy! the varmints didn't get ye."

"And you, Tom?" I answered, looking up at him, bewildered with happiness.

"They was nearer than I suspicioned when I went off," he said, and looked at me curiously. "Drat the little deevil," he said affectionately, and his voice trembled, "he took care of Polly Ann, I'll warrant."

He carried me to the top of the bank, where we were surrounded by the whole band of backwoodsmen.

"That he did!" cried Polly Ann, "and fetched a redskin yonder as clean as you could have done it, Tom."

"The little deevil!" exclaimed Tom again.

The Crossing, Vol. 1

I looked up, burning with this praise from Tom (for I had never thought of praise nor of anything save his happiness and Polly Ann's). I looked up, and my eyes were caught and held with a strange fascination by fearless blue ones that gazed down into them. I give you but a poor description of the owner of these blue eyes, for personal magnetism springs not from one feature or another. He was a young man,—perhaps five and twenty as I now know age,— woodsman-clad, square-built, sun-reddened. His hair might have been orange in one light and sand-colored in another. With a boy's sense of such things I knew that the other woodsmen were waiting for him to speak, for they glanced at him expectantly.

"You had a near call, McChesney," said he, at length; "fortunate for you we were after this band,—shot some of it to pieces yesterday morning." He paused, looking at Tom with that quality of tribute which comes naturally to a leader of men. "By God," he said, "I didn't think you'd try it."

"My word is good, Colonel Clark," answered Tom, simply.

Young Colonel Clark glanced at the lithe figure of Polly Ann. He seemed a man of few words, for he did not add to his praise of Tom's achievement by complimenting her as Captain Sevier had done. In fact, he said nothing more, but leaped down the bank and strode into the water where the body of Weldon lay, and dragged it out himself. We gathered around it silently, and two great tears rolled down Polly Ann's cheeks as she parted the hair with tenderness and loosened the clenched hands. Nor did any of the tall woodsmen speak. Poor Weldon! The tragedy of his life and death was the tragedy of Kentucky herself. They buried him by the waterside, where he had fallen.

But there was little time for mourning on the border. The burial finished, the Kentuckians splashed across the creek, and one of them, stooping with a shout at the mouth of the run, lifted out of the brambles a painted body with drooping head and feathers trailing.

"Ay, Mac," he cried, "here's a sculp for ye."

"It's Davy's," exclaimed Polly Ann from the top of the bank; "Davy shot that one."

"Hooray for Davy," cried a huge, strapping backwoodsman who stood beside her, and the others laughingly took up the shout. "Hooray for Davy. Bring him over, Cowan." The giant threw me on his shoulder as though I had been a fox, leaped down, and took the stream in two strides. I little thought how often he was to carry me in days to come, but I felt a great awe at the strength of him, as I stared into his rough features and his veined and weathered skin. He stood me down beside the Indian's body, smiled as he whipped my hunting knife from my belt, and said, "Now, Davy, take the sculp."

Nothing loath, I seized the Indian by the long scalp-lock, while my big friend guided my hand, and amid laughter and cheers I cut off my first trophy of war. Nor did I have any other feeling than fierce hatred of the race which had killed my father.

Those who have known armies in their discipline will find it difficult to understand the leadership of the border. Such leadership was granted only to those whose force and individuality compelled men to obey them. I had my first glimpse of it that day. This Colonel Clark to whom Tom delivered Mr. Robertson's letter was perchance the youngest man in the company that had rescued us, saving only a slim lad of seventeen whom I noticed and envied, and whose name was James Ray. Colonel Clark, so I was told by my friend Cowan, held that title in Kentucky by reason of his prowess.

Clark had been standing quietly on the bank while I had scalped my first redskin. Then he called Tom McChesney to him and questioned him closely about our journey, the signs we had seen, and, finally, the news in the Watauga settlements. While this was going on the others gathered round them.

"What now?" asked Cowan, when he had finished.

"Back to Harrodstown," answered the Colonel, shortly.

There was a brief silence, followed by a hoarse murmur from a thick-set man at the edge of the crowd, who shouldered his way to the centre of it.

"We set out to hunt a fight, and my pluck is to clean up. We ain't finished 'em yet."

The man had a deep, coarse voice that was a piece with his roughness.

"I reckon this band ain't a-goin' to harry the station any more, McGary," cried Cowan.

"By Job, what did we come out for? Who'll take the trail with me?"

There were some who answered him, and straightway they began to quarrel among themselves, filling the woods with a babel of voices. While I stood listening to these disputes with a boy's awe of a man's quarrel, what was my astonishment to feel a hand on my shoulder. It was Colonel Clark's, and he was not paying the least attention to the dispute.

"Davy," said he, "you look as if you could make a fire."

"Yes, sir," I answered, gasping.

"Well," said he, "make one."

I lighted a piece of punk with the flint, and, wrapping it up in some dry brush, soon had a blaze started. Looking up, I caught his eye on me again.

"Mrs. McChesney," said Colonel Clark to Polly Ann, "you look as if you could make johnny-cake. Have you any meal?"

"That I have," cried Polly Ann, "though it's fair mouldy. Davy, run and fetch it."

I ran to the pack on the sorrel mare. When I returned Mr. Clark said:—

"That seems a handy boy, Mrs. McChesney."

"Handy!" cried Polly Ann, "I reckon he's more than handy. Didn't he save my life twice on our way out here?"

"And how was that?" said the Colonel.

"Run and fetch some water, Davy," said Polly Ann, and straightway launched forth into a vivid description of my exploits, as she mixed the meal. Nay, she went so far as to tell how she came by me. The young Colonel listened gravely, though with a gleam now and then in his blue eyes. Leaning on his long rifle, he paid no manner of attention to the angry voices near by,—which conduct to me was little short of the marvellous.

"Now, Davy," said he, at length, "the rest of your history."

"There is little of it, sir," I answered. "I was born in the Yadkin country, lived alone with my father, who was a Scotchman. He hated a man named Cameron, took me to Charlestown, and left me with some kin of his who had a place called Temple Bow, and went off to fight Cameron and the Cherokees." There I gulped. "He was killed at Cherokee Ford, and—and I ran away from Temple Bow, and found Polly Ann."

This time I caught something of surprise on the Colonel's face.

"By thunder, Davy," said he, "but you have a clean gift for brief narrative. Where did you learn it?"

"My father was a gentleman once, and taught me to speak and read," I answered, as I brought a flat piece of limestone for Polly Ann's baking.

"And what would you like best to be when you grow up, Davy?" he asked.

"Six feet," said I, so promptly that he laughed.

"Faith," said Polly Ann, looking at me comically, "he may be many things, but I'll warrant he'll never be that."

I have often thought since that young Mr. Clark showed much of the wisdom of the famous king of Israel on that day. Polly Ann cooked a piece of a deer which one of the woodsmen had with him, and the quarrel died of itself when we sat down to this and the johnny-cake. By noon we had taken up the trace for Harrodstown, marching with scouts ahead and behind. Mr. Clark walked mostly alone, seemingly wrapped in thought. At times he had short talks with different men, oftenest—I noted with pride—with Tom McChesney. And more than once when he halted he called me to him, my answers to his questions seeming to amuse him. Indeed, I became a kind of pet with the backwoodsmen, Cowan often flinging me to his shoulder as he swung along. The pack was taken from the sorrel mare and divided among the party, and Polly Ann made to ride that we might move the faster.

It must have been the next afternoon, about four, that the rough stockade of Harrodstown greeted our eyes as we stole cautiously to the edge of the forest. And the sight of no roofs and spires could have been more welcome than that of these logs and cabins, broiling in the midsummer sun. At a little distance from the fort, a silent testimony of siege, the stumpy, cleared fields were overgrown with weeds, tall and rank, the corn choked. Nearer the stockade, where the keepers of the fort might venture out at times, a more orderly growth met the eye. It was young James Ray whom Colonel Clark singled to creep with our message to the gates. At six, when the smoke was rising from the stone chimneys behind the palisades, Ray came back to say that all was well. Then we went forward quickly, hands waved a welcome above the logs, the great wooden gates swung open, and at last we had reached the haven for which we had suffered so much. Mangy dogs barked at our feet, men and women ran forward joyfully to seize our hands and greet us.

And so we came to Kaintuckee.

CHAPTER X

HARRODSTOWN

THE old forts like Harrodstown and Boonesboro and Logan's at St. Asaph's have long since passed away. It is many, many years since I lived through that summer of siege in Harrodstown, the horrors of it are faded and dim, the discomforts lost to a boy thrilled with a new experience. I have read in my old age the books of travellers in Kentucky, English and French, who wrote much of squalor and strife and sin and little of those qualities that go to the conquest of an empire and the making of a people. Perchance my own pages may be colored by gratitude and love for the pioneers amongst whom I found myself, and thankfulness to God that we had reached them alive.

I know not how many had been cooped up in the little fort since the early spring, awaiting the chance to go back to their weed-choked clearings. The fort at Harrodstown was like an hundred others I have since seen, but sufficiently surprising to me then. Imagine a great parallelogram made of log cabins set end to end, their common outside wall being the wall of the fort, and loopholed. At the four corners of the parallelogram the cabins jutted out, with ports in the angle in order to give a flanking fire in case the savages reached the palisade. And then there were huge log gates with watch-towers on either side where sentries sat day and night scanning the forest line. Within the fort was a big common dotted with forest trees, where such cattle as had been saved browsed on the scanty grass. There had been but the one scrawny horse before our arrival.

And the settlers! How shall I describe them as they crowded around us inside the gate? Some stared at us with sallow faces and eyes brightened by the fever, yet others had the red glow of health. Many of the men wore rough beards, unkempt, and yellow, weather-worn hunting shirts, often stained with blood. The barefooted women wore sunbonnets and loose homespun gowns, some of linen made from nettles, while the children swarmed here and there and everywhere in any costume that chance had given them. All seemingly talking at once, they plied us with question after question of the trace, the Watauga settlements, the news in the Carolinys, and how the war went.

"A lad is it, this one," said an Irish voice near me, "and a woman! The dear help us, and who'd 'ave thought to see a woman come over the mountain this year! Where did ye find them, Bill Cowan?"

"Near the Crab Orchard, and the lad killed and sculped a six-foot brave."

"The saints save us! And what 'll be his name?"

"Davy," said my friend.

"Is it Davy? Sure his namesake killed a giant, too."

"And is he come along, also?" said another. His shy blue eyes and stiff blond hair gave him a strange appearance in a hunting shirt.

"Hist to him! Who will ye be talkin' about, Poulsson? Is it King David ye mane?"

There was a roar of laughter, and this was my introduction to Terence McCann and Swein Poulsson. The fort being crowded, we were put into a cabin with Terence and Cowan and Cowan's wife — a tall, gaunt woman with a sharp tongue and a kind heart — and her four brats, "All hugemsmug together," as Cowan said. And that night we supped upon dried buffalo meat and boiled nettle-tops, for of such was the fare in Harrodstown that summer.

"Tom McChesney kept his faith." One other man was to keep his faith with the little community — George Rogers Clark. And I soon learned that trustworthiness is held in greater esteem in a border community than anywhere else. Of course, the love of the frontier was in the grain of these men. But what did they come back to? Day after day would the sun rise over the forest and beat down upon the little enclosure in which we were penned. The row of cabins leaning against the stockade marked the boundaries of our diminutive world. Beyond them, invisible, lurked a relentless foe. Within, the greater souls alone were calm, and a man's worth was set down to a hair's breadth. Some were always to be found squatting on their door-steps cursing the hour which had seen them depart for this land; some wrestled and fought on the common, for a fist fight with a fair field and no favor was a favorite amusement of the backwoodsmen. My big friend, Cowan, was the champion of these, and often of an evening the whole of the inhabitants would gather near the spring to see him fight those who had the courage to stand up to him. His muscles were like hickory wood, and I have known a man insensible for a quarter of an hour after one of his blows. Strangely enough, he never fought in anger, and was the first to the spring for a gourd of water after the fight was over. But Tom McChesney was the best wrestler of the lot, and could make a wider leap than any other man in Harrodstown.

Tom's reputation did not end there, for he became one of the two bread-winners of the station. I would better have said *meat*winners. Woe be to the incautious who, lulled by a week of fancied security, ventured out into the dishevelled field for a little food! In the early days of the siege man after man had gone forth for game, never to return. Until Tom came, one only had been successful,—that lad of seventeen, whose achievements were the envy of my boyish soul, James Ray. He slept in the cabin next to Cowan's, and long before the dawn had revealed the forest line had been wont to steal out of the gates on the one scrawny horse the Indians had left them, gain the Salt River, and make his way thence through the water to some distant place where the listening savages could not hear his shot. And now Tom took his turn. Often did I sit with Polly Ann till midnight in the sentry's tower, straining my ears for the owl's hoot that warned us of his coming. Sometimes he was empty-handed, but sometimes a deer hung limp and black across his saddle, or a pair of turkeys swung from his shoulder.

"Arrah, darlin'," said Terence to Polly Ann, "'tis yer husband and James is the jools av the fort. Sure I niver loved me father as I do thim."

I would have given kingdoms in those days to have been seventeen and James Ray. When he was in the fort I dogged his footsteps, and listened with a painful yearning to the stories of his escapes from the roving bands. And as many a character is watered in its growth by hero-worship, so my own grew firmer in the contemplation of Ray's resourcefulness. My strange life had far removed me from lads of my own age, and he took a fancy to me, perhaps because of the very persistence of my devotion to him. I cleaned his gun, filled his powder flask, and ran to do his every bidding.

I used in the hot summer days to lie under the elm tree and listen to the settlers' talk about a man named Henderson, who had bought a great part of Kentucky from the Indians, and had gone out with Boone to found Boonesboro some two years before. They spoke of much that I did not understand concerning the discountenance by Virginia of these claims, speculating as to whether Henderson's grants were good. For some of them held these grants, and others Virginia grants—a fruitful source of quarrel between them. Some spoke, too, of Washington and his ragged soldiers going up and down the old colonies and fighting for a freedom which there seemed little chance of getting. But their anger seemed to blaze most fiercely when they spoke of a mysterious British general named Hamilton, whom they called "the ha'r buyer," and who from his stronghold in the north country across the great Ohio sent down these hordes of savages to harry us. I learned to hate Hamilton with the rest, and pictured him with the visage of a fiend. We laid at his door every outrage that had happened at the three stations, and put upon him the blood of those who had been carried off to torture in the Indian villages of the northern forests. And when—amidst great excitement—a spent runner would arrive from Boonesboro or St. Asaph's and beg Mr. Clark for a squad, it was commonly with the first breath that came into his body that he cursed Hamilton.

So the summer wore away, while we lived from hand to mouth on such scanty fare as the two of them shot and what we could venture to gather in the unkempt fields near the gates. A winter of famine lurked ahead, and men were goaded near to madness at the thought of clearings made and corn planted in the spring within reach of their hands, as it were, and they might not harvest it. At length, when a fortnight had passed, and Tom and Ray had gone forth day after day without sight or fresh sign of Indians, the weight lifted from our hearts. There were many things that might yet be planted and come to maturity before the late Kentucky frosts.

The pressure within the fort, like a flood, opened the gates of it, despite the sturdily disapproving figure of a young man who stood silent under the sentry box, leaning on his Deckard. He was Colonel

George Rogers Clark,[1] Commander-in-chief of the backwoodsmen of Kentucky, whose power was reënforced by that strange thing called an education. It was this, no doubt, gave him command of words when he chose to use them.

[1] It appears that Mr. Clark had not yet received the title of Colonel, though he held command. — EDITOR.

"Faith," said Terence, as we passed him, "'tis a foine man he is, and a gintleman born. Wasn't it him gathered the Convintion here in Harrodstown last year that chose him and another to go to the Virginia legislatoor? And him but a lad, ye might say. The divil fly away wid his caution! Sure the redskins is as toired as us, and gone home to the wives and childher, bad cess to thim."

And so the first day the gates were opened we went into the fields a little way; and the next day a little farther. They had once seemed to me an unexplored and forbidden country as I searched them with my eyes from the sentry boxes. And yet I felt a shame to go with Polly Ann and Mrs. Cowan and the women while James Ray and Tom sat with the guard of men between us and the forest line. Like a child on a holiday, Polly Ann ran hither and thither among the stalks, her black hair flying and a song on her lips.

"Soon we'll be having a little home of our own, Davy," she cried; "Tom has the place chose on a knoll by the river, and the land is rich with hickory and pawpaw. I reckon we may be going there next week."

Caution being born into me with all the strength of a vice, I said nothing. Whereupon she seized me in her strong hands and shook me.

"Ye little imp!" said she, while the women paused in their work to laugh at us.

"The boy is right, Polly Ann," said Mrs. Harrod, "and he's got more sense than most of the men in the fort."

"Ay, that he has," the gaunt Mrs. Cowan put in, eying me fiercely, while she gave one of her own offsprings a slap that sent him spinning.

Whatever Polly Ann might have said would have been to the point, but it was lost, for just then the sound of a shot came down the wind, and a half a score of women stampeded through the stalks, carrying me down like a reed before them. When I staggered to my feet Polly Ann and Mrs. Cowan and Mrs. Harrod were standing alone. For there was little of fear in those three.

"Shucks!" said Mrs. Cowan, "I reckon it's that Jim Ray shooting at a mark," and she began to pick nettles again.

"Vimmen is a shy critter," remarked Swein Poulsson, coming up. I had a shrewd notion that he had run with the others.

"Wimmen!" Mrs. Cowan fairly roared. "Wimmen! Tell us how ye went in March with the boys to fight the varmints at the Sugar Orchard, Swein!"

We all laughed, for we loved him none the less. His little blue eyes were perfectly solemn as he answered:—

"Ve send you fight Injuns mit your tongue, Mrs. Cowan. Then we haf no more troubles."

"Land of Canaan!" cried she, "I reckon I could do more harm with it than you with a gun."

There were many such false alarms in the bright days following, and never a bullet sped from the shadow of the forest. Each day we went farther afield, and each night trooped merrily in through the gates with hopes of homes and clearings rising in our hearts—until the motionless figure of the young Virginian met our eye. It was then that men began to scoff at him behind his back, though some spoke with sufficient backwoods bluntness to his face. And yet he gave no sign of anger or impatience. Not so the other leaders. No sooner did the danger seem past than bitter strife sprang up within the walls. Even the two captains were mortal enemies. One was Harrod, a tall, spare, dark-haired man of great endurance,—a type of the best that conquered the land for the nation; the other, that Hugh McGary of whom I have spoken, coarse and brutal, if you like, but fearless and a leader of men withal.

A certain Sunday morning, I remember, broke with a cloud-flecked sky, and as we were preparing to go afield with such ploughs as could be got together (we were to sow turnips) the loud sounds of a quarrel came from the elm at the spring. With one accord men and women and children flocked thither, and as we ran we heard McGary's voice above the rest. Worming my way, boylike, through the crowd, I came upon McGary and Harrod glaring at each other in the centre of it.

"By Job! there's no devil if I'll stand back from my clearing and waste the rest of the summer for the fears of a pack of cowards. I'll take a posse and march to Shawanee Springs this day, and see any man a fair fight that tries to stop me."

"And who's in command here?" demanded Harrod.

"I am, for one," said McGary, with an oath, "and my corn's on the ear. I've held back long enough, I tell you, and I'll starve this winter for you nor any one else."

Harrod turned.

"Where's Clark?" he said to Bowman.

"Clark!" roared McGary, "Clark be d—d. Ye'd think he was a woman." He strode up to Harrod until their faces almost touched, and his voice shook with the intensity of his anger. "By G—d, you nor Clark nor any one else will stop me, I say!" He swung around and faced the people. "Come on, boys! We'll fetch that corn, or know the reason why."

A responding murmur showed that the bulk of them were with him. Weary of the pent-up life, longing for action, and starved for a good meal, the anger of his many followers against Clark and Harrod was nigh as great as his. He started roughly to shoulder his way out, and whether from accident or design Captain Harrod slipped in front of him, I never knew. The thing that followed happened quickly as the catching of my breath. I saw McGary powdering his pan, and Harrod his, and felt the crowd giving back like buffalo. All at once the circle had vanished, and the two men were standing not five paces apart with their rifles clutched across their bodies, each watching, catlike, for the other to level. It was a cry that startled us— and them. There was a vision of a woman flying across the common, and we saw the dauntless Mrs. Harrod snatching her husband's gun from his resisting hands. So she saved his life and McGary's.

At this point Colonel Clark was seen coming from the gate. When he got to Harrod and McGary the quarrel blazed up again, but now it was between the three of them, and Clark took Harrod's rifle from Mrs. Harrod and held it. However, it was presently decided that McGary should wait one more day before going to his clearing; whereupon the gates were opened, the picked men going ahead to take station as a guard, and soon we were hard at work, ploughing here and mowing there, and in another place putting seed in the ground: in the cheer of the work hardships were forgotten, and we paused now and again to laugh at some sally of Terence McCann's or odd word of Swein Poulsson's. As the day wore on to afternoon a blue haze—harbinger of autumn—settled over fort and forest. Bees hummed in the air as they searched hither and thither amongst the flowers, or shot straight as a bullet for a distant hive. But presently a rifle cracked, and we raised our heads.

"Hist!" said Terence, "the bhoys on watch is that warlike! Whin there's no redskins to kill they must be wastin' good powdher on a three."

I leaped upon a stump and scanned the line of sentries between us and the woods; only their heads and shoulders appeared above the rank growth. I saw them looking from one to another questioningly, some shouting words I could not hear. Then I saw some running; and next, as I stood there wondering, came another crack, and then a volley like the noise of a great fire licking into dry wood, and things that were not bees humming round about. A distant man in a yellow hunting shirt stumbled, and was drowned in the tangle as in water. Around me men dropped plough-handles and women baskets, and as we ran our legs grew numb and our bodies cold at a sound which had haunted us in dreams by night—the war-whoop. The deep and guttural song of it rose and fell with a horrid fierceness. An agonized voice was in my ears, and I halted, ashamed. It was Polly Ann's.

"Davy!" she cried, "Davy, have ye seen Tom?"

Two men dashed by. I seized one by the fringe of his shirt, and he flung me from my feet. The other leaped me as I knelt.

"Run, ye fools!" he shouted. But we stood still, with yearning eyes staring back through the frantic forms for a sight of Tom's.

"I'll go back!" I cried, "I'll go back for him. Do you run to the fort." For suddenly I seemed to forget my fear, nor did even the hideous notes of the scalp halloo disturb me. Before Polly Ann could catch me I had turned and started, stumbled,—I thought on a stump,—and fallen headlong among the nettles with a stinging pain in my leg. Staggering to my feet, I tried to run on, fell again, and putting down my hand found it smeared with blood. A man came by, paused an instant while his eye caught me, and ran on again. I shall remember his face and name to my dying day; but there is no reason to put it down here. In a few seconds' space as I lay I suffered all the pains of captivity and of death by torture, that cry of savage man an hundred times more frightful than savage beast sounding in my ears, and plainly nearer now by half the first distance. Nearer, and nearer yet—and then I heard my name called. I was lifted from the ground, and found myself in the lithe arms of Polly Ann.

"Set me down!" I screamed, "set me down!" and must have added some of the curses I had heard in the fort. But she clutched me tightly (God bless the memory of those frontier women!), and flew like a deer toward the gates. Over her shoulder I glanced back. A spare three hundred yards away in a ragged line a hundred red devils were bounding after us with feathers flying and mouths open as they yelled. Again I cried to her to set me down; but though her heart beat faster and her breath came shorter, she held me the tighter. Second by second they gained on us, relentlessly. Were we near the fort? Hoarse shouts answered the question, but they seemed distant—too distant. The savages were gaining, and Polly Ann's breath quicker still. She staggered, but the brave soul had no thought of faltering. I had a sight of a man on a plough horse with dangling harness coming up from somewhere, of the man leaping off, of ourselves being pitched on the animal's bony back and clinging there at the gallop, the man running at the side. Shots whistled over our heads, and here was the brown fort. Its big gates swung together as we dashed through the narrowed opening. Then, as he lifted us off, I knew that the man who had saved us was Tom himself. The gates closed with a bang, and a patter of bullets beat against them like rain.

Through the shouting and confusion came a cry in a voice I knew, now pleading, now commanding.

"Open, open! For God's sake open!"

"It's Ray! Open for Ray! Ray's out!"

Some were seizing the bar to thrust it back when the heavy figure of McGary crushed into the crowd beside it.

"By Job, I'll shoot the man that touches it!" he shouted, as he tore them away. But the sturdiest of them went again to it, and cursed him. And while they fought backward and forward, the lad's mother, Mrs. Ray, cried out to them to open in tones to rend their hearts. But McGary had gained the bar and swore (perhaps wisely) that he would not sacrifice the station for one man. Where was Ray?

Where was Ray, indeed? It seemed as if no man might live in the hellish storm that raged without the walls: as if the very impetus of hate and fury would carry the savages over the stockade to murder us. Into the turmoil at the gate came Colonel Clark, sending the disputants this way and that to defend the fort, McGary to command one quarter, Harrod and Bowman another, and every man that could be found to a loophole, while Mrs. Ray continued to run up and down, wringing her hands, now facing one man, now another. Some of her words came to me, shrilly, above the noise.

"He fed you—he fed you. Oh, my God, and you are grateful— grateful! When you were starving he risked his life—"

Torn by anxiety for my friend, I dragged myself into the nearest cabin, and a man was fighting there in the half-light at the port. The huge figure I knew to be my friend Cowan's, and when he drew back to load I seized his arm, shouting Ray's name. Although the lead was pattering on the other side of the logs, Cowan lifted me to the port. And there, stretched on the ground behind a stump, within twenty feet of the walls, was James. Even as I looked the puffs of dust at his side showed that the savages knew his refuge. I saw him level and fire, and then Bill Cowan set me down and began to ram in a charge with tremendous energy.

Was there no way to save Ray? I stood turning this problem in my mind, subconsciously aware of Cowan's movements: of his yells when he thought he had made a shot, when Polly Ann appeared at the doorway. Darting in, she fairly hauled me to the shake-down in the far corner.

"Will ye bleed to death, Davy?" she cried, as she slipped off my legging and bent over the wound. Her eye lighting on a gourdful of water on the puncheon table, she tore a strip from her dress and washed and bound me deftly. The bullet was in the flesh, and gave me no great pain.

"Lie there, ye imp!" she commanded, when she had finished.

"Some one's under the bed," said I, for I had heard a movement.

In an instant we were down on our knees on the hard dirt floor, and there was a man's foot in a moccasin! We both grabbed it and pulled, bringing to life a person with little blue eyes and stiff blond hair.

"Swein Poulsson!" exclaimed Polly Ann, giving him an involuntary kick, "may the devil give ye shame!"

Swein Poulsson rose to a sitting position and clasped his knees in his hands.

"I haf one great fright," said he.

"Send him into the common with the women in yere place, Mis' McChesney," growled Cowan, who was loading.

"By tam!" said Swein Poulsson, leaping to his feet, "I vill stay here und fight. I am prave once again." Stooping down, he searched under the bed, pulled out his rifle, powdered the pan, and flying to the other port, fired. At that Cowan left his post and snatched the rifle from Poulsson's hands.

"Ye're but wasting powder," he cried angrily.

"Then, by tam, I am as vell under the bed," said Poulsson. "Vat can I do?"

I had it.

"Dig!" I shouted; and seizing the astonished Cowan's tomahawk from his belt I set to work furiously chopping at the dirt beneath the log wall. "Dig, so that James can get under."

Cowan gave me the one look, swore a mighty oath, and leaping to the port shouted to Ray in a thundering voice what we were doing.

"Dig!" roared Cowan. "Dig, for the love of God, for he can't hear me."

The three of us set to work with all our might, Poulsson making great holes in the ground at every stroke, Polly Ann scraping at the dirt with the gourd. Two feet below the surface we struck the edge of the lowest log, and then it was Poulsson who got into the hole with his hunting knife—perspiring, muttering to himself, working as one possessed with a fury, while we scraped out the dirt from under him. At length, after what seemed an age of staring at his legs, the ground caved on him, and he would have smothered if we had not dragged him out by the heels, sputtering and all powdered brown. But there was the daylight under the log.

Again Cowan shouted at Ray, and again, but he did not understand. It was then the miracle happened. I have seen brave men and cowards since, and I am as far as ever from distinguishing them. Before we knew it Poulsson was in the hole once more—had wriggled out of it on the other side, and was squirming in a hail of bullets towards Ray. There was a full minute of suspense—perhaps two—during which the very rifles of the fort were silent (though the popping in the weeds was redoubled), and then the barrel of a Deckard was poked through the hole. After it came James Ray himself, and lastly Poulsson, and a great shout went out from the loopholes and was taken up by the women in the common.

Swein Poulsson had become a hero, nor was he willing to lose any of the glamour which was a hero's right. As the Indians' fire slackened, he went from cabin to cabin, and if its occupants failed to mention the exploit (some did fail so to do, out of mischief), Swein would say:—

"You did not see me safe James, no? I vill tell you joost how."

It never leaked out that Swein was first of all under the bed, for Polly Ann and Bill Cowan and myself swore to keep the secret. But they told how I had thought of digging the hole under the logs—a happy circumstance which got me a reputation for wisdom beyond my years. There was a certain Scotchman at Harrodstown called McAndrew, and it was he gave me the nickname "Canny Davy," and I grew to have a sort of precocious fame in the station. Often Captain Harrod or Bowman or some of the others would pause in their arguments and say gravely, "What does Davy think of it?" This was not good for a boy, and the wonder of it is that it did not make me altogether insupportable. One effect it had on me—to make me long even more earnestly to be a man.

The impulse of my reputation led me farther. A fortnight of more inactivity followed, and then we ventured out into the fields once more. But I went with the guard this time, not with the women,— thanks to a whim the men had for humoring me.

"Arrah, and beant he a man all but two feet," said Terence, "wid more brain than me an' Bill Cowan and Poulsson togither? 'Tis a fox's nose Davy has for the divils, Bill. Sure he can smell thim the same as you an' me kin see the red paint on their faces."

"I reckon that's true," said Bill Cowan, with solemnity, and so he carried me off.

At length the cattle were turned out to browse greedily through the clearing, while we lay in the woods by the forest and listened to the sound of their bells, but when they strayed too far, I was often sent to drive them back. Once when this happened I followed them to the shade at the edge of the woods, for it was noon, and the sun beat down fiercely. And there I sat for some time watching them as they lashed their sides with their tails and pawed the ground, for experience is a good master. Whether or not the flies were all that troubled them I could not tell, and no sound save the tinkle of their bells broke the noonday stillness. Making a circle I drove them back toward the fort, much troubled in mind. I told Cowan, but he laughed and said it was the flies. Yet I was not satisfied, and finally stole back again to the place where I had found them. I sat a long time hidden at the edge of the forest, listening until my imagination tricked me into hearing those noises which I feared and yet longed for. Trembling, I stole a little farther in the shade of the woods, and then a little farther still. The leaves rustled in the summer's breeze, patches of sunlight flickered on the mould, the birds twittered, and the squirrels scolded. A chipmunk frightened me as he flew chattering along a log. And yet I went on. I came to the creek as it flowed silently in the shade, stepped in, and made my way slowly down it, I know not how far, walking in the water, my eye alert to every movement about me. At length I stopped and caught my breath. Before me, in a glade opening out under great trees, what seemed a myriad of forked sticks were piled against one another, three by three, and it struck me all in a heap that I had come upon a great encampment. But the skeletons of the pyramid tents alone remained. Where were the skins? Was the camp deserted?

For a while I stared through the brier leaves, then I took a venture, pushed on, and found myself in the midst of the place. It must have held near a thousand warriors. All about me were gray heaps of ashes, and bones of deer and elk and buffalo scattered, some picked clean, some with the meat and hide sticking to them. Impelled by a strong fascination, I went hither and thither until a sound brought me to a stand — the echoing crack of a distant rifle. On the heels of it came another, then several together, and a faint shouting borne on the light wind. Terrorized, I sought for shelter. A pile of brush underlain by ashes was by, and I crept into that. The sounds continued, but seemed to come no nearer, and my courage returning, I got out again and ran wildly through the camp toward the briers on the creek, expecting every moment to be tumbled headlong by a bullet. And when I reached the briers, what between panting and the thumping of my heart I could for a few moments hear nothing. Then I ran on again up the creek, heedless of cover, stumbling over logs and trailing vines, when all at once a dozen bronze forms glided with the speed of deer across my path ahead. They splashed over the creek and were gone. Bewildered with fear, I dropped under a fallen tree. Shouts were in my ears, and the noise of men running. I stood up, and there, not twenty paces away, was Colonel Clark himself rushing toward me. He halted with a cry, raised his rifle, and dropped it at the sight of my queer little figure covered with ashes.

"My God!" he cried, "it's Davy."

"They crossed the creek," I shouted, pointing the way, "they crossed the creek, some twelve of them."

"Ay," he said, staring at me, and by this time the rest of the guard were come up. They too stared, with different exclamations on their lips,—Cowan and Bowman and Tom McChesney and Terence McCann in front.

"And there's a great camp below," I went on, "deserted, where a thousand men have been."

"A camp—deserted?" said Clark, quickly.

"Yes," I said, "yes." But he had already started forward and seized me by the arm.

"Lead on," he cried, "show it to us." He went ahead with me, travelling so fast that I must needs run to keep up, and fairly lifting me over the logs. But when we came in sight of the place he darted forward alone and went through it like a hound on the trail. The others followed him, crying out at the size of the place and poking among the ashes. At length they all took up the trail for a way down the creek. Presently Clark called a halt.

"I reckon that they've made for the Ohio," he said. And at this judgment from him the guard gave a cheer that might almost have been heard in the fields around the fort. The terror that had hovered over us all that long summer was lifted at last.

You may be sure that Cowan carried me back to the station. "To think it was Davy that found it!" he cried again and again, "to think it was Davy found it!"

"And wasn't it me that said he could smell the divils," said Terence, as he circled around us in a mimic war dance. And when from the fort they saw us coming across the fields they opened the gates in astonishment, and on hearing the news gave themselves over to the wildest rejoicing. For the backwoodsmen were children of nature. Bill Cowan ran for the fiddle which he had carried so carefully over the mountain, and that night we had jigs and reels on the common while the big fellow played "Billy of the Wild Woods" and "Jump Juba," with all his might, and the pine knots threw their fitful, red light on the wild scenes of merriment. I must have cut a queer little figure as I sat between Cowan and Tom watching the dance, for presently Colonel Clark came up to us, laughing in his quiet way.

"Davy," said he, "there is another great man here who would like to see you," and led me away wondering. I went with him toward the gate, burning all over with pride at this attention, and beside a torch there a broad-shouldered figure was standing, at sight of whom I had a start of remembrance.

"Do you know who that is, Davy?" said Colonel Clark.

"It's Mr. Daniel Boone," said I.

"By thunder," said Clark, "I believe the boy *is* a wizard," while Mr. Boone's broad mouth was creased into a smile, and there was a trace of astonishment, too, in his kindly eye.

"Mr. Boone came to my father's cabin on the Yadkin once," I said; "he taught me to skin a deer."

"Ay, that I did," exclaimed Mr. Boone, "and I said ye'd make a woodsman sometime."

Mr. Boone, it seemed, had come over from Boonesboro to consult with Colonel Clark on certain matters, and had but just arrived. But so modest was he that he would not let it be known that he was in the station, for fear of interrupting the pleasure. He was much the same as I had known him, only grown older and his reputation now increased to vastness. He and Clark sat on a door log talking for a long time on Kentucky matters, the strength of the forts, the prospect of new settlers that autumn, of the British policy, and finally of a journey which Colonel Clark was soon to make back to Virginia across the mountains. They seemed not to mind my presence. At length Colonel Clark turned to me with that quiet, jocose way he had when relaxed.

"Davy," said he, "we'll see how much of a general you are. What would you do if a scoundrel named Hamilton far away at Detroit was bribing all the redskins he could find north of the Ohio to come down and scalp your men?"

"I'd go for Hamilton," I answered.

"By God!" exclaimed Clark, striking Mr. Boone on the knee, "that's what I'd do."

CHAPTER XI

FRAGMENTARY

MR. BOONE'S visit lasted but a day. I was a great deal with Colonel Clark in the few weeks that followed before his departure for Virginia. He held himself a little aloof (as a leader should) from the captains in the station, without seeming to offend them. But he had a fancy for James Ray and for me, and he often took me into the woods with him by day, and talked with me of an evening.

"I'm going away to Virginia, Davy," he said; "will you not go with me? We'll see Williamsburg, and come back in the spring, and I'll have you a little rifle made."

My look must have been wistful.

"I can't leave Polly Ann and Tom," I answered.

"Well," he said, "I like that. Faith to your friends is a big equipment for life."

"But why are you going?" I asked.

"Because I love Kentucky best of all things in the world," he answered, smiling.

"And what are you going to do?" I insisted.

"Ah," he said, "that I can't tell even to you."

"To catch Hamilton?" I ventured at random.

He looked at me queerly.

"Would you go along, Davy?" said he, laughing now.

"Would you take Tom?"

"Among the first," answered Colonel Clark, heartily.

We were seated under the elm near the spring, and at that instant I saw Tom coming toward us. I jumped up, thinking to please him by this intelligence, when Colonel Clark pulled me down again.

"Davy," said he, almost roughly, I thought, "remember that we have been joking. Do you understand?—joking. You have a tongue in your mouth, but sense enough in your head, I believe, to hold it." He turned to Tom. "McChesney, this is a queer lad you brought us," said he.

"He's a little deevil," agreed Tom, for that had become a formula with him.

It was all very mysterious to me, and I lay awake many a night with curiosity, trying to solve a puzzle that was none of my business. And one day, to cap the matter, two woodsmen arrived at Harrodstown with clothes frayed and bodies lean from a long journey. Not one of the hundred questions with which they were beset would they answer, nor say where they had been or why, save that they had carried out certain orders of Clark, who was locked up with them in a cabin for several hours.

The first of October, the day of Colonel Clark's departure, dawned crisp and clear. He was to take with him the disheartened and the cowed, the weaklings who loved neither work nor exposure nor danger. And before he set out of the gate he made a little speech to the assembled people.

"My friends," he said, "you know me. I put the interests of Kentucky before my own. Last year when I left to represent her at Williamsburg there were some who said I would desert her. It was for her sake I made that journey, suffered the tortures of hell from scalded feet, was near to dying in the mountains. It was for her sake that I importuned the governor and council for powder and lead, and when they refused it I said to them, 'Gentlemen, a country that is not worth defending is not worth claiming.'"

At these words the settlers gave a great shout, waving their coonskin hats in the air.

"Ay, that ye did," cried Bill Cowan, "and got the amminition."

"I made that journey for her sake, I say," Colonel Clark continued, "and even so I am making this one. I pray you trust me, and God bless and keep you while I am gone."

He did not forget to speak to me as he walked between our lines, and told me to be a good boy and that he would see me in the spring. Some of the women shed tears as he passed through the gate, and many of us climbed to sentry box and cabin roof that we might see the last of the little company wending its way across the fields. A motley company it was, the refuse of the station, headed by its cherished captain. So they started back over the weary road that led to that now far-away land of civilization and safety.

During the balmy Indian summer, when the sharper lines of nature are softened by the haze, some came to us from across the mountains to make up for the deserters. From time to time a little group would straggle to the gates of the station, weary and footsore, but overjoyed at the sight of white faces again: the fathers walking ahead with watchful eyes, the women and older children driving the horses, and the babies slung to the pack in hickory withes. Nay, some of our best citizens came to Kentucky swinging to the tail of a patient animal. The Indians were still abroad, and in small war parties darted hither and thither with incredible swiftness. And at night we would gather at the fire around our new emigrants to listen to the stories they had to tell,—familiar stories to all of us. Sometimes it had been the gobble of a wild turkey that had lured to danger, again a wood-owl had cried strangely in the night.

Winter came, and passed—somehow. I cannot dwell here on the tediousness of it, and the one bright spot it has left in my memory concerns Polly Ann. Did man, woman, or child fall sick, it was Polly Ann who nursed them. She had by nature the God-given gift of healing, knew by heart all the simple remedies that backwoods lore had inherited from the north of Ireland or borrowed from the Indians. Her sympathy and loving-kindness did more than these, her never tiring and ever cheerful watchfulness. She was deft, too, was Polly Ann, and spun from nettle bark many a cut of linen that could scarce be told from flax. Before the sap began to run again in the maples there was not a soul in Harrodstown who did not love her, and I truly believe that most of them would have risked their lives to do her bidding.

Then came the sugaring, the warm days and the freezing nights when the earth stirs in her sleep and the taps drip from red sunrise to red sunset. Old and young went to the camps, the women and children boiling and graining, the squads of men posted in guards round about. And after that the days flew so quickly that it seemed as if the woods had burst suddenly into white flower, and it was spring again. And then—a joy to be long remembered—I went on a hunting trip with Tom and Cowan and three others where the Kentucky tumbles between its darkly wooded cliffs. And other wonders of that strange land I saw then for the first time: great licks, trampled down for acres by the wild herds, where the salt water oozes out of the hoofprints. On the edge of one of these licks we paused and stared breathless at giant bones sticking here and there in the black mud, and great skulls of fearful beasts half-embedded. This was called the Big Bone Lick, and some travellers that went before us had made their tents with the thighs of these monsters of a past age.

A danger past is oft a danger forgotten. Men went out to build the homes of which they had dreamed through the long winter. Axes rang amidst the white dogwoods and the crabs and redbuds, and there were riotous log-raisings in the clearings. But I think the building of Tom's house was the most joyous occasion of all, and for none in the settlement would men work more willingly than for him and Polly Ann. The cabin went up as if by magic. It stood on a rise upon the bank of the river in a grove of oaks and hickories, with a big persimmon tree in front of the door. It was in the shade of this tree that Polly Ann sat watching Tom and me through the mild spring days as we barked the roof, and none ever felt greater joy and pride in a home than she. We had our first supper on a wide puncheon under the persimmon tree on the few pewter plates we had fetched across the mountain, the blue smoke from our own hearth rising in the valley until the cold night air spread it out in a line above us, while the horses grazed at the river's edge.

After that we went to ploughing, an occupation which Tom fancied but little, for he loved the life of a hunter best of all. But there was corn to be raised and fodder for the horses, and a truck-patch to be cleared near the house.

One day a great event happened,—and after the manner of many great events, it began in mystery. Leaping on the roan mare, I was riding like mad for Harrodstown to fetch Mrs. Cowan. And she, when she heard the summons, abandoned a turkey on the spit, pitched her brats out of the door, seized the mare, and dashing through the gates at a gallop left me to make my way back afoot. Scenting a sensation, I hurried along the wooded trace at a dog trot, and when I came in sight of the cabin there was Mrs. Cowan sitting on the step, holding in her long but motherly arms something bundled up in nettle linen, while Tom stood sheepishly by, staring at it.

"Shucks," Mrs. Cowan was saying loudly, "I reckon ye're as little use to-day as Swein Poulsson,—standin' there on one foot. Ye anger me—just grinning at it like a fool—and yer own doin'. Have ye forgot how to talk?"

Tom grinned the more, but was saved the effort of a reply by a loud noise from the bundle.

"Here's another," cried Mrs. Cowan to me. "Ye needn't act as if it was an animal. Faith, yereself was like that once, all red an' crinkled. But I warrant ye didn't have the heft," and she lifted it, judicially. "A grand baby," attacking Tom again, "and ye're no more worthy to be his father than Davy here."

Then I heard a voice calling me, and pushing past Mrs. Cowan, I ran into the cabin. Polly Ann lay on the log bedstead, and she turned to mine a face radiant with a happiness I had not imagined.

"Oh, Davy, have ye seen him? Have ye seen little Tom? Davy, I reckon I'll never be so happy again. Fetch him here, Mrs. Cowan."

Mrs. Cowan, with a glance of contempt at Tom and me, put the bundle tenderly down on the coarse brown sheet beside her.

Poor little Tom! Only the first fortnight of his existence was spent in peace. I have a pathetic memory of it all—of our little home, of our hopes for it, of our days of labor and nights of planning to make it complete. And then, one morning when the three of us were turning over the black loam in the patch, while the baby slept peacefully in the shade, a sound came to our ears that made us pause and listen with bated breath. It was the sound of many guns, muffled in the distant forest. With a cry Polly Ann flew to the hickory cradle under the tree, Tom sprang for the rifle that was never far from his side, while with a kind of instinct I ran to catch the spancelled horses by the river. In silence and sorrow we fled through the tall cane, nor dared to take one last look at the cabin, or the fields lying black in the spring sunlight. The shots had ceased, but ere we had reached the little clearing McCann had made they began again, though as distant as before. Tom went ahead, while I led the mare and Polly Ann clutched the child to her breast. But when we came in sight of the fort across the clearings the gates were closed. There was nothing to do but cower in the thicket, listening while the battle went on afar, Polly Ann trying to still the cries of the child, lest they should bring death upon us. At length the shooting ceased; stillness reigned; then came a faint halloo, and out of the forest beyond us a man rode, waving his hat at the fort. After him came others. The gates opened, and we rushed pell-mell across the fields to safety.

The Indians had shot at a party shelling corn at Captain Bowman's plantation, and killed two, while the others had taken refuge in the crib. Fired at from every brake, James Ray had ridden to Harrodstown for succor, and the savages had been beaten off. But only the foolhardy returned to their clearings now. We were on the edge of another dreaded summer of siege, the prospect of banishment from the homes we could almost see, staring us in the face, and the labors of the spring lost again. There was bitter talk within the gates that night, and many declared angrily that Colonel Clark had abandoned us. But I remembered what he had said, and had faith in him.

It was that very night, too, I sat with Cowan, who had duty in one of the sentry boxes, and we heard a voice calling softly under us. Fearing treachery, Cowan cried out for a sign. Then the answer came back loudly to open to a runner with a message from Colonel Clark to Captain Harrod. Cowan let the man in, while I ran for the captain, and in five minutes it seemed as if every man and woman and child in the fort were awake and crowding around the man by the gates, their eager faces reddened by the smoking pine knots. Where was Clark? What had he been doing? Had he deserted them?

"Deserted ye!" cried the runner, and swore a great oath. Wasn't Clark even then on the Ohio raising a great army with authority from the Commonwealth of Virginia to rid them of the red scourge? And would they desert him? Or would they be men and bring from Harrodstown the company he asked for? Then Captain Harrod read the letter asking him to raise the company, and before day had dawned they were ready for the word to march—ready to leave cabin and clearing, and wife and child, trusting in Clark's judgment for time and place. Never were volunteers mustered more quickly than in that cool April night by the gates of Harrodstown Station.

"And we'll fetch Davy along, for luck," cried Cowan, catching sight of me beside him.

"Sure we'll be wanting a dhrummer b'y," said McCann.

And so they enrolled me.

CHAPTER XII

THE CAMPAIGN BEGINS

"DAVY, take care of my Tom," cried Polly Ann.

I can see her now, standing among the women by the great hewn gateposts, with little Tom in her arms, holding him out to us as we filed by. And the vision of his little, round face haunted Tom and me for many weary miles of our tramp through the wilderness. I have often thought since that that march of the volunteer company to join Clark at the Falls of the Ohio was a superb example of confidence in one man, and scarce to be equalled in history.

In less than a week we of Captain Harrod's little company stood on a forest-clad bank, gazing spellbound at the troubled waters of a mighty river. That river was the Ohio, and it divided us from the strange north country whence the savages came. From below, the angry voice of the Great Falls cried out to us unceasingly. Smoke rose through the tree-tops of the island opposite, and through the new gaps of its forest cabins could be seen. And presently, at a signal from us, a big flatboat left its shore, swung out and circled on the polished current, and grounded at length in the mud below us. A dozen tall boatmen, buckskin-clad, dropped the big oars and leaped out on the bank with a yell of greeting. At the head of them was a man of huge frame, and long, light hair falling down over the collar of his hunting shirt. He wrung Captain Harrod's hand.

"That there's Simon Kenton, Davy," said Cowan, as we stood watching them.

I ran forward for a better look at the backwoods Hercules, the tales of whose prowess had helped to while away many a winter's night in Harrodstown Station. Big-featured and stern, yet he had the kindly eye of the most indomitable of frontier fighters, and I doubted not the truth of what was said of him—that he could kill any redskin hand-to-hand.

"Clark's thar," he was saying to Captain Harrod. "God knows what his pluck is. He ain't said a word."

"He doesn't say whar he's going?" said Harrod.

"Not a notion," answered Kenton. "He's the greatest man to keep his mouth shut I ever saw. He kept at the governor of Virginny till he gave him twelve hundred pounds in Continentals and power to raise troops. Then Clark fetched a circle for Fort Pitt, raised some troops thar and in Virginny and some about Red Stone, and come down the Ohio here with 'em in a lot of flatboats. Now that ye've got here the Kentucky boys is all in. I come over with Montgomery, and Dillard's here from the Holston country with a company."

"Well," said Captain Harrod, "I reckon we'll report."

I went among the first boat-load, and as the men strained against the current, Kenton explained that Colonel Clark had brought a number of emigrants down the river with him; that he purposed to leave them on this island with a little force, that they might raise corn and provisions during the summer; and that he had called the place Corn Island.

"Sure, there's the Colonel himself," cried Terence McCann, who was in the bow, and indeed I could pick out the familiar figure among the hundred frontiersmen that gathered among the stumps at the landing-place. As our keel scraped they gave a shout that rattled in the forest behind them, and Clark came down to the waterside.

"I knew that Harrodstown wouldn't fail me," he said, and called every man by name as we waded ashore. When I came splashing along after Tom he pulled me from the water with his two hands.

"Colonel," said Terence McCann, "we've brought ye a dhrummer b'y."

"We'd have no luck at all without him," said Cowan, and the men laughed.

"Can you walk an hundred miles without food, Davy?" asked Colonel Clark, eying me gravely.

"Faith he's lean as a wolf, and no stomach to hinder him," said Terence, seeing me look troubled. "I'll not be missing the bit of food the likes of him would eat."

"And as for the heft of him," added Cowan, "Mac and I'll not feel it."

Colonel Clark laughed. "Well, boys," he said, "if you must have him, you must. His Excellency gave me no instructions about a drummer, but we'll take you, Davy."

In those days he was a man that wasted no time, was Colonel Clark, and within the hour our little detachment had joined the others, felling trees and shaping the log-ends for the cabins. That night, as Tom and Cowan and McCann and James Ray lay around their fire, taking a well-earned rest, a man broke excitedly into the light with a kettle-shaped object balanced on his head, which he set down in front of us. The man proved to be Swein Poulsson, and the object a big drum, and he straightway began to beat upon it a tattoo with improvised drumsticks.

"A Red Stone man," he cried, "a Red Stone man, he have it in the flatboat. It is for Tavy."

"The saints be good to us," said Terence, "if it isn't the King's own drum he has." And sure enough, on the head of it gleamed the royal arms of England, and on the other side, as we turned it over, the device of a regiment. They flung the sling about my neck, and the next day, when the little army drew up for parade among the stumps, there I was at the end of the line, and prouder than any man in the ranks. And Colonel Clark coming to my end of the line paused and smiled and patted me kindly on the cheek.

"Have you put this man on the roll, Harrod?" says he.

"No, Colonel," answers Captain Harrod, amid the laughter of the men at my end.

"What!" says the Colonel, "what an oversight! From this day he is drummer boy and orderly to the Commander-in-chief. Beat the retreat, my man."

I did my best, and as the men broke ranks they crowded around me, laughing and joking, and Cowan picked me up, drum and all, and carried me off, I rapping furiously the while.

And so I became a kind of handy boy for the whole regiment from the Colonel down, for I was willing and glad to work. I cooked the Colonel's meals, roasting the turkey breasts and saddles of venison that the hunters brought in from the mainland, and even made him journey-cake, a trick which Polly Ann had taught me. And when I went about the island, if a man were loafing, he would seize his axe and cry, "Here's Davy, he'll tell the Colonel on me." Thanks to the jokes of Terence McCann, I gained an owl-like reputation for wisdom amongst these superstitious backwoodsmen, and they came verily to believe that upon my existence depended the success of the campaign. But day after day passed, and no sign from Colonel Clark of his intentions.

"There's a good lad," said Terence. "He'll be telling us where we're going."

I was asked the same question by a score or more, but Colonel Clark kept his own counsel. He himself was everywhere during the days that followed, superintending the work on the blockhouse we were building, and eying the men. Rumor had it that he was sorting out the sheep from the goats, silently choosing those who were to remain on the island and those who were to take part in the campaign.

At length the blockhouse stood finished amid the yellow stumps of the great trees, the trunks of which were in its walls. And suddenly the order went forth for the men to draw up in front of it by companies, with the families of the emigrants behind them. It was a picture to fix itself in a boy's mind, and one that I have never forgotten. The line of backwoodsmen, as fine a lot of men as I ever wish to see, bronzed by the June sun, strong and tireless as the wild animals of the forest, stood expectant with rifles grounded. And beside the tallest, at the end of the line, was a diminutive figure with a drum hung in front of it. The early summer wind rustled in the forest, and the never ending song of the Great Falls sounded from afar. Apart, square-shouldered and indomitable, stood a young man of twenty-six.

"My friends and neighbors," he said in a firm voice, "there is scarce a man standing among you to-day who has not suffered at the hands of savages. Some of you have seen wives and children killed before your eyes—or dragged into captivity. None of you can to-day call the home for which he has risked so much his own. And who, I ask you, is to blame for this hideous war? Whose gold is it that buys guns and powder and lead to send the Shawnee and the Iroquois and Algonquin on the warpath?"

He paused, and a hoarse murmur of anger ran along the ranks.

"Whose gold but George's, by the grace of God King of Great Britain and Ireland? And what minions distribute it? Abbott at Kaskaskia, for one, and Hamilton at Detroit, the Hair Buyer, for another!"

When he spoke Hamilton's name his voice was nearly drowned by imprecations.

"Silence!" cried Clark, sternly, and they were silent. "My friends, the best way for a man to defend himself is to maim his enemy. One year since, when you did me the honor to choose me Commander-in-chief of your militia in Kentucky, I sent two scouts to Kaskaskia. A dozen years ago the French owned that place, and St. Vincent, and Detroit, and the people there are still French. My men brought back word that the French feared the Long Knives, as the Indians call us. On the first of October I went to Virginia, and some of you thought again that I had deserted you. I went to Williamsburg and wrestled with Governor Patrick Henry and his council, with Mr. Jefferson and Mr. Mason and Mr. Wythe. Virginia had no troops to send us, and her men were fighting barefoot with Washington against the armies of the British king. But the governor gave me twelve hundred pounds in paper, and with it I have raised the little force that we have here. And with it we will carry the war into Hamilton's country. On the swift waters of this great river which flows past us have come tidings to-day, and God Himself has sent them. To-morrow would have been too late. The ships and armies of the French king are on their way across the ocean to help us fight the tyrant, and this is the news that we bear to the Kaskaskias. When they hear this, the French of those towns will not fight against us. My friends, we are going to conquer an empire for liberty, and I can look onward," he cried in a burst of inspired eloquence, sweeping his arm to the northward toward the forests on the far side of the Ohio, "I can look onward to the day when these lands will be filled with the cities of a Great Republic. And who among you will falter at such a call?"

There was a brief silence, and then a shout went up from the ranks that drowned the noise of the Falls, and many fell into antics, some throwing their coonskin hats in the air, and others cursing and scalping Hamilton in mockery, while I pounded on the drum with all my might. But when we had broken ranks the rumor was whispered about that the Holston company had not cheered, and indeed the rest of the day these men went about plainly morose and discontented,—some saying openly (and with much justice, though we failed to see it then) that they had their own families and settlements to defend from the Southern Indians and Chickamauga bandits, and could not undertake Kentucky's fight at that time. And when the enthusiasm had burned away a little the disaffection spread, and some even of the Kentuckians began to murmur against Clark, for faith or genius was needful to inspire men to his plan. One of the malcontents from Boonesboro came to our fire to argue.

"He's mad as a medicine man, is Clark, to go into that country with less than two hundred rifles. And he'll force us, will he? I'd as lief have the King for a master."

He brought every man in our circle to his feet,—Ray, McCann, Cowan, and Tom. But Tom was nearest, and words not coming easily to him he fell on the Boonesboro man instead, and they fought it out for ten minutes in the firelight with half the regiment around them. At the end of it, when the malcontents were carrying their champion away, they were stopped suddenly at the sight of one bursting through the circle into the light, and a hush fell upon the quarrel. It was Colonel Clark.

"Are you hurt, McChesney?" he demanded.

"I reckon not much, Colonel," said Tom, grinning, as he wiped his face.

"If any man deserts this camp to-night," cried Colonel Clark, swinging around, "I swear by God to have him chased and brought back and punished as he deserves. Captain Harrod, set a guard."

I pass quickly over the rest of the incident. How the Holston men and some others escaped in the night in spite of our guard, and swam the river on logs. How at dawn we found them gone, and Kenton and Harrod and brave Captain Montgomery set out in pursuit, with Cowan and Tom and Ray. All day they rode, relentless, and the next evening returned with but eight weary and sullen fugitives of all those who had deserted.

The next day the sun rose on a smiling world, the polished reaches of the river golden mirrors reflecting the forest's green. And we were astir with the light, preparing for our journey into the unknown country. At seven we embarked by companies in the flatboats, waving a farewell to those who were to be left behind. Some stayed through inclination and disaffection: others because Colonel Clark did not deem them equal to the task. But Swein Poulsson came. With tears in his little blue eyes he had begged the Colonel to take him, and I remember him well on that June morning, his red face perspiring under the white bristles of his hair as he strained at the big oar. For we must needs pull a mile up the stream ere we could reach the passage in which to shoot downward to the Falls. Suddenly Poulsson dropped his handle, causing the boat to swing round in the stream, while the men damned him. Paying them no attention, he stood pointing into the blinding disk of the sun. Across the edge of it a piece was bitten out in blackness.

"Mein Gott!" he cried, "the world is being ended just now."

"The holy saints remember us this day!" said McCann, missing a stroke to cross himself. "Will ye pull, ye damned Dutchman? Or we'll be the first to slide into hell. This is no kind of a place at all at all."

By this time the men all along the line of boats had seen it, and many faltered. Clark's voice could be heard across the waters urging them to pull, while the bows swept across the current. They obeyed him, but steadily the blackness ate out the light, and a weird gloaming overspread the scene. River and forest became stern, the men silent. The more ignorant were in fear of a cataclysm, the others taking it for an omen.

"Shucks!" said Tom, when appealed to, "I've seed it afore, and it come all right again."

Clark's boat rounded the shoal: next our turn came, and then the whole line was gliding down the river, the rising roar of the angry waters with which we were soon to grapple coming to us with an added grimness. And now but a faint rim of light saved us from utter darkness. Big Bill Cowan, undaunted in war, stared at me with fright written on his face.

"And what 'll ye think of it, Davy?" he said.

I glanced at the figure of our commander in the boat ahead, and took courage.

"It's Hamilton's scalp hanging by a lock," I answered, pointing to what was left of the sun. "Soon it will be off, and then we'll have light again."

To my surprise he snatched me from the thwart and held me up with a shout, and I saw Colonel Clark turn and look back.

"Davy says the Ha'r Buyer's sculp hangs by the lock, boys," he shouted, pointing at the sun.

The word was cried from boat to boat, and we could see the men pointing upwards and laughing. And then, as the light began to grow, we were in the midst of the tumbling waters, the steersmen straining now right, now left, to keep the prows in the smooth reaches between rock and bar. We gained the still pools below, the sun came out once more and smiled on the landscape, and the spirits of the men, reviving, burst all bounds.

Thus I earned my reputation as a prophet.

Four days and nights we rowed down the great river, our oars double-manned, for fear that our coming might be heralded to the French towns. We made our first camp on a green little island at the mouth of the Cherokee, as we then called the Tennessee, and there I set about cooking a turkey for Colonel Clark, which Ray had shot. Chancing to look up, I saw the Colonel himself watching me.

"How is this, Davy?" said he. "I hear that you have saved my army for me before we have met the enemy."

"I did not know it, sir," I answered.

"Well," said he, "if you have learned to turn an evil omen into a good sign, you know more than some generals. What ails you now?"

"There's a pirogue, sir," I cried, staring and pointing.

"Where?" said he, alert all at once. "Here, McChesney, take a crew and put out after them."

He had scarcely spoken ere Tom and his men were rowing into the sunset, the whole of our little army watching from the bank. Presently the other boat was seen coming back with ours, and five strange woodsmen stepped ashore, our men pressing around them. But Clark flew to the spot, the men giving back.

"Who's the leader here?" he demanded.

A tall man stepped forward.

"I am," said he, bewildered but defiant.

"Your name?"

"John Duff," he answered, as though against his will.

"Your business?"

"Hunters," said Duff; "and I reckon we're in our rights."

"I'll judge of that," said our Colonel. "Where are you from?"

"That's no secret, neither. Kaskasky, ten days gone."

At that there was a murmur of surprise from our companies. Clark turned.

"Get your men back," he said to the captains, who stood about them. And all of them not moving: "Get your men back, I say. I'll have it known who's in command here."

At that the men retired. "Who commands at Kaskaskia?" he demanded of Duff.

"Monseer Rocheblave, a Frenchy holding a British commission," said Duff. "And the British Governor Abbott has left Post St. Vincent and gone to Detroit. Who be you?" he added suspiciously. "Be you Rebels?"

"Colonel Clark is my name, and I am in the service of the Commonwealth of Virginia."

Duff uttered an exclamatory oath and his manner changed. "Be you Clark?" he said with respect. "And you're going after Kaskasky? Wal, the mility is prime, and the Injun scouts is keeping a good lookout. But, Colonel, I'll tell ye something: the Frenchies is etarnal afeard of the Long Knives. My God! they've got the notion that if you ketch 'em you'll burn and scalp 'em same as the Red Sticks."

"Good," was all that Clark answered.

"I reckon I don't know much about what the Rebels is fighting for," said John Duff; "but I like your looks, Colonel, and wherever you're going there'll be a fight. Me and my boys would kinder like to go along."

Clark did not answer at once, but looked John Duff and his men over carefully.

"Will you take the oath of allegiance to Virginia and the Continental Congress?" he asked at length.

"I reckon it won't pizen us," said John Duff.

"Hold up your hands," said Clark, and they took the oath. "Now, my men," said he, "you will be assigned to companies. Does any one among you know the old French trail from Massacre to Kaskaskia?"

"Why," exclaimed John Duff, "why, Johnny Saunders here can tread it in the dark like the road to the grogshop."

John Saunders, loose limbed, grinning sheepishly, shuffled forward, and Clark shot a dozen questions at him one after another. Yes, the trail had been blazed the Lord knew how long ago by the French, and given up when they left Massacre.

"Look you," said Clark to him, "I am not a man to stand trifling. If there is any deception in this, you will be shot without mercy."

"And good riddance," said John Duff. "Boys, we're Rebels now. Steer clear of the Ha'r Buyer."

CHAPTER XIII

Kaskaskia

For one more day we floated downward on the face of the waters between the forest walls of the wilderness, and at length we landed in a little gully on the north shore of the river, and there we hid our boats.

"Davy," said Colonel Clark, "let's walk about a bit. Tell me where you learned to be so silent?"

"My father did not like to be talked to," I answered, "except when he was drinking."

He gave me a strange look. Many the stroll I took with him afterwards, when he sought to relax himself from the cares which the campaign had put upon him. This night was still and clear, the west all yellow with the departing light, and the mists coming on the river. And presently, as we strayed down the shore we came upon a strange sight, the same being a huge fort rising from the waterside, all overgrown with brush and saplings and tall weeds. The palisades that held its earthenwork were rotten and crumbling, and the mighty bastions of its corners sliding away. Behind the fort, at the end farthest from the river, we came upon gravelled walks hidden by the rank growth, where the soldiers of his most Christian Majesty once paraded. Lost in thought, Clark stood on the parapet, watching the water gliding by until the darkness hid it,—nay, until the stars came and made golden dimples upon its surface. But as we went back to the camp again he told me how the French had tried once to conquer this vast country and failed, leaving to the Spaniards the endless stretch beyond the Mississippi called Louisiana, and this part to the English. And he told me likewise that this fort in the days of its glory had been called *Massacre*, from a bloody event which had happened there more than threescore years before.

"Threescore years!" I exclaimed, longing to see the men of this race which had set up these monuments only to abandon them.

"Ay, lad," he answered, "before you or I were born, and before our fathers were born, the French missionaries and soldiers threaded this wilderness. And they called this river 'La Belle Rivière,'—the Beautiful River."

"And shall I see that race at Kaskaskia?" I asked, wondering.

"That you shall," he cried, with a force that left no doubt in my mind.

In the morning we broke camp and started off for the strange place which we hoped to capture. A hundred miles it was across the trackless wilds, and each man was ordered to carry on his back provisions for four days only.

"*Herr Gott!*" cried Swein Poulsson, from the bottom of a flatboat, whence he was tossing out venison flitches, "four day, und vat is it ve eat then?"

"Frenchies, sure," said Terence; "there'll be plenty av thim for a season. Faith, I do hear they're tinder as lambs."

"You'll no set tooth in the Frenchies," the pessimistic McAndrew put in, "wi' five thousand redskins aboot, and they lying in wait. The Colonel's no vera mindful of that, I'm thinking."

"Will ye hush, ye ill-omened hound!" cried Cowan, angrily. "Pitch him in the crick, Mac!"

Tom was diverted from this duty by a loud quarrel between Captain Harrod and five men of the company who wanted scout duty, and on the heels of that came another turmoil occasioned by Cowan's dropping my drum into the water. While he and McCann and Tom were fishing it out, Colonel Clark himself appeared, quelled the mutiny that Harrod had on his hands, and bade the men sternly to get into ranks.

"What foolishness is this?" he said, eying the dripping drum.

"Sure, Colonel," said McCann, swinging it on his back, "we'd have no heart in us at Kaskasky widout the rattle of it in our ears. Bill Cowan and me will not be feeling the heft of it bechune us."

"Get into ranks," said the Colonel, amusement struggling with the anger in his face as he turned on his heel. His wisdom well knew when to humor a man, and when to chastise.

"Arrah," said Terence, as he took his place, "I'd as soon l'ave me gun behind as Davy and the dhrum."

Methinks I can see now, as I write, the long file of woodsmen with their swinging stride, planting one foot before the other, even as the Indian himself threaded the wilderness. Though my legs were short, I had both sinew and training, and now I was at one end of the line and now at the other. And often with a laugh some giant would hand his gun to a neighbor, swing me to his shoulder, and so give me a lift for a weary mile or two; and perchance whisper to me to put down my hand into the wallet of his shirt, where I would find a choice morsel which he had saved for his supper. Sometimes I trotted beside the Colonel himself, listening as he talked to this man or that, and thus I got the gravest notion of the daring of this undertaking, and of the dangers ahead of us. This north country was infested with Indians, allies of the English and friends of the French their subjects; and the fact was never for an instant absent from our minds that our little band might at any moment run into a thousand warriors, be overpowered and massacred; or, worst of all, that our coming might have been heralded to Kaskaskia.

For three days we marched in the green shade of the primeval wood, nor saw the sky save in blue patches here and there. Again we toiled for hours through the coffee-colored waters of the swamps. But the third day brought us to the first of those strange clearings which the French call prairies, where the long grass ripples like a lake in the summer wind. Here we first knew raging thirst, and longed for the loam-specked water we had scorned, as our tired feet tore through the grass. For Saunders, our guide, took a line across the open in plain sight of any eye that might be watching from the forest cover. But at length our column wavered and halted by reason of some disturbance at the head of it. Conjectures in our company, the rear guard, became rife at once.

"Run, Davy darlin,' an' see what the throuble is," said Terence.

Nothing loath, I made my way to the head of the column, where Bowman's company had broken ranks and stood in a ring up to their thighs in the grass. In the centre of the ring, standing on one foot before our angry Colonel, was Saunders.

"Now, what does this mean?" demanded Clark; "my eye is on you, and you've boxed the compass in this last hour."

Saunders' jaw dropped.

"I'm guiding you right," he answered, with that sullenness which comes to his kind from fear, "but a man will slip his bearings sometimes in this country."

Clark's eyes shot fire, and he brought down the stock of his rifle with a thud.

"By the eternal God!" he cried, "I believe you are a traitor. I've been watching you every step, and you've acted strangely this morning."

"Ay, ay," came from the men round him.

"Silence!" cried Clark, and turned again to the cowering Saunders. "You pretend to know the way to Kaskaskia, you bring us to the middle of the Indian country where we may be wiped out at any time, and now you have the damned effrontery to tell me that you have lost your way. I am a man of my word," he added with a vibrant intensity, and pointed to the limbs of a giant tree which stood at the edge of the distant forest. "I will give you half an hour, but as I live, I will leave you hanging there."

The man's brown hand trembled as he clutched his rifle barrel.

"'Tis a hard country, sir," he said. "I'm lost. I swear it on the evangels."

"A hard country!" cried Clark. "A man would have to walk over it but once to know it. I believe you are a damned traitor and perjurer,—in spite of your oath, a British spy."

Saunders wiped the sweat from his brow on his buckskin sleeve.

"I reckon I could get the trace, Colonel, if you'd let me go a little way into the prairie."

"Half an hour," said Clark, "and you'll not go alone." Sweeping his eye over Bowman's company, he picked out a man here and a man there to go with Saunders. Then his eye lighted on me. "Where's McChesney?" he said. "Fetch McChesney."

I ran to get Tom, and seven of them went away, with Saunders in the middle, Clark watching them like a hawk, while the men sat down in the grass to wait. Fifteen minutes went by, and twenty, and twenty-five, and Clark was calling for a rope, when some one caught sight of the squad in the distance returning at a run. And when they came within hail it was Saunders' voice we heard, shouting brokenly:—

"I've struck it, Colonel, I've struck the trace. There's a pecan at the edge of the bottom with my own blaze on it."

"May you never be as near death again," said the Colonel, grimly, as he gave the order to march.

The fourth day passed, and we left behind us the patches of forest and came into the open prairie,—as far as the eye could reach a long, level sea of waving green. The scanty provisions ran out, hunger was added to the pangs of thirst and weariness, and here and there in the straggling file discontent smouldered and angry undertone was heard. Kaskaskia was somewhere to the west and north; but how far? Clark had misled them. And in addition it were foolish to believe that the garrison had not been warned. English soldiers and French militia and Indian allies stood ready for our reception. Of such was the talk as we lay down in the grass under the stars on the fifth night. For in the rank and file an empty stomach is not hopeful.

The next morning we took up our march silently with the dawn, the prairie grouse whirring ahead of us. At last, as afternoon drew on, a dark line of green edged the prairie to the westward, and our spirits rose. From mouth to mouth ran the word that these were the woods which fringed the bluff above Kaskaskia itself. We pressed ahead, and the destiny of the new Republic for which we had fought made us walk unseen. Excitement keyed us high; we reached the shade, plunged into it, and presently came out staring at the bastioned corners of a fort which rose from the centre of a clearing. It had once defended the place, but now stood abandoned and dismantled. Beyond it, at the edge of the bluff, we halted, astonished. The sun was falling in the west, and below us was the goal for the sight of which we had suffered so much. At our feet, across the wooded bottom, was the Kaskaskia River, and beyond, the peaceful little French village with its low houses and orchards and gardens colored by the touch of the evening light. In the centre of it stood a stone church with its belfry; but our searching eyes alighted on the spot to the southward of it, near the river. There stood a rambling stone building with the shingles of its roof weathered black, and all around it a palisade of pointed sticks thrust in the ground, and with a pair of gates and watch-towers. Drooping on its staff was the standard of England. North and south of the village the emerald common gleamed in the slanting light, speckled red and white and black by grazing cattle. Here and there, in untidy brown patches, were Indian settlements, and far away to the westward the tawny Father of Waters gleamed through the cottonwoods.

Through the waning day the men lay resting under the trees, talking in undertones. Some cleaned their rifles, and others lost themselves in conjectures of the attack. But Clark himself, tireless, stood with folded arms gazing at the scene below, and the sunlight on his face illumined him (to the lad standing at his side) as the servant of destiny. At length, at eventide, the sweet-toned bell of the little cathedral rang to vespers,—a gentle message of peace to war. Colonel Clark looked into my upturned face.

"Davy, do you know what day this is?" he asked.

"No, sir," I answered.

"Two years have gone since the bells pealed for the birth of a new nation—your nation, Davy, and mine—the nation that is to be the refuge of the oppressed of this earth—the nation which is to be made of all peoples, out of all time. And this land for which you and I shall fight to-night will belong to it, and the lands beyond," he pointed to the west, "until the sun sets on the sea again." He put his hand on my head. "You will remember this when I am dead and gone," he said.

I was silent, awed by the power of his words.

Darkness fell, and still we waited, impatient for the order. And when at last it came the men bustled hither and thither to find their commands, and we picked our way on the unseen road that led down the bluff, our hearts thumping. The lights of the village twinkled at our feet, and now and then a voice from below was caught and borne upward to us. Once another noise startled us, followed by an exclamation, *"Donnerblitzen"* and a volley of low curses from the company. Poor Swein Poulsson had loosed a stone, which had taken a reverberating flight riverward.

We reached the bottom, and the long file turned and hurried silently northward, searching for a crossing. I try to recall my feelings as I trotted beside the tall forms that loomed above me in the night. The sense of protection they gave me stripped me of fear, and I was not troubled with that. My thoughts were chiefly on Polly Ann and the child we had left in the fort now so far to the south of us, and in my fancy I saw her cheerful, ever helpful to those around her, despite the load that must rest on her heart. I saw her simple joy at our return. But should we return? My chest tightened, and I sped along the ranks to Harrod's company and caught Tom by the wrist.

"Davy," he murmured, and, seizing my hand in his strong grip, pulled me along with him. For it was not given to him to say what he felt; but as I hurried to keep pace with his stride, Polly Ann's words rang in my ears, "Davy, take care of my Tom," and I knew that he, too, was thinking of her.

A hail aroused me, the sound of a loud rapping, and I saw in black relief a cabin ahead. The door opened, a man came out with a horde of children cowering at his heels, a volley of frightened words pouring from his mouth in a strange tongue. John Duff was plying him with questions in French, and presently the man became calmer and lapsed into broken English.

"Kaskaskia—yes, she is prepare. Many spy is gone out—cross *la rivière*. But now they all sleep."

Even as he spoke a shout came faintly from the distant town.

"What is that?" demanded Clark, sharply.

The man shrugged his shoulders. "*Une fête des nègres, peut-être*,—the negro, he dance maybe."

"Are you the ferryman?" said Clark.

"*Oui*—I have some boat."

We crossed the hundred and fifty yards of sluggish water, squad by squad, and in the silence of the night stood gathered, expectant, on the farther bank. Midnight was at hand. Commands were passed about, and men ran this way and that, jostling one another to find their places in a new order. But at length our little force stood in three detachments on the river's bank, their captains repeating again and again the part which each was to play, that none might mistake his duty. The two larger ones were to surround the town, while the picked force under Simon Kenton himself was to storm the fort. Should he gain it by surprise and without battle, three shots were to be fired in quick succession, the other detachments were to start the war-whoop, while Duff and some with a smattering of French were to run up and down the streets proclaiming that every *habitan* who left his house would be shot. No provision being made for the drummer boy (I had left my drum on the heights above), I chose the favored column, at the head of which Tom and Cowan and Ray and McCann were striding behind Kenton and Colonel Clark. Not a word was spoken. There was a kind of cow-path that rose and fell and twisted along the river-bank. This we followed, and in ten minutes we must have covered the mile to the now darkened village. The starlight alone outlined against the sky the houses of it as we climbed the bank. Then we halted, breathless, in a street, but there was no sound save that of the crickets and the frogs. Forward again, and twisting a corner, we beheld the indented edge of the stockade. Still no hail, nor had our moccasined feet betrayed us as we sought the river side of the fort and drew up before the big river gates of it. Simon Kenton bore against them, and tried the little postern that was set there, but both were fast. The spikes towered a dozen feet overhead.

"Quick!" muttered Clark, "a light man to go over and open the postern."

Before I guessed what was in his mind, Cowan seized me.

"Send the lad, Colonel," said he.

"Ay, ay," said Simon Kenton, hoarsely.

In a second Tom was on Kenton's shoulders, and they passed me up with as little trouble as though I had been my own drum. Feverishly searching with my foot for Tom's shoulder, I seized the spikes at the top, clambered over them, paused, surveyed the empty area below me, destitute even of a sentry, and then let myself down with the aid of the cross-bars inside. As I was feeling vainly for the bolt of the postern, rays of light suddenly shot my shadow against the door. And next, as I got my hand on the bolt-head, I felt the weight of another on my shoulder, and a voice behind me said in English:—

"In the devil's name!"

I gave the one frantic pull, the bolt slipped, and caught again. Then Colonel Clark's voice rang out in the night:—

"Open the gate! Open the gate in the name of Virginia and the Continental Congress!"

Before I could cry out the man gave a grunt, leaned his gun against the gate, and tore my fingers from the bolt-handle. Astonishment robbed me of breath as he threw open the postern.

"In the name of the Continental Congress," he cried, and seized his gun. Clark and Kenton stepped in instantly, no doubt as astounded as I, and had the man in their grasp.

"Who are you?" said Clark.

"Name o' Skene, from Pennsylvanya," said the man, "and by the Lord God ye shall have the fort."

"You looked for us?" said Clark.

"Faith, never less," said the Pennsylvanian. "The one sentry is at the main gate."

"And the governor?"

"Rocheblave?" said the Pennsylvanian. "He sleeps yonder in the old Jesuit house in the middle."

Clark turned to Tom McChesney, who was at his elbow.

"Corporal!" said he, swiftly, "secure the sentry at the main gate! You," he added, turning to the Pennsylvanian, "lead us to the governor. But mind, if you betray me, I'll be the first to blow out your brains."

The man seized a lantern and made swiftly over the level ground until the rubble-work of the old Jesuit house showed in the light, nor Clark nor any of them stopped to think of the danger our little handful ran at the mercy of a stranger. The house was silent. We halted, and Clark threw himself against the rude panels of the door, which gave to inward blackness. Our men filled the little passage, and suddenly we found ourselves in a low-ceiled room in front of a great four-poster bed. And in it, upright, blinking at the light, were two odd Frenchified figures in tasselled nightcaps. Astonishment and anger and fear struggled in the faces of Monsieur de Rocheblave and his lady. A regard for truth compels me to admit that it was madame who first found her voice, and no uncertain one it was.

First came a shriek that might have roused the garrison.

"Villains! Murderers! Outragers of decency!" she cried with spirit, pouring a heap of invectives, now in French, now in English, much to the discomfiture of our backwoodsmen, who peered at her helplessly.

"*Nom du diable!*" cried the commandant, when his lady's breath was gone, "what does this mean?"

"It means, sir," answered Clark, promptly, "that you are my prisoner."

"And who are you?" gasped the commandant.

"George Rogers Clark, Colonel in the service of the Commonwealth of Virginia." He held out his hand restrainingly, for the furious Monsieur Rocheblave made an attempt to rise. "You will oblige me by remaining in bed, sir, for a moment."

"*Coquins! Canailles! Cochons!*" shrieked the lady.

"Madame," said Colonel Clark, politely, "the necessities of war are often cruel."

He made a bow, and paying no further attention to the torrent of her reproaches or the threats of the helpless commandant, he calmly searched the room with the lantern, and finally pulled out from under the bed a metal despatch box. Then he lighted a candle in a brass candlestick that stood on the simple walnut dresser, and bowed again to the outraged couple in the four-poster.

"Now, sir," he said, "you may dress. We will retire."

"*Pardieu!*" said the commandant in French, "a hundred thousand thanks."

We had scarcely closed the bedroom door when three shots were heard.

"The signal!" exclaimed Clark.

Immediately a pandemonium broke on the silence of the night that must have struck cold terror in the hearts of the poor Creoles sleeping in their beds. The war-whoop, the scalp halloo in the dead of the morning, with the hideous winding notes of them that reached the bluff beyond and echoed back, were enough to frighten a man from his senses. In the intervals, in backwoods French, John Duff and his companions were heard in terrifying tones crying out to the *habitans* to venture out at the peril of their lives. Within the fort a score of lights flew up and down like will-o'-the-wisps, and Colonel Clark, standing on the steps of the governor's house, gave out his orders and despatched his messengers. Me he sent speeding through the village to tell Captain Bowman to patrol the outskirts of the town, that no runner might get through to warn Fort Chartres and Cohos, as some called Cahokia. None stirred save the few Indians left in the place, and these were brought before Clark in the fort, sullen and defiant, and put in the guard-house there. And Rocheblave, when he appeared, was no better, and was put back in his house under guard.

As for the papers in the despatch box, they revealed I know not what briberies of the savage nations and plans of the English. But of other papers we found none, though there must have been more. Madame Rocheblave was suspected of having hidden some in the inviolable portions of her dress.

At length the cocks crowing for day proclaimed the morning, and while yet the blue shadow of the bluff was on the town, Colonel Clark sallied out of the gate and walked abroad. Strange it seemed that war had come to this village, so peaceful and remote. And even stranger it seemed to me to see these Arcadian homes in the midst of the fierce wilderness. The little houses with their sloping roofs and wide porches, the gardens ablaze with color, the neat palings,—all were a restful sight for our weary eyes. And now I scarcely knew our commander. For we had not gone far ere, timidly, a door opened and a mild-visaged man, in the simple workaday smock that the French wore, stood, hesitating, on the steps. The odd thing was that he should have bowed to Clark, who was dressed no differently from Bowman and Harrod and Duff; and the man's voice trembled piteously as he spoke. It needed not John Duff to tell us that he was pleading for the lives of his family.

"He will sell himself as a slave if your Excellency will spare them," said Duff, translating.

But Clark stared at the man sternly.

"I will tell them my plans at the proper time," he said and when Duff had translated this the man turned and went silently into his house again, closing the door behind him. And before we had traversed the village the same thing had happened many times. We gained the fort again, I wondering greatly why he had not reassured these simple people. It was Bowman who asked this question, he being closer to Clark than any of the other captains. Clark said nothing then, and began to give out directions for the day. But presently he called the Captain aside.

"Bowman," I heard him say, "we have one hundred and fifty men to hold a province bigger than the whole of France, and filled with treacherous tribes in the King's pay. I must work out the problem for myself."

Bowman was silent. Clark, with that touch which made men love him and die for him, laid his hand on the Captain's shoulder.

"Have the men called in by detachments," he said, "and fed. God knows they must be hungry,—and you."

Suddenly I remembered that he himself had had nothing. Running around the commandant's house to the kitchen door, I came unexpectedly upon Swein Poulsson, who was face to face with the linsey-woolsey-clad figure of Monsieur Rocheblave's negro cook. The early sun cast long shadows of them on the ground.

"By tam," my friend was saying, "so I vill eat. I am choost like an ox for three days, und chew grass. Prairie grass, is it?"

"*Mo pas capab'*, Michié," said the cook, with a terrified roll of his white eyes.

"*Herr Gott!*" cried Swein Poulsson, "I am red face. *Aber Herr Gott*, I thank thee I am not a nigger. Und my hair is bristles, yes. Davy" (spying me), "I thank *Herr Gott* it is not vool. Let us in the kitchen go."

"I am come to get something for the Colonel's breakfast," said I, pushing past the slave, through the open doorway. Swein Poulsson followed, and here I struck another contradiction in his strange nature. He helped me light the fire in the great stone chimney-place, and we soon had a pot of hominy on the crane, and turning on the spit a piece of buffalo steak which we found in the larder. Nor did a mouthful pass his lips until I had sped away with a steaming portion to find the Colonel. By this time the men had broken into the storehouse, and the open place was dotted with their breakfast fires. Clark was standing alone by the flagstaff, his face careworn. But he smiled as he saw me coming.

"What's this?" says he.

"Your breakfast, sir," I answered. I set down the plate and the pot before him and pressed the pewter spoon into his hand.

"Davy," said he.

"Sir?" said I.

"What did you have for your breakfast?"

My lip trembled, for I was very hungry, and the rich steam from the hominy was as much as I could stand. Then the Colonel took me by the arms, as gently as a woman might, set me down on the ground beside him, and taking a spoonful of the hominy forced it between my lips. I was near to fainting at the taste of it. Then he took a bit himself, and divided the buffalo steak with his own hands. And when from the camp-fires they perceived the Colonel and the drummer boy eating together in plain sight of all, they gave a rousing cheer.

"Swein Poulsson helped get your breakfast, sir, and would eat nothing either," I ventured.

"Davy," said Colonel Clark, gravely, "I hope you will be younger when you are twenty."

"I hope I shall be bigger, sir," I answered gravely.

CHAPTER XIV

How the Kaskaskians were made Citizens

NEVER before had such a day dawned upon Kaskaskia. With July fierceness the sun beat down upon the village, but man nor woman nor child stirred from the darkened houses. What they awaited at the hands of the Long Knives they knew not,—captivity, torture, death perhaps. Through the deserted streets stalked a squad of backwoodsmen headed by John Duff and two American traders found in the town, who were bestirring themselves in our behalf, knocking now at this door and anon at that.

"The Colonel bids you come to the fort," he said, and was gone.

The church bell rang with slow, ominous strokes, far different from its gentle vesper peal of yesterday. Two companies were drawn up in the sun before the old Jesuit house, and presently through the gate a procession came, grave and mournful. The tone of it was sombre in the white glare, for men had donned their best (as they thought) for the last time,—cloth of camlet and Cadiz and Limbourg, white cotton stockings, and brass-buckled shoes. They came like captives led to execution. But at their head a figure held our eye,—a figure that spoke of dignity and courage, of trials borne for others. It was the village priest in his robes. He had a receding forehead and a strong, pointed chin; but benevolence was in the curve of his great nose. I have many times since seen his type of face in the French prints. He and his flock halted before our young Colonel, even as the citizens of Calais in a bygone century must have stood before the English king.

The scene comes back to me. On the one side, not the warriors of a nation that has made its mark in war, but peaceful peasants who had sought this place for its remoteness from persecution, to live and die in harmony with all mankind. On the other, the sinewy advance guard of a race that knows not peace, whose goddess of liberty carries in her hand a sword. The plough might have been graven on our arms, but always the rifle.

The silence of the trackless wilds reigned while Clark gazed at them sternly. And when he spoke it was with the voice of a conqueror, and they listened as the conquered listen, with heads bowed—all save the priest.

Clark told them first that they had been given a false and a wicked notion of the American cause, and he spoke of the tyranny of the English king, which had become past endurance to a free people. As for ourselves, the Long Knives, we came in truth to conquer, and because of their hasty judgment the Kaskaskians were at our mercy. The British had told them that the Kentuckians were a barbarous people, and they had believed.

He paused that John Duff might translate and the gist of what he had said sink in. But suddenly the priest had stepped out from the ranks, faced his people, and was himself translating in a strong voice. When he had finished a tremor shook the group. But he turned calmly and faced Clark once more.

"Citizens of Kaskaskia," Colonel Clark went on, "the king whom you renounced when the English conquered you, the great King of France, has judged for you and the French people. Knowing that the American cause is just, he is sending his fleets and regiments to fight for it against the British King, who until now has been your sovereign."

Again he paused, and when the priest had told them this, a murmur of astonishment came from the boldest.

"Citizens of Kaskaskia, know you that the Long Knives come not to massacre, as you foolishly believed, but to release from bondage. We are come not against you, who have been deceived, but against those soldiers of the British King who have bribed the savages to slaughter our wives and children. You have but to take the oath of allegiance to the Continental Congress to become free, even as we are, to enjoy the blessings of that American government under which we live and for which we fight."

The face of the good priest kindled as he glanced at Clark. He turned once more, and though we could not understand his words, the thrill of his eloquence moved us. And when he had finished there was a moment's hush of inarticulate joy among his flock, and then such transports as moved strangely the sternest men in our ranks. The simple people fell to embracing each other and praising God, the tears running on their cheeks. Out of the group came an old man. A skullcap rested on his silvered hair, and he felt the ground uncertainly with his gold-headed stick.

"Monsieur," he said tremulously "you will pardon an old man if he show feeling. I am born seventy year ago in Gascon. I inhabit this country thirty year, and last night I think I not live any longer. Last night we make our peace with the good God, and come here to-day to die. But we know you not," he cried, with a sudden and surprising vigor; "ha, we know you not! They told us lies, and we were humble and believed. But now we are *Américains*," he cried, his voice pitched high, as he pointed with a trembling arm to the stars and stripes above him. "*Mes enfants, vive les Bostonnais! Vive les Américains! Vive Monsieur le Colonel Clark, sauveur de Kaskaskia!*"

The listening village heard the shout and wondered. And when it had died down Colonel Clark took the old Gascon by the hand, and not a man of his but saw that this was a master-stroke of his genius.

"My friends," he said simply, "I thank you. I would not force you, and you will have some days to think over the oath of allegiance to the Republic. Go now to your homes, and tell those who are awaiting you what I have said. And if any man of French birth wish to leave this place, he may go of his own free will, save only three whom I suspect are not our friends."

They turned, and in an ecstasy of joy quite pitiful to see went trooping out of the gate. But scarce could they have reached the street and we have broken ranks, when we saw them coming back again, the priest leading them as before. They drew near to the spot where Clark stood, talking to the captains, and halted expectantly.

"What is it, my friends?" asked the Colonel.

The priest came forward and bowed gravely.

"I am Père Gibault, sir," he said, "curé of Kaskaskia." He paused, surveying our commander with a clear eye. "There is something that still troubles the good citizens."

"And what is that, sir?" said Clark.

The priest hesitated.

"If your Excellency will only allow the church to be opened—" he ventured.

The group stood wistful, fearful that their boldness had displeased, expectant of reprimand.

"My good Father," said Colonel Clark, "an American commander has but one relation to any church. And that is" (he added with force) "to protect it. For all religions are equal before the Republic."

The priest gazed at him intently.

"By that answer," said he, "your Excellency has made for your government loyal citizens in Kaskaskia."

Then the Colonel stepped up to the priest and took him likewise by the hand.

"I have arranged for a house in town," said he. "Monsieur Rocheblave has refused to dine with me there. Will you do me that honor, Father?"

"With all my heart, your Excellency," said Father Gibault. And turning to the people, he translated what the Colonel had said. Then their cup of happiness was indeed full, and some ran to Clark and would have thrown their arms about him had he been a man to embrace. Hurrying out of the gate, they spread the news like wildfire, and presently the church bell clanged in tones of unmistakable joy.

"Sure, Davy dear, it puts me in mind of the Saints' day at home," said Terence, as he stood leaning against a picket fence that bordered the street, "savin' the presence of the naygurs and thim red divils wid blankets an' scowls as wud turrn the milk sour in the pail."

He had stopped beside two Kaskaskia warriors in scarlet blankets who stood at the corner, watching with silent contempt the antics of the French inhabitants. Now and again one or the other gave a grunt and wrapped his blanket more tightly about him.

"Umrrhh!" said Terence. "Faith, I talk that langwidge mesilf when I have throuble." The warriors stared at him with what might be called a stoical surprise. "Umrrh! Does the holy father praych to ye wid thim wurrds, ye haythens? Begorra, 'tis a wondher ye wuddent wash yereselves," he added, making a face, "wid muddy wather to be had for the askin'."

We moved on, through such a scene as I have seldom beheld. The village had donned its best: women in cap and gown were hurrying hither and thither, some laughing and some weeping; grown men embraced each other; children of all colors flung themselves against Terence's legs,—dark-haired Creoles, little negroes with woolly pates, and naked Indian lads with bow and arrow. Terence dashed at them now and then, and they fled screaming into dooryards to come out again and mimic him when he had passed, while mothers and fathers and grandfathers smiled at the good nature in his Irish face. Presently he looked down at me comically.

"Why wuddent ye be doin' the like, Davy?" he asked. "Amusha! 'tis mesilf that wants to run and hop and skip wid the childher. Ye put me in mind of a wizened old man that sat all day makin' shoes in Killarney,—all savin' the fringe he had on his chin."

"A soldier must be dignified," I answered.

"The saints bar that wurrd from hiven," said Terence, trying to pronounce it. "Come, we'll go to mass, or me mother will be visitin' me this night."

We crossed the square and went into the darkened church, where the candles were burning. It was the first church I had ever entered, and I heard with awe the voice of the priest and the fervent responses, but I understood not a word of what was said. Afterwards Father Gibault mounted to the pulpit and stood for a moment with his hand raised above his flock, and then began to speak. What he told them I have learned since. And this I know, that when they came out again into the sunlit square they were Americans. It matters not when they took the oath.

As we walked back towards the fort we came to a little house with a flower garden in front of it, and there stood Colonel Clark himself by the gate. He stopped us with a motion of his hand.

"Davy," said he, "we are to live here for a while, you and I. What do you think of our headquarters?" He did not wait for me to reply, but continued, "Can you suggest any improvement?"

"You will be needing a soldier to be on guard in front, sir," said I.

"Ah," said the Colonel, "McChesney is too valuable a man. I am sending him with Captain Bowman to take Cahokia."

"Would you have Terence, sir?" I ventured, while Terence grinned. Whereupon Colonel Clark sent him to report to his captain that he was detailed for orderly duty to the commanding officer. And within half an hour he was standing guard in the flower garden, making grimaces at the children in the street. Colonel Clark sat at a table in the little front room, and while two of Monsieur Rocheblave's negroes cooked his dinner, he was busy with a score of visitors, organizing, advising, planning, and commanding. There were disputes to settle now that alarm had subsided, and at noon three excitable gentlemen came in to inform against a certain Monsieur Cerre, merchant and trader, then absent at St. Louis. When at length the Colonel had succeeded in bringing their denunciations to an end and they had departed, he looked at me comically as I stood in the doorway.

"Davy," said he, "all I ask of the good Lord is that He will frighten me incontinently for a month before I die."

"I think He would find that difficult, sir," I answered.

"Then there's no hope for me," he answered, laughing, "for I have observed that fright alone brings a man into a fit spiritual state to enter heaven. What would you say of those slanderers of Monsieur Cerre?"

Not expecting an answer, he dipped his quill into the ink-pot and turned to his papers.

"I should say that they owed Monsieur Cerre money," I replied.

The Colonel dropped his quill and stared. As for me, I was puzzled to know why.

"Egad," said Colonel Clark, "most of us get by hard knocks what you seem to have been born with." He fell to musing, a worried look coming on his face that was no stranger to me later, and his hand fell heavily on the loose pile of paper before him. "Davy," says he, "I need a commissary-general."

"What would that be, sir," I asked.

"A John Law, who will make something out of nothing, who will make money out of this blank paper, who will wheedle the Creole traders into believing they are doing us a favor and making their everlasting fortune by advancing us flour and bacon."

"And doesn't Congress make money, sir?" I asked.

"That they do, Davy, by the ton," he replied, "and so must we, as the rulers of a great province. For mark me, though the men are happy to-day, in four days they will be grumbling and trying to desert in dozens."

We were interrupted by a knock at the door, and there stood Terence McCann.

"His riverence!" he announced, and bowed low as the priest came into the room.

I was bid by Colonel Clark to sit down and dine with them on the good things which Monsieur Rocheblave's cook had prepared. After dinner they went into the little orchard behind the house and sat drinking (in the French fashion) the commandant's precious coffee which had been sent to him from far-away New Orleans. Colonel Clark plied the priest with questions of the French towns under English rule: and Father Gibault, speaking for his simple people, said that the English had led them easily to believe that the Kentuckians were cutthroats.

"Ah, monsieur," he said, "if they but knew you! If they but knew the principles of that government for which you fight, they would renounce the English allegiance, and the whole of this territory would be yours. I know them, from Quebec to Detroit and Michilimackinac and Saint Vincennes. Listen, monsieur," he cried, his homely face alight; "I myself will go to Saint Vincennes for you. I will tell them the truth, and you shall have the post for the asking."

"You will go to Vincennes!" exclaimed Clark; "a hard and dangerous journey of a hundred leagues!"

"Monsieur," answered the priest, simply, "the journey is nothing. For a century the missionaries of the Church have walked this wilderness alone with God. Often they have suffered, and often died in tortures—but gladly."

Colonel Clark regarded the man intently.

"The cause of liberty, both religious and civil, is our cause," Father Gibault continued. "Men have died for it, and will die for it, and it will prosper. Furthermore, Monsieur, my life has not known many wants. I have saved something to keep my old age, with which to buy a little house and an orchard in this peaceful place. The sum I have is at your service. The good Congress will repay me. And you need the money."

Colonel Clark was not an impulsive man, but he felt none the less deeply, as I know well. His reply to this generous offer was almost brusque, but it did not deceive the priest.

"Nay, monsieur," he said, "it is for mankind I give it, in remembrance of Him who gave everything. And though I receive nothing in return, I shall have my reward an hundred fold."

In due time, I know not how, the talk swung round again to lightness, for the Colonel loved a good story, and the priest had many which he told with wit in his quaint French accent. As he was rising to take his leave, Père Gibault put his hand on my head.

"I saw your Excellency's son in the church this morning," he said.

Colonel Clark laughed and gave me a pinch.

"My dear sir," he said, "the boy is old enough to be my father."

The priest looked down at me with a puzzled expression in his brown eyes.

"I would I had him for my son," said Colonel Clark, kindly; "but the lad is eleven, and I shall not be twenty-six until next November."

"Your Excellency not twenty-six!" cried Father Gibault, in astonishment. "What will you be when you are thirty?"

The young Colonel's face clouded.

"God knows!" he said.

Father Gibault dropped his eyes and turned to me with native tact.

"What would you like best to do, my son?" he asked.

"I should like to learn to speak French," said I, for I had been much irritated at not understanding what was said in the streets.

"And so you shall," said Father Gibault; "I myself will teach you. You must come to my house to-day."

"And Davy will teach me," said the Colonel.

CHAPTER XV

Days of Trial

But I was not immediately to take up the study of French. Things began to happen in Kaskaskia. In the first place, Captain Bowman's company, with a few scouts, of which Tom was one, set out that very afternoon for the capture of Cohos, or Cahokia, and this despite the fact that they had had no sleep for two nights. If you will look at the map,[1] you will see, dotted along the bottoms and the bluffs beside the great Mississippi, the string of villages, Kaskaskia, La Prairie du Rocher, Fort Chartres, St. Philip, and Cahokia. Some few miles from Cahokia, on the western bank of the Father of Waters, was the little French village of St. Louis, in the Spanish territory of Louisiana. From thence eastward stretched the great waste of prairie and forest inhabited by roving bands of the forty Indian nations. Then you come to Vincennes on the Wabash, Fort St. Vincent, the English and Canadians called it, for there were a few of the latter who had settled in Kaskaskia since the English occupation.

[1]The best map which the editor has found of this district is in vol. VI, Part 11, of Winsor's "Narrative and Critical History of America," p. 721.

We gathered on the western skirts of the village to give Bowman's company a cheer, and every man, woman, and child in the place watched the little column as it wound snakelike over the prairie on the road to Fort Chartres, until it was lost in the cottonwoods to the westward.

Things began to happen in Kaskaskia. It would have been strange indeed if things had not happened. One hundred and seventy-five men had marched into that territory out of which now are carved the great states of Ohio, Indiana, and Illinois, and to most of them the thing was a picnic, a jaunt which would soon be finished. Many had left families in the frontier forts without protection. The time of their enlistment had almost expired.

There was a store in the village kept by a great citizen,—not a citizen of Kaskaskia alone, but a citizen of the world. This, I am aware, sounds like fiction, like an attempt to get an effect which was not there. But it is true as gospel. The owner of this store had many others scattered about in this foreign country: at Vincennes, at St. Louis, where he resided, at Cahokia. He knew Michilimackinac and Quebec and New Orleans. He had been born some thirty-one years before in Sardinia, had served in the Spanish army, and was still a Spanish subject. The name of this famous gentleman was Monsieur François Vigo, and he was the Rothschild of the country north of the Ohio. Monsieur Vigo, though he merited it, I had not room to mention in the last chapter. Clark had routed him from his bed on the morning of our arrival, and whether or not he had been in the secret of frightening the inhabitants into making their wills, and then throwing them into transports of joy, I know not.

Monsieur Vigo's store was the village club. It had neither glass in the window nor an attractive display of goods; it was merely a log cabin set down on a weedy, sun-baked plot. The stuffy smell of skins and furs came out of the doorway. Within, when he was in Kaskaskia, Monsieur Vigo was wont to sit behind his rough walnut table, writing with a fine quill, or dispensing the news of the villages to the priest and other prominent citizens, or haggling with persistent blanketed braves over canoe-loads of ill-smelling pelts which they brought down from the green forests of the north. Monsieur Vigo's clothes were the color of the tobacco he gave in exchange; his eyes were not unlike the black beads he traded, but shrewd and kindly withal, set in a square saffron face that had the contradiction of a small chin. As the days wore into months, Monsieur Vigo's place very naturally became the headquarters for our army, if army it might be called. Of a morning a dozen would be sitting against the logs in the black shadow, and in the midst of them always squatted an unsavory Indian squaw. A few braves usually stood like statues at the corner, and in front of the door another group of hunting shirts. Without was the paper money of the Continental Congress, within the good *tafia* and tobacco of Monsieur Vigo. One day Monsieur Vigo's young Creole clerk stood shrugging his shoulders in the doorway. I stopped.

"By tam!" Swein Poulsson was crying to the clerk, as he waved a worthless scrip above his head. "Vat is money?"

This definition the clerk, not being a Doctor Johnson, was unable to give offhand.

"Vat are you, choost? Is it America?" demanded Poulsson, while the others looked on, some laughing, some serious. "And vich citizen are you since you are ours? You vill please to give me one carrot of tobacco." And he thrust the scrip under the clerk's nose.

The clerk stared at the uneven lettering on the scrip with disdain.

"Money," he exclaimed scornfully, "she is not money. *Piastre*—Spanish dollare—then I give you carrot."

"By God!" shouted Bill Cowan, "ye will take Virginny paper, and Congress paper, or else I reckon we'll have a drink and tobaccy, boys, take or no take."

"Hooray, Bill, ye're right," cried several of our men.

"Lemme in here," said Cowan. But the frightened Creole blocked the doorway.

"*Sacré!*" he screamed, and then, "*Voleurs!*"

The excitement drew a number of people from the neighborhood. Nay, it seemed as if the whole town was ringed about us.

"*Bravo, Jules!*" they cried, "*garde-tu la porte. À bas les Bostonnais! À bas les voleurs!*"

"Damn such monkey talk," said Cowan, facing them suddenly. I knew him well, and when the giant lost his temper it was gone irrevocably until a fight was over. "Call a man a squar' name."

"Hey, Frenchy," another of our men put in, stalking up to the clerk, "I reckon this here store's ourn, ef we've a mind to tek it. I 'low you'll give us the rum and the 'baccy. Come on, boys!"

In between him and the clerk leaped a little, robin-like man with a red waistcoat, beside himself with rage. Bill Cowan and his friends stared at this diminutive Frenchman, open-mouthed, as he poured forth a veritable torrent of unintelligible words, plentifully mixed with *sacrés*, which he ripped out like snarls. I would as soon have touched him as a ball of angry bees or a pair of fighting wildcats. Not so Bill Cowan. When that worthy recovered from his first surprise he seized hold of some of the man's twisting arms and legs and lifted him bodily from the ground, as he would have taken a perverse and struggling child. There was no question of a fight. Cowan picked him up, I say, and before any one knew what happened, he flung him on to the hot roof of the store (the eaves were but two feet above his head), and there the man stuck, clinging to a loose shingle, purpling and coughing and spitting with rage. There was a loud gust of guffaws from the woodsmen, and oaths like whip-cracks from the circle around us, menacing growls as it surged inward and our men turned to face it. A few citizens pushed through the outskirts of it and ran away, and in the hush that followed we heard them calling wildly the names of Father Gibault and Clark and of Vigo himself. Cowan thrust me past the clerk into the store, where I stood listening to the little man on the roof, scratching and clutching at the shingles, and coughing still.

But there was no fight. Shouts of *"Monsieur Vigo! Voici Monsieur Vigo!"* were heard, the crowd parted respectfully, and Monsieur Vigo in his snuff-colored suit stood glancing from Cowan to his pallid clerk. He was not in the least excited.

"Come in, my frens," he said; "it is too hot in the sun." And he set the example by stepping over the sill on to the hard-baked earth of the floor within. Then he spied me. "Ah," he said, "the boy of Monsieur le Colonel! And how are you called, my son?" he added, patting me kindly.

"Davy, sir," I answered.

"Ha," he said, "and a brave soldier, no doubt."

I was flattered as well as astonished by this attention. But Monsieur Vigo knew men, and he had given them time to turn around. By this time Bill Cowan and some of my friends had stooped through the doorway, followed by a prying Kaskaskian brave and as many Creoles as could crowd behind them. Monsieur Vigo was surprisingly calm.

"It make hot weather, my frens," said he. "How can I serve you, messieurs?"

"Hain't the Congress got authority here?" said one.

"I am happy to say," answered Monsieur Vigo, rubbing his hands, "for I think much of your principle."

"Then," said the man, "we come here to trade with Congress money. Hain't that money good in Kaskasky?"

There was an anxious pause. Then Monsieur Vigo's eyes twinkled, and he looked at me.

"And what you say, Davy?" he asked.

"The money would be good if you took it, sir," I said, not knowing what else to answer.

"*Sapristi!*" exclaimed Monsieur Vigo, looking hard at me. "Who teach you that?"

"No one, sir," said I, staring in my turn.

"And if Congress lose, and not pay, where am I, *mon petit maître de la haute finance?*" demanded Monsieur Vigo, with the palms of his hands outward.

"You will be in good company, sir," said I.

At that he threw back his head and laughed, and Bill Cowan and my friends laughed with him.

"Good company—*c'est la plupart de la vie,*" said Monsieur Vigo. "*Et quel garçon*—what a boy it is!"

"I never seed his beat fer wisdom, Mister Vigo," said Bill Cowan, now in good humor once more at the prospect of rum and tobacco. And I found out later that he and the others had actually given to me the credit of this coup. "He never failed us yet. Hain't that truth, boys? Hain't we a-goin' on to St. Vincent because he seen the Ha'r Buyer sculped on the Ohio?"

The rest assented so heartily but withal so gravely, that I am between laughter and tears over the remembrance of it.

"At noon you come back," said Monsieur Vigo. "I think till then about rate of exchange, and talk with your Colonel. Davy, you stay here."

I remained, while the others filed out, and at length I was alone with him and Jules, his clerk.

"Davy, how you like to be trader?" asked Monsieur Vigo.

It was a new thought to me, and I turned it over in my mind. To see the strange places of the world, and the stranger people; to become a man of wealth and influence such as Monsieur Vigo; and (I fear I loved it best) to match my brains with others at a bargain,—I turned it all over slowly, gravely, in my boyish mind, rubbing the hard dirt on the floor with the toe of my moccasin. And suddenly the thought came to me that I was a traitor to my friends, a deserter from the little army that loved me so well.

"*Eh bien?*" said Monsieur Vigo.

I shook my head, but in spite of me I felt the tears welling into my eyes and brushed them away shamefully. At such times of stress some of my paternal Scotch crept into my speech.

"I will no be leaving Colonel Clark and the boys," I cried, "not for all the money in the world."

"Congress money?" said Monsieur Vigo, with a queer expression.

It was then I laughed through my tears, and that cemented the friendship between us. It was a lifelong friendship, though I little suspected it then.

In the days that followed he never met me on the street that he did not stop to pass the time of day, and ask me if I had changed my mind. He came every morning to headquarters, where he and Colonel Clark sat by the hour with brows knit. Monsieur Vigo was as good as his word, and took the Congress money, though not at such a value as many would have had him. I have often thought that we were all children then, and knew nothing of the ingratitude of republics. Monsieur Vigo took the money, and was all his life many, many thousand dollars the poorer. Father Gibault advanced his little store, and lived to feel the pangs of want. And Colonel Clark? But I must not go beyond the troubles of that summer, and the problems that vexed our commander. One night I missed him from the room where we slept, and walking into the orchard found him pacing there, where the moon cast filmy shadows on the grass. By day as he went around among the men his brow was unclouded, though his face was stern. But now I surprised the man so strangely moved that I yearned to comfort him. He had taken three turns before he perceived me.

"Davy," he said, "what are you doing here?"

"I missed you, sir," I answered, staring at the furrows in his face.

"Come!" he said almost roughly, and seizing my hand, led me back and forth swiftly through the wet grass for I know not how long. The moon dipped to the uneven line of the ridge-pole and slipped behind the stone chimney. All at once he stopped, dropped my hand, and smote both of his together.

"I *will* hold on, by the eternal!" he cried. "I will let no American read his history and say that I abandoned this land. Let them desert! If ten men be found who will stay, I will hold the place for the Republic."

"Will not Virginia and the Congress send you men, sir?" I asked wonderingly.

He laughed a laugh that was all bitterness.

"Virginia and the Continental Congress know little and care less about me," he answered. "Some day you will learn that foresight sometimes comes to men, but never to assemblies. But it is often given to one man to work out the salvation of a people, and be destroyed for it. Davy, we have been up too long."

At the morning parade, from my wonted place at the end of the line, I watched him with astonishment, reviewing the troops as usual. For the very first day I had crossed the river with Terence, climbed the heights to the old fort, and returned with my drum. But no sooner had I beaten the retreat than the men gathered here and there in groups that smouldered with mutiny, and I noted that some of the officers were amongst these. Once in a while a sentence like a flaming brand was flung out. Their time was up, their wives and children for all they knew sculped by the red varmints, and, by the etarnal, Clark or no man living could keep them.

"Hi," said one, as I passed, "here's Davy with his drum. He'll be leadin' us back to Kaintuck in the morning."

"Ay, ay," cried another man in the group, "I reckon he's had his full of tyranny, too."

I stopped, my face blazing red.

"Shame on you for those words!" I shouted shrilly. "Shame on you, you fools, to desert the man who would save your wives and children. How are the redskins to be beaten if they are not cowed in their own country?" For I had learned much at headquarters.

They stood silent, astonished, no doubt, at the sight of my small figure a-tremble with anger. I heard Bill Cowan's voice behind me.

"There's truth for ye," he said, "that will slink home when a thing's half done."

"Ye needn't talk, Bill Cowan; it's well enough for ye. I reckon your wife'd scare any redskin off her clearin'."

"Many the time she scart me," said Bill Cowan.

And so the matter went by with a laugh. But the grumbling continued, and the danger was that the French would learn of it. The day passed, yet the embers blazed not into the flame of open mutiny. But he who has seen service knows how ominous is the gathering of men here and there, the low humming talk, the silence when a dissenter passes. There were fights, too, that had to be quelled by company captains, and no man knew when the loud quarrel between the two races at Vigo's store would grow into an ugly battle.

What did Clark intend to do? This was the question that hung in the minds of mutineer and faithful alike. They knew the desperation of his case. Without money, save that which the generous Creoles had advanced upon his personal credit; without apparent resources; without authority, save that which the weight of his character exerted,—how could he prevent desertion? They eyed him as he went from place to place about his business,—erect, thoughtful, undisturbed. Few men dare to set their will against a multitude when there are no fruits to be won. Columbus persisted, and found a new world; Clark persisted, and won an empire for thoughtless generations to enjoy.

That night he slept not at all, but sat, while the candles flickered in their sockets, poring over maps and papers. I dared not disturb him, but lay the darkness through with staring eyes. And when the windows on the orchard side showed a gray square of light, he flung down the parchment he was reading on the table. It rolled up of itself, and he pushed back his chair. I heard him call my name, and leaping out of bed, I stood before him.

"You sleep lightly, Davy," he said, I think to try me.

I did not answer, fearing to tell him that I had been awake watching him.

"I have one friend, at least," said the Colonel.

"You have many, sir," I answered, "as you will find when the time comes."

"The time has come," said he; "to-day I shall be able to count them. Davy, I want you to do something for me."

"Now, sir?" I answered, overjoyed.

"As soon as the sun strikes that orchard," he said, pointing out of the window. "You have learned how to keep things to yourself. Now I want you to impart them to others. Go out, and tell the village that I am going away."

"That you are going away, sir?" I repeated.

"That I am going away," he said, "with my army, (save the mark!), with my army and my drummer boy and my paper money. Such is my faith in the loyalty of the good people of these villages to the American cause, that I can safely leave the flag flying over their heads with the assurance that they will protect it."

I stared at him doubtfully, for at times a pleasantry came out of his bitterness.

"Ay," he said, "go! Have you any love for me?"

"I have, sir," I answered.

"By the Lord, I believe you," he said, and picking up my small hunting shirt, he flung it at me. "Put it on, and go when the sun rises."

As the first shaft of light over the bluff revealed the diamonds in the orchard grass I went out, wondering. *Suspecting* would be a better word for the nature I had inherited. But I had my orders. Terence was pacing the garden, his leggings turned black with the dew. I looked at him. Here was a vessel to disseminate.

"Terence, the Colonel is going back to Virginia with the army."

"Him!" cried Terence, dropping the stock of his Deckard to the ground. "And back to Kaintuckee! Arrah, 'tis a sin to be jokin' before a man has a bit in his sthummick. Bad cess to yere plisantry before breakfast."

"I'm telling you what the Colonel himself told me," I answered, and ran on. "Davy, darlin'!" I heard him calling after me as I turned the corner, but I looked not back.

There was a single sound in the street. A thin, bronzed Indian lad squatted against the pickets with his fingers on a reed, his cheeks distended. He broke off with a wild, mournful note to stare at me. A wisp of smoke stole from a stone chimney, and the smell that cornpone and bacon leave was in the air. A bolt was slammed back, a door creaked and stuck, was flung open, and with a *"Va t'en, méchant!"* a cotton-clad urchin was cast out of the house, and fled into the dusty street. Breathing the morning air in the doorway, stood a young woman in a cotton gown, a saucepan in hand. She had inquisitive eyes, a pointed, prying nose, and I knew her to be the village gossip, the wife of Jules, Monsieur Vigo's clerk. She had the same smattering of English as her husband. Now she stood regarding me narrowly between half-closed lids.

"A la bonne heure! Que fais-tu donc? What do you do so early?"

"The garrison is getting ready to leave for Kentucky to-day," I answered.

"Ha! Jules! Écoute-toi! Nom de dieu! Is it true what you say?"

The visage of Jules, surmounted by a nightcap and heavy with sleep, appeared behind her.

"Ha, e'est Daveed!" he said. "What news have you?"

I repeated, whereupon they both began to lament.

"And why is it?" persisted Jules.

"He has such faith in the loyalty of the Kaskaskians," I answered, parrot-like.

"Diable!" cried Jules, "we shall perish. We shall be as the Acadians. And loyalty—she will not save us, no."

Other doors creaked. Other inhabitants came in varied costumes into the street to hear the news, lamenting. If Clark left, the day of judgment was at hand for them, that was certain. Between the savage and the Briton not one stone would be left standing on another. Madame Jules forgot her breakfast, and fled up the street with the tidings. And then I made my way to the fort, where the men were gathering about the camp-fires, talking excitedly. Terence, relieved from duty, had done the work here.

"And he as little as a fox, wid all that in him," he cried, when he perceived me walking demurely past the sentry. "Davy, dear, come here an' tell the b'ys am I a liar."

"Davy's monstrous cute," said Bill Cowan; "I reckon he knows as well as me the Colonel hain't a-goin' to do no such tomfool thing as leave."

"He is," I cried, for the benefit of some others, "he's fair sick of grumblers that haven't got the grit to stand by him in trouble."

"By the Lord!" said Bill Cowan, "and I'll not blame him." He turned fiercely, his face reddening. "Shame on ye all yere lives," he shouted. "Ye're making the best man that ever led a regiment take the back trail. Ye'll fetch back to Kaintuck, and draw every redskin in the north woods suckin' after ye like leaves in a harricane wind. There hain't a man of ye has the pluck of this little shaver that beats the drum. I wish to God McChesney was here."

He turned away to cross the parade ground, followed by the faithful Terence and myself. Others gathered about him: McAndrew, who, for all his sourness, was true; Swein Poulsson, who would have died for the Colonel; John Duff, and some twenty more, including Saunders, whose affection had not been killed, though Clark had nearly hanged him among the prairies.

"Begob!" said Terence, "Davy has inflooence wid his Excellency. It's Davy we'll sind, prayin' him not to lave the Frinch alone wid their loyalty."

It was agreed, and I was to repeat the name of every man that sent me.

Departing on this embassy, I sped out of the gates of the fort. But, as I approached the little house where Clark lived, the humming of a crowd came to my ears, and I saw with astonishment that the street was blocked. It appeared that the whole of the inhabitants of Kaskaskia were packed in front of the place. Wriggling my way through the people, I had barely reached the gate when I saw Monsieur Vigo and the priest, three Creole gentlemen in uniform, and several others coming out of the door. They stopped, and Monsieur Vigo, raising his hand for silence, made a speech in French to the people. What he said I could not understand, and when he had finished they broke up into groups, and many of them departed. Before I could gain the house, Colonel Clark himself came out with Captain Helm and Captain Harrod. The Colonel glanced at me and smiled.

"Parade, Davy," he said, and walked on.

I ran back to the fort, and when I had gotten my drum the three companies were falling into line, the men murmuring in undertones among themselves. They were brought to attention. Colonel Clark was seen to come out of the commandant's house, and we watched him furtively as he walked slowly to his place in front of the line. A tremor of excitement went from sergeant to drummer boy. The sentries closed the big gates of the fort.

The Colonel stood for a full minute surveying us calmly,—a disquieting way he had when matters were at a crisis. Then he began to talk.

"I have heard from many sources that you are dissatisfied, that you wish to go back to Kentucky. If that be so, I say to you, 'Go, and God be with you.' I will hinder no man. We have taken a brave and generous people into the fold of the Republic, and they have shown their patriotism by giving us freely of their money and stores." He raised his voice. "They have given the last proof of that patriotism this day. Yes, they have come to me and offered to take your places, to finish the campaign which you have so well begun and wish to abandon. To-day I shall enroll their militia under the flag for which you have fought."

When he had ceased speaking a murmur ran through the ranks.

"But if there be any," he said, "who have faith in me and in the cause for which we have come here, who have the perseverance and the courage to remain, I will reënlist them. The rest of you shall march for Kentucky," he cried, "as soon as Captain Bowman's company can be relieved at Cahokia. The regiment is dismissed."

For a moment they remained in ranks, as though stupefied. It was Cowan who stepped out first, snatched his coonskin hat from his head, and waved it in the air.

"Huzzay for Colonel Clark!" he roared. "I'll foller him into Canady, and stand up to my lick log."

They surrounded Bill Cowan, not the twenty which had flocked to him in the morning, but four times twenty, and they marched in a body to the commandant's house to be reënlisted. The Colonel stood by the door, and there came a light in his eyes as he regarded us. They cheered him again.

"Thank you, lads," he said; "remember, we may have to whistle for our pay."

"Damn the pay!" cried Bill Cowan, and we echoed the sentiment.

"We'll see what can be done about land grants," said the Colonel, and he turned away.

At dusk that evening I sat on the back door-step, by the orchard, cleaning his rifle. The sound of steps came from the little passage behind me, and a hand was on my head.

"Davee," said a voice (it was Monsieur Vigo's), "do you know what is *un coup d' é'tat?*"

"No, sir."

"Ha! You execute one to-day. Is it not so, Monsieur le Colonel?"

"I reckon he was in the secret," said Colonel Clark. "Did you think I meant to leave Kaskaskia, Davy?"

"No, sir."

"He is not so easy fool," Monsieur Vigo put in. "He tell me paper money good if I take it. *C'est la haute finance!*"

Colonel Clark laughed.

"And why didn't you think I meant to leave?" said he.

"Because you bade me go out and tell everybody," I answered. "What you really mean to do you tell no one."

"*Nom du bon Dieu!*" exclaimed Monsieur Vigo.

Yesterday Colonel Clark had stood alone, the enterprise for which he had risked all on the verge of failure. By a master-stroke his ranks were repleted, his position recovered, his authority secured once more.

Few men recognize genius when they see it. Monsieur Vigo was not one of these.

The Crossing, Vol. 1

CHAPTER XVI

Davy goes to Cahokia

I should make but a poor historian, for I have not stuck to my chronology. But as I write, the vivid recollections are those that I set down. I have forgotten two things of great importance. First, the departure of Father Gibault with several Creole gentlemen and a spy of Colonel Clark's for Vincennes, and their triumphant return in August. The sacrifice of the good priest had not been in vain, and he came back with the joyous news of a peaceful conquest. The stars and stripes now waved over the fort, and the French themselves had put it there. And the vast stretch of country from that place westward to the Father of Waters was now American.

And that brings me to the second oversight. The surprise and conquest of Cahokia by Bowman and his men was like that of Kaskaskia. And the French there were loyal, too, offering their militia for service in the place of those men of Bowman's company who would not reënlist. These came to Kaskaskia to join our home-goers, and no sooner had the hundred marched out of the gate and taken up their way for Kentucky than Colonel Clark began the drilling of the new troops.

Captain Leonard Helm was sent to take charge of Vincennes, and Captain Montgomery set out across the mountains for Williamsburg with letters praying the governor of Virginia to come to our assistance.

For another cloud had risen in the horizon: another problem for Clark to face of greater portent than all the others. A messenger from Captain Bowman at Cohos came riding down the street on a scraggly French pony, and pulled up before headquarters. The messenger was Sergeant Thomas McChesney, and his long legs almost reached the ground on either side of the little beast. Leaping from the saddle, he seized me in his arms, set me down, and bade me tell Colonel Clark of his arrival.

It was a sultry August morning. Within the hour Colonel Clark and Tom and myself were riding over the dusty trace that wound westward across the common lands of the village, which was known as the Fort Chartres road. The heat-haze shimmered in the distance, and there was no sound in plain or village save the tinkle of a cowbell from the clumps of shade. Colonel Clark rode twenty paces in front, alone, his head bowed with thinking.

"They're coming into Cahokia as thick as bees out'n a gum, Davy," said Tom; "seems like there's thousands of 'em. Nothin' will do 'em but they must see the Colonel,—the varmints. And they've got patience, they'll wait thar till the b'ars git fat. I reckon they 'low Clark's got the armies of Congress behind him. If they knowed," said Tom, with a chuckle, "if they knowed that we'd only got seventy of the boys and some hundred Frenchies in the army! I reckon the Colonel's too cute for 'em."

The savages in Cahokia were as the leaves of the forest. Curiosity, that mainspring of the Indian character, had brought the chiefs, big and little, to see with their own eyes the great Captain of the Long Knives. In vain had the faithful Bowman put them off. They would wait. Clark must come. And Clark was coming, for he was not the man to quail at such a crisis. For the crux of the whole matter was here. And if he failed to impress them with his power, with the might of the Congress for which he fought, no man of his would ever see Kentucky again.

As we rode through the bottom under the pecan trees we talked of Polly Ann, Tom and I, and of our little home by the Salt River far to the southward, where we would live in peace when the campaign was over. Tom had written her, painfully enough, an affectionate scrawl, which he sent by one of Captain Linn's men. And I, too, had written. My letter had been about Tom, and how he had become a sergeant, and what a favorite he was with Bowman and the Colonel. Poor Polly Ann! She could not write, but a runner from Harrodstown who was a friend of Tom's had carried all the way to Cahokia, in the pocket with his despatches, a fold of nettle-bark linen. Tom pulled it from the bosom of his hunting shirt to show me, and in it was a little ring of hair like unto the finest spun red-gold. This was the message Polly Ann had sent,—a message from little Tom as well.

At Prairie du Rocher, at St. Philippe, the inhabitants lined the streets to do homage to this man of strange power who rode, unattended and unafraid, to the council of the savage tribes which had terrorized his people of Kentucky. From the ramparts of Fort Chartres (once one of the mighty chain of strongholds to protect a new France, and now deserted like Massacre), I gazed for the first time in awe at the turgid flood of the Mississippi, and at the lands of the Spanish king beyond. With never ceasing fury the river tore at his clay banks and worried the green islands that braved his charge. And my boyish fancy pictured to itself the monsters which might lie hidden in his muddy depths.

We lay that night in the open at a spring on the bluffs, and the next morning beheld the church tower of Cahokia. A little way from the town we perceived an odd gathering on the road, the yellowed and weathered hunting shirts of Bowman's company mixed with the motley dress of the Creole volunteers. Some of these gentlemen wore the costume of *coureurs du bois*, others had odd regimental coats and hats which had seen much service. Besides the military was a sober deputation of citizens, and hovering behind the whole a horde of curious, blanketed braves, come to get a first glimpse of the great white captain. So escorted, we crossed at the mill, came to a shady street that faced the little river, and stopped at the stone house where Colonel Clark was to abide.

On that day, and for many days more, that street was thronged with warriors. Chiefs in gala dress strutted up and down, feathered and plumed and blanketed, smeared with paint, bedecked with rude jewellery,—earrings and bracelets. From the remote forests of the north they had come, where the cold winds blow off the blue lakes; from the prairies to the east; from the upper running waters, where the Mississippi flows clear and undefiled by the muddy flood; from the villages and wigwams of the sluggish Wabash; and from the sandy, piny country between the great northern seas where Michilimackinac stands guard alone,—Sacs and Foxes, Chippeways and Maumies and Missesogies, Puans and Pottawattomies, chiefs and medicine men.

Well might the sleep of the good citizens be disturbed, and the women fear to venture to the creek with their linen and their paddles!

The lives of these people hung in truth upon a slender thing—the bearing of one man. All day long the great chiefs sought an audience with him, but he sent them word that matters would be settled in the council that was to come. All day long the warriors lined the picket fence in front of the house, and more than once Tom McChesney roughly shouldered a lane through them that timid visitors might pass. Like a pack of wolves, they watched narrowly for any sign of weakness. As for Tom, they were to him as so many dogs.

"Ye varmints!" he cried, "I'll take a blizz'rd at ye if ye don't keep the way clear."

At that they would give back grudgingly with a chorus of grunts, only to close in again as tightly as before. But they came to have a wholesome regard for the sun-browned man with the red hair who guarded the Colonel's privacy. The boy who sat on the door-step, the son of the great Pale Face Chief (as they called me), was a never ending source of comment among them. Once Colonel Clark sent for me. The little front room of this house was not unlike the one we had occupied at Kaskaskia. It had bare walls, a plain table and chairs, and a crucifix in the corner. It served as dining room, parlor, bedroom, for there was a pallet too. Now the table was covered with parchments and papers, and beside Colonel Clark sat a grave gentleman of about his own age. As I came into the room Colonel Clark relaxed, turned toward this gentleman, and said:—

"Monsieur Gratiot, behold my commissary-general, my strategist, my financier." And Monsieur Gratiot smiled. He struck me as a man who never let himself go sufficiently to laugh.

"Ah," he said, "Vigo has told me how he settled the question of paper money. He might do something for the Congress in the East."

"Davy is a Scotchman, like John Law," said the Colonel, "and he is a master at perceiving a man's character and business."

"What would you call me, at a venture, Davy?" asked Monsieur Gratiot.

He spoke excellent English, with only a slight accent.

"A citizen of the world, like Monsieur Vigo," I answered at a hazard.

"*Pardieu!*" said Monsieur Gratiot, "you are not far away. Like Monsieur Vigo I keep a store here at Cahokia. Like Monsieur Vigo, I have travelled much in my day. Do you know where Switzerland is, Davy?"

I did not.

"It is a country set like a cluster of jewels in the heart of Europe," said Monsieur Gratiot, "and there are mountains there that rise amon the clouds and are covered with perpetual snows. And when the sun sets on those snows they are rubies, and the skies above them sapphire."

"I was born amongst the mountains, sir," I answered, my pulse quickening at his description, "but they were not so high as those you speak of."

"Then," said Monsieur Gratiot, "you can understand a little my sorrow as a lad when I left it. From Switzerland I went to a foggy place called London, and thence I crossed the ocean to the solemn forests of the north of Canada, where I was many years, learning the characters of these gentlemen who are looking in upon us." And he waved his arm at the line of peering red faces by the pickets. Monsieur Gratiot smiled at Clark. "And there's another point of resemblance between myself and Monsieur Vigo."

"Have you taken the paper money?" I demanded.

Monsieur Gratiot slapped his linen breeches. "That I have," and this time I thought he was going to laugh. But he did not, though his eyes sparkled. "And do you think that the good Congress will ever repay me, Davy?"

"No, sir," said I.

"*Peste!*" exclaimed Monsieur Gratiot, but he did not seem to be offended or shaken.

"Davy," said Colonel Clark, "we have had enough of predictions fo the present. Fetch this letter to Captain Bowman at the garrison up the street." He handed me the letter. "Are you afraid of the Indians?"

"If I were, sir, I would not show it," I said, for he had encouraged me to talk freely to him.

"Avast!" cried the Colonel, as I was going out. "And why not?"

"If I show that I am not afraid of them, sir, they will think that you are the less so."

"There you are for strategy, Gratiot," said Colonel Clark, laughing. "Get out, you rascal."

Tom was more concerned when I appeared.

"Don't pester 'em, Davy," said he; "fer God's sake don't pester 'em. They're spoilin' fer a fight. Stand back thar, ye critters," he shouted, brandishing his rifle in their faces. "Ugh, I reckon it wouldn't take a horse or a dog to scent ye to-day. Rank b'ar's oil! Kite along, Davy."

Clutching the letter tightly, I slipped between the narrowed ranks, and gained the middle of the street, not without a quickened beat of my heart. Thence I sped, dodging this group and that, until I came to the long log house that was called the garrison. Here our men were stationed, where formerly a squad from an English regiment was quartered. I found Captain Bowman, delivered the letter, and started back again through the brown, dusty street, which lay in the shade of the great forest trees that still lined it, doubling now and again to avoid an idling brave that looked bent upon mischief. For a single mischance might set the tide running to massacre.

I was nearing the gate again, the dust flying from my moccasined feet, the sight of the stalwart Tom giving me courage again. Suddenly, with the deftness of a panther, an Indian shot forward and lifted me high in his arms. To this day I recall my terror as I dangled in mid-air, staring into a hideous face. By intuition I kicked him in the stomach with all my might, and with a howl of surprise and rage his fingers gripped into my flesh. The next thing I remember was being in the dust, suffocated by that odor which he who has known it can never forget. A medley of discordant cries was in my ears. Then I was snatched up, bumped against heads and shoulders, and deposited somewhere. Now it was Tom's face that was close to mine, and the light of a fierce anger was in his blue eyes.

"Did they hurt ye, Davy?" he asked.

I shook my head. Before I could speak he was at the gate again, confronting the mob of savages that swayed against the fence, and the street was filled with running figures. A voice of command that I knew well came from behind me. It was Colonel Clark's.

"Stay where you are, McChesney!" he shouted, and Tom halted with his hand on the latch.

"With your permission, I will speak to them," said Monsieur Gratiot, who had come out also.

I looked up at him, and he was as calm as when he had joked with me a quarter of an hour since.

"Very well," said Clark, briefly.

Monsieur Gratiot surveyed them scornfully.

"Where is the Hungry Wolf, who speaks English?" he said.

There was a stir in the rear ranks, and a lean savage with abnormal cheek bones pushed forward.

"Hungry Wolf here," he said with a grunt.

"The Hungry Wolf knew the French trader at Michilimackinac," said Monsieur Gratiot. "He knows that the French trader's word is a true word. Let the Hungry Wolf tell his companions that the Chief of the Long Knives is very angry."

The Hungry Wolf turned, and began to speak. His words, hoarse and resonant, seemed to come from the depths of his body. Presently he paused, and there came an answer from the fiend who had seized me. After that there were many grunts, and the Hungry Wolf turned again.

"The North Wind mean no harm," he answered. "He play with the son of the Great White Chief, and his belly is very sore where the Chief's son kicked him."

"The Chief of the Long Knives will consider the offence," said Monsieur Gratiot, and retired into the house with Colonel Clark. For a full five minutes the Indians waited, impassive. And then Monsieur Gratiot reappeared, alone.

"The Chief of the Long Knives is mercifully inclined to forgive," he said. "It was in play. But there must be no more play with the Chief's son. And the path to the Great Chief's presence must be kept clear."

Again the Hungry Wolf translated. The North Wind grunted and departed in silence, followed by many of his friends. And indeed for a while after that the others kept a passage clear to the gate.

As for the son of the Great White Chief, he sat for a long time that afternoon beside the truck patch of the house. And presently he slipped out by a byway into the street again, among the savages. His heart was bumping in his throat, but a boyish reasoning told him that he must show no fear. And that day he found what his Colonel had long since learned to be true—that in courage is the greater safety. The power of the Great White Chief was such that he allowed his son to go forth alone, and feared not for his life. Even so Clark himself walked among them, nor looked to right or left.

Two nights Colonel Clark sat through, calling now on this man and now on that, and conning the treaties which the English had made with the various tribes—ay, and French and Spanish treaties too—until he knew them all by heart. There was no haste in what he did, no uneasiness in his manner. He listened to the advice of Monsieur Gratiot and other Creole gentlemen of weight, to the Spanish officers who came in their regimentals from St. Louis out of curiosity to see how this man would treat with the tribes. For he spoke of his intentions to none of them, and gained the more respect by it. Within the week the council began; and the scene of the great drama was a field near the village, the background of forest trees. Few plays on the world's stage have held such suspense, few battles such excitement for those who watched. Here was the spectacle of one strong man's brain pitted against the combined craft of the wilderness. In the midst of a stretch of waving grass was a table, and a young man of six-and-twenty sat there alone. Around him were ringed the gathered tribes, each chief in the order of his importance squatted in the inner circle, their blankets making patches of bright color against the green. Behind the tribes was the little group of hunting shirts, the men leaning on the barrels of their long rifles, indolent but watchful. Here and there a gay uniform of a Spanish or Creole officer, and behind these all the population of the village that dared to show itself.

The ceremonies began with the kindling of the council fire,—a rite handed down through unknown centuries of Indian usage. By it nations had been made and unmade, broad lands passed, even as they now might pass. The yellow of its crackling flames was shamed by the summer sun, and the black smoke of it was wafted by the south wind over the forest. Then for three days the chiefs spoke, and a man listened, unmoved. The sound of these orations, wild and fearful to my boyish ear, comes back to me now. Yet there was a cadence in it, a music of notes now falling, now rising to a passion and intensity that thrilled us.

Bad birds flying through the land (the British agents) had besought them to take up the bloody hatchet. They had sinned. They had listened to the lies which the bad birds had told of the Big Knives, they had taken their presents. But now the Great Spirit in His wisdom had brought themselves and the Chief of the Big Knives together. Therefore (suiting the action to the word) they stamped on the bloody belt, and rent in pieces the emblems of the White King across the water. So said the interpreters, as the chiefs one after another tore the miniature British flags which had been given them into bits. On the evening of the third day the White Chief rose in his chair, gazing haughtily about him. There was a deep silence.

"Tell your chiefs," he said, "tell your chiefs that to-morrow I will give them an answer. And upon the manner in which they receive that answer depends the fate of your nations. Good night."

They rose and, thronging around him, sought to take his hand. But Clark turned from them.

"Peace is not yet come," he said sternly. "It is time to take the hand when the heart is given with it."

A feathered headsman of one of the tribes gave back with dignity and spoke.

"It is well said by the Great Chief of the Pale Faces," he answered; "these in truth are not the words of a man with a double tongue."

So they sought their quarters for the night, and suspense hung breathless over the village.

There were many callers at the stone house that evening,—Spanish officers, Creole gentlemen, an English Canadian trader or two. With my elbow on the sill of the open window I watched them awhile, listening with a boy's eagerness to what they had to say of the day's doings. They disputed amongst themselves in various degrees of English as to the manner of treating the red man,—now gesticulating, now threatening, now seizing a rolled parchment treaty from the table. Clark sat alone, a little apart, silent save a word now and then in a low tone to Monsieur Gratiot or Captain Bowman. Here was an odd assortment of the races which had overrun the new world. At intervals some disputant would pause in his talk to kill a mosquito or fight away a moth or a June-bug, but presently the argument reached such a pitch that the mosquitoes fed undisturbed.

"You have done much, sir," said the Spanish commandant of St. Louis, "but the savage, he will never be content without present. He will never be won without present."

Clark was one of those men who are perforce listened to when they begin to speak.

"Captain de Leyba," said he, "I know not what may be the present policy of his Spanish Majesty with McGillivray and his Creeks in the south, but this I do believe," and he brought down his fist among the papers, "that the old French and Spanish treaties were right in principle. Here are copies of the English treaties that I have secured, and in them thousands of sovereigns have been thrown away. They are so much waste paper. Gentlemen, the Indians are children. If you give them presents, they believe you to be afraid of them. I will deal with them without presents; and if I had the gold of the Bank of England stored in the garrison there, they should not touch a piece of it."

But Captain de Leyba, incredulous, raised his eyebrows and shrugged.

"*Por Dios,*" he cried, "whoever hear of one man and fifty militia subduing the northern tribes without a *piastre?*"

After a while the Colonel called me in, and sent me speeding across the little river with a note to a certain Mr. Brady, whose house was not far away. Like many another citizen of Cahokia, Mr. Brady was terror-ridden. A party of young Puan bucks had decreed it to be their pleasure to encamp in Mr. Brady's yard, to peer through the shutters into Mr. Brady's house, to enjoy themselves by annoying Mr. Brady's family and others as much as possible. During the Indian occupation of Cahokia this band had gained a well-deserved reputation for mischief; and chief among them was the North Wind himself, whom I had done the honor to kick in the stomach. To-night they had made a fire in this Mr. Brady's flower-garden, over which they were cooking venison steaks. And, as I reached the door, the North Wind spied me, grinned, rubbed his stomach, made a false dash at me that frightened me out of my wits, and finally went through the pantomime of scalping me. I stood looking at him with my legs apart, for the son of the Great Chief must not run away. And I marked that the North Wind had two great ornamental daubs like shutter-fastenings painted on his cheeks. I sniffed preparation, too, on his followers, and I was sure they were getting ready for some new deviltry. I handed the note to Mr. Brady through the crack of the door that he vouchsafed to me, and when he had slammed and bolted me out, I ran into the street and stood for some time behind the trunk of a big hickory, watching the followers of the North Wind. Some were painting themselves, others cleaning their rifles and sharpening their scalping knives. All jabbered unceasingly. Now and again a silent brave passed, paused a moment to survey them gravely, grunted an answer to something they would fling at him, and went on. At length arrived three chiefs whom I knew to be high in the councils. The North Wind came out to them, and the four blanketed forms stood silhouetted between me and the fire for a quarter of an hour. By this time I was sure of a plot, and fled away to another tree for fear of detection. At length stalked through the street the Hungry Wolf, the interpreter. I knew this man to be friendly to Clark, and I acted on impulse. He gave a grunt of surprise when I halted before him. I made up my mind.

"The son of the Great Chief knows that the Puans have wickedness in their hearts to-night," I said; "the tongue of the Hungry Wolf does not lie."

The big Indian drew back with another grunt, and the distant firelight flashed on his eyes as on polished black flints.

"Umrrhh! Is the Pale Face Chief's son a prophet?"

"The anger of the Pale Face Chief and of his countrymen is as the hurricane," I said, scarce believing my own ears. For a lad is imitative by nature, and I had not listened to the interpreters for three days without profit.

The Hungry Wolf grunted again, after which he was silent for a long time. Then he said:—

"Let the Chief of the Long Knives have guard tonight." And suddenly he was gone into the darkness.

I waded the creek and sped to Clark. He was alone now, the shutters of the room closed. And as I came in I could scarce believe that he was the same masterful man I had seen at the council that day, and at the conference an hour gone. He was once more the friend at whose feet I sat in private, who talked to me as a companion and a father.

"Where have you been, Davy?" he asked. And then, "What is it, my lad?"

I crept close to him and told him in a breathless undertone, and I knew that I was shaking the while. He listened gravely, and when I had finished laid a firm hand on my head.

"There," he said, "you are a brave lad, and a canny."

He thought a minute, his hand still resting on my head, and then rose and led me to the back door of the house. It was near midnight, and the sounds of the place were stilling, the crickets chirping in the grass.

"Run to Captain Bowman and tell him to send ten men to this door. But they must come man by man, to escape detection. Do you understand?" I nodded and was starting, but he still held me. "God bless you, Davy, you are a brave boy."

He closed the door softly and I sped away, my moccasins making no sound on the soft dirt. I reached the garrison, was challenged by Jack Terrill, the guard, and brought by him to Bowman's room. The Captain sat, undressed, at the edge of his bed. But he was a man of action, and strode into the long room where his company was sleeping and gave his orders without delay.

Half an hour later there was no light in the village. The Colonel's headquarters were dark, but in the kitchen a dozen tall men were waiting.

CHAPTER XVII

THE SACRIFICE

SO far as the world knew, the Chief of the Long Knives slept peacefully in his house. And such was his sense of power that not even a sentry paced the street without. For by these things is the Indian mind impressed. In the tiny kitchen a dozen men and a boy tried to hush their breathing, and sweltered. For it was very hot, and the pent-up odor of past cookings was stifling to men used to the open. In a corner, hooded under a box, was a lighted lantern, and Tom McChesney stood ready to seize it at the first alarm. On such occasions the current of time runs sluggish. Thrice our muscles were startled into tenseness by the baying of a hound, and once a cock crew out of all season. For the night was cloudy and pitchy black, and the dawn as far away as eternity.

Suddenly I knew that every man in the room was on the alert, for the skilled frontiersman, when watchful, has a sixth sense. None of them might have told you what he had heard. The next sound was the faint creaking of Colonel Clark's door as it opened. Wrapping a blanket around the lantern, Tom led the way, and we massed ourselves behind the front door. Another breathing space, and then the war-cry of the Puans broke hideously on the night, and children woke, crying, from their sleep. In two bounds our little detachment was in the street, the fire spouting red from the Deckards, faint, shadowy forms fading along the line of trees. After that an uproar of awakening, cries here and there, a drum beating madly for the militia. The dozen flung themselves across the stream, I hot in their wake, through Mr. Brady's gate, which was open; and there was a scene of sweet tranquillity under the lantern's rays, — the North Wind and his friends wrapped in their blankets and sleeping the sleep of the just.

"Damn the sly varmints," cried Tom, and he turned over the North Wind with his foot, as a log.

With a grunt of fury the Indian shed his blanket and scrambled to his feet, and stood glaring at us through his paint. But suddenly he met the fixed sternness of Clark's gaze, and his own shifted. By this time his followers were up. The North Wind raised his hands to heaven in token of his innocence, and then spread his palms outward. Where was the proof?

"Look!" I cried, quivering with excitement; "look, their leggings and moccasins are wet!"

"There's no devil if they beant!" said Tom, and there was a murmur of approval from the other men.

"The boy is right," said the Colonel, and turned to Tom. "Sergeant, have the chiefs put in irons." He swung on his heel, and without more ado went back to his house to bed. The North Wind and two others were easily singled out as the leaders, and were straightway escorted to the garrison house, their air of injured innocence availing them not a whit. The militia was dismissed, and the village was hushed once more.

But all night long the chiefs went to and fro, taking counsel among themselves. What would the Chief of the Pale Faces do?

The morning came with a cloudy, damp dawning. Within a decent time (for the Indian is decorous) blanketed deputations filled the archways under the trees and waited there as the minutes ran into hours. The Chief of the Long Knives surveyed the morning from his door-step, and his eyes rested on a solemn figure at the gate. It was the Hungry Wolf. Sorrow was in his voice, and he bore messages from the twenty great chiefs who stood beyond. They were come to express their abhorrence of the night's doings, of which they were as innocent as the deer of the forest.

"Let the Hungry Wolf tell the chiefs," said Colonel Clark, briefly, "that the council is the place for talk." And he went back into the house again.

Then he bade me run to Captain Bowman with an order to bring the North Wind and his confederates to the council field in irons.

The day followed the promise of the dawn. The clouds hung low, and now and again great drops struck the faces of the people in the field. And like the heavens, the assembly itself was charged with we knew not what. Was it peace or war? As before, a white man sat with supreme indifference at a table, and in front of him three most unhappy chiefs squatted in the grass, the shame of their irons hidden under the blanket folds. Audacity is truly a part of the equipment of genius. To have rescued the North Wind and his friends would have been child's play; to have retired from the council with threats of war, as easy.

And yet they craved pardon.

One chief after another rose with dignity in the ring and came to the table to plead. An argument deserving mention was that the North Wind had desired to test the friendship of the French for the Big Knives,—set forth without a smile. To all pleaders Colonel Clark shook his head. He, being a warrior, cared little whether such people were friends or foes. He held them in the hollow of his hand. And at length they came no more.

The very clouds seemed to hang motionless when he rose to speak, and you who will may read in his memoir what he said. The Hungry Wolf caught the spirit of it, and was eloquent in his own tongue, and no word of it was lost. First he told them of the causes of war, of the thirteen council fires with the English, and in terms that the Indian mind might grasp, and how their old father, the French King, had joined the Big Knives in this righteous fight.

"Warriors," said he, "here is a bloody belt and a white one; take which you choose. But behave like men. Should it be the bloody path, you may leave this town in safety to join the English, and we shall then see which of us can stain our shirts with the most blood. But, should it be the path of peace as brothers of the Big Knives and of their friends the French, and then you go to your homes and listen to the bad birds, you will then no longer deserve to be called men and warriors,—but creatures of two tongues, which ought to be destroyed. Let us then part this evening in the hope that the Great Spirit will bring us together again with the sun as brothers.

So the council broke up. White man and red went trooping into town, staring curiously at the guard which was leading the North Wind and his friends to another night of meditation. What their fate would be no man knew. Many thought the tomahawk.

That night the citizens of the little village of *Pain Court*, as St. Louis was called, might have seen the sky reddened in the eastward. It was the loom of many fires at Cahokia, and around them the chiefs of the forty tribes—all save the three in durance vile—were gathered in solemn talk. Would they take the bloody belt or the white one? No man cared so little as the Pale Face Chief. When their eyes were turned from the fitful blaze of the logs, the gala light of many candles greeted them. And above the sound of their own speeches rose the merrier note of the fiddle. The garrison windows shone like lanterns, and behind these Creole and backwoodsman swung the village ladies in the gay French dances. The man at whose bidding this merrymaking was held stood in a corner watching with folded arms, and none to look at him might know that he was playing for a stake.

The troubled fires of the Indians had died to embers long before the candles were snuffed in the garrison house and the music ceased.

The sun himself was pleased to hail that last morning of the great council, and beamed with torrid tolerance upon the ceremony of kindling the greatest of the fires. On this morning Colonel Clark did not sit alone, but was surrounded by men of weight,—by Monsieur Gratiot and other citizens, Captain Bowman and the Spanish officers. And when at length the brush crackled and the flames caught the logs, three of the mightiest chiefs arose. The greatest, victor in fifty tribal wars, held in his hand the white belt of peace. The second bore a long-stemmed pipe with a huge bowl. And after him, with measured steps, a third came with a smoking censer,—the sacred fire with which to kindle the pipe. Halting before Clark, he first swung the censer to the heavens, then to the earth, then to all the spirits of the air,—calling these to witness that peace was come at last,—and finally to the Chief of the Long Knives and to the gentlemen of dignity about his person. Next the Indian turned, and spoke to his brethren in measured, sonorous tones. He bade them thank that Great Spirit who had cleared the sky and opened their ears and hearts that they might receive the truth,—who had laid bare to their understanding the lies of the English. Even as these English had served the Big Knives, so might they one day serve the Indians. Therefore he commanded them to cast the tomahawk into the river, and when they should return to their land to drive the evil birds from it. And they must send their wise men to Kaskaskia to hear the words of wisdom of the Great White Chief, Clark. He thanked the Great Spirit for this council fire which He had kindled at Cahokia.

Lifting the bowl of the censer, in the eyes of all the people he drew in a long whiff to bear witness of peace. After him the pipe went the interminable rounds of the chiefs. Colonel Clark took it, and puffed; Captain Bowman puffed, — everybody puffed.

"Davy must have a pull," cried Tom; and even the chiefs smiled as I coughed and sputtered, while my friends roared with laughter. It gave me no great notion of the fragrance of tobacco. And then came such a hand-shaking and grunting as a man rarely sees in a lifetime.

There was but one disquieting question left: What was to become of the North Wind and his friends? None dared mention the matter at such a time. But at length, as the day wore on to afternoon, the Colonel was seen to speak quietly to Captain Bowman, and several backwoodsmen went off toward the town. And presently a silence fell on the company as they beheld the dejected three crossing the field with a guard. They were led before Clark, and when he saw them his face hardened to sternness.

"It is only women who watch to catch a bear sleeping," he said. "The Big Knives do not kill women. I shall give you meat for your journey home, for women cannot hunt. If you remain here, you shall be treated as squaws. Set the women free."

Tom McChesney cast off their irons. As for Clark, he began to talk immediately with Monsieur Gratiot, as though he had dismissed them from his mind. And their agitation was a pitiful thing to see. In vain they pressed about him, in vain they even pulled the fringe of his shirt to gain his attention. And then they went about among the other chiefs, but these dared not intercede. Uneasiness was written on every man's face, and the talk went haltingly. But Clark was serenity itself. At length with a supreme effort they plucked up courage to come again to the table, one holding out the belt of peace, and the other the still smouldering pipe.

Clark paused in his talk. He took the belt, and flung it away over the heads of those around him. He seized the pipe, and taking up his sword from the table drew it, and with one blow clave the stem in half. There was no anger in either act, but much deliberation.

"The Big Knives," he said scornfully, "do not treat with women."

The pleading began again, the Hungry Wolf interpreting with tremors of earnestness. Their lives were spared, but to what purpose, since the White Chief looked with disfavor upon them? Let him know that bad men from Michilimackinac put the deed into their hearts.

"When the Big Knives come upon such people in the wilderness," Clark answered, "they shoot them down that they may not eat the deer. But they have never talked of it."

He turned from them once more; they went away in a dejection to wring our compassion, and we thought the matter ended at last. The sun was falling low, the people beginning to move away, when, to the astonishment of all, the culprits were seen coming back again. With them were two young men of their own nation. The Indians opened up a path for them to pass through, and they came as men go to the grave. So mournful, so impressive withal, that the crowd fell into silence again, and the Colonel turned his eyes. The two young men sank down on the ground before him and shrouded their heads in their blankets.

"What is this?" Clark demanded.

The North Wind spoke in a voice of sorrow:—

"An atonement to the Great White Chief for the sins of our nation. Perchance the Great Chief will deign to strike a tomahawk into their heads, that our nation may be saved in war by the Big Knives." And the North Wind held forth the pipe once more.

"I have nothing to say to you," said Clark.

Still they stood irresolute, their minds now bereft of expedients. And the young men sat motionless on the ground. As Clark talked they peered out from under their blankets, once, twice, thrice. He was still talking to the wondering Monsieur Gratiot. But no other voice was heard, and the eyes of all were turned on him in amazement. But at last, when the drama had risen to the pitch of unbearable suspense, he looked down upon the two miserable pyramids at his feet, and touched them. The blankets quivered.

"Stand up," said the Colonel, "and uncover."

They rose, cast the blankets from them, and stood with a stoic dignity awaiting his pleasure. Wonderful, fine-limbed men they were, and for the first time Clark's eyes were seen to kindle.

"I thank the Great Spirit," said he, in a loud voice, "that I have found men among your nation. That I have at last discovered the real chiefs of your people. Had they sent such as you to treat with me in the beginning all might have been well. Go back to your people as their chiefs, and tell them that through you the Big Knives have granted peace to your nation."

Stepping forward, he grasped them each by the hand, and, despite training, joy shone in their faces, while a long-drawn murmur arose from the assemblage. But Clark did not stop there. He presented them to Captain Bowman and to the French and Spanish gentlemen present, and they were hailed by their own kind as chiefs of their nation. To cap it all our troops, backwoodsmen and Creole militia, paraded in line on the common, and fired a salute in their honor.

Thus did Clark gain the friendship of the forty tribes in the Northwest country.

CHAPTER XVIII

"An' ye had been where I had been"

WE went back to Kaskaskia, Colonel Clark, Tom, and myself, and a great weight was lifted from our hearts.

A peaceful autumn passed, and we were happy save when we thought of those we had left at home. There is no space here to tell of many incidents. Great chiefs who had not been to the council came hundreds of leagues across wide rivers that they might see with their own eyes this man who had made peace without gold, and these had to be amused and entertained.

The apples ripened, and were shaken to the ground by the winds. The good Father Gibault, true to his promise, strove to teach me French. Indeed, I picked up much of that language in my intercourse with the inhabitants of Kaskaskia. How well I recall that simple life,—its dances, its songs, and the games with the laughing boys and girls on the common! And the good people were very kind to the orphan that dwelt with Colonel Clark, the drummer boy of his regiment.

But winter brought forebodings. When the garden patches grew bare and brown, and the bleak winds from across the Mississippi swept over the common, untoward tidings came like water dripping from a roof, bit by bit. And day by day Colonel Clark looked graver. The messengers he had sent to Vincennes came not back, and the *coureurs* and traders from time to time brought rumors of a British force gathering like a thundercloud in the northeast. Monsieur Vigo himself, who had gone to Vincennes on his own business, did not return. As for the inhabitants, some of them who had once bowed to us with a smile now passed with faces averted.

The cold set the miry roads like cement, in ruts and ridges. A flurry of snow came and powdered the roofs even as the French loaves are powdered.

It was January. There was Colonel Clark on a runt of an Indian pony; Tom McChesney on another, riding ahead, several French gentlemen seated on stools in a two-wheeled cart, and myself. We were going to

Cahokia, and it was very cold, and when the tireless wheels bumped from ridge to gully, the gentlemen grabbed each other as they slid about, and laughed.

All at once the merriment ceased, and looking forward we saw that Tom had leaped from his saddle and was bending over something in the snow. These chanced to be the footprints of some twenty men.

The immediate result of this alarming discovery was that Tom went on express to warn Captain Bowman, and the rest of us returned to a painful scene at Kaskaskia. We reached the village, the French gentlemen leaped down from their stools in the cart, and in ten minutes the streets were filled with frenzied, hooded figures. Hamilton, called the Hair Buyer, was upon them with no less than six hundred, and he would hang them to their own gateposts for listening to the Long Knives. These were but a handful after all was said. There was Father Gibault, for example. Father Gibault would doubtless be exposed to the crows in the belfry of his own church because he had busied himself at Vincennes and with other matters. Father Gibault was human, and therefore lovable. He bade his parishioners a hasty and tearful farewell, and he made a cold and painful journey to the territories of his Spanish Majesty across the Mississippi.

Father Gibault looked back, and against the gray of the winter's twilight there were flames like red maple leaves. In the fort the men stood to their guns, their faces flushed with staring at the burning houses. Only a few were burned,—enough to give no cover for Hamilton and his six hundred if they came.

But they did not come. The faithful Bowman and his men arrived instead, with the news that there had been only a roving party of forty, and these were now in full retreat.

Father Gibault came back. But where was Hamilton? This was the disquieting thing.

One bitter day, when the sun smiled mockingly on the powdered common, a horseman was perceived on the Fort Chartres road. It was Monsieur Vigo returning from Vincennes, but he had been first to St. Louis by reason of the value he set upon his head. Yes, Monsieur Vigo had been to Vincennes, remaining a little longer than he expected, the guest of Governor Hamilton. So Governor Hamilton had recaptured that place! Monsieur Vigo was no spy, hence he had gone first to St. Louis. Governor Hamilton was at Vincennes with much of King George's gold, and many supplies, and certain Indians who had not been at the council. Eight hundred in all, said Monsieur Vigo, using his fingers. And it was Governor Hamilton's design to march upon Kaskaskia and Cahokia and sweep over Kentucky; nay, he had already sent certain emissaries to McGillivray and his Creeks and the Southern Indians with presents, and these were to press forward on their side. The Governor could do nothing now, but would move as soon as the rigors of winter had somewhat relented. Monsieur Vigo shook his head and shrugged his shoulders. He loved *les Américains*. What would *Monsieur le Colonel* do now?

Monsieur le Colonel was grave, but this was his usual manner. He did not tear his hair, but the ways of the Long Knives were past understanding. He asked many questions. How was it with the garrison at Vincennes? Monsieur Vigo was exact, as a business man should be. They were now reduced to eighty men, and five hundred savages had gone out to ravage. There was no chance, then, of Hamilton moving at present? Monsieur Vigo threw up his hands. Never had he made such a trip, and he had been forced to come back by a northern route. The Wabash was as the Great Lakes, and the forests grew out of the water. A fox could not go to Vincennes in this weather. A fish? Monsieur Vigo laughed heartily. Yes, a fish might.

"Then," said Colonel Clark, "we will be fish."

Monsieur Vigo stared, and passed his hand from his forehead backwards over his long hair. I leaned forward in my corner by the hickory fire.

"Then we will be fish," said Colonel Clark. "Better that than food for the crows. For, if we stay here, we shall be caught like bears in a trap, and Kentucky will be at Hamilton's mercy."

"*Sacré!*" exclaimed Monsieur Vigo, "you are mad, *mon ami*. I know what this country is, and you cannot get to Vincennes."

"I *will* get to Vincennes," said Colonel Clark, so gently that Monsieur Vigo knew he meant it. "I will *swim* to Vincennes."

Monsieur Vigo raised his hands to heaven. The three of us went out of the door and walked. There was a snowy place in front of the church all party-colored like a clown's coat,—scarlet capotes, yellow capotes, and blue capotes, and bright silk handkerchiefs. They surrounded the Colonel. *Pardieu*, what was he to do now? For the British governor and his savages were coming to take revenge on them because, in their necessity, they had declared for Congress. Colonel Clark went silently on his way to the gate; but Monsieur Vigo stopped, and Kaskaskia heard, with a shock, that this man of iron was to march against Vincennes.

The gates of the fort were shut, and the captains summoned. Undaunted woodsmen as they were, they were lukewarm, at first, at the idea of this march through the floods. Who can blame them? They had, indeed, sacrificed much. But in ten minutes they had caught his enthusiasm (which is one of the mysteries of genius). And the men paraded in the snow likewise caught it, and swung their hats at the notion of taking the Hair Buyer.

"'Tis no news to me," said Terence, stamping his feet on the flinty ground; "wasn't it Davy that pointed him out to us and the hair liftin' from his head six months since?"

"Und you like schwimmin', yes?" said Swein Poulsson, his face like the rising sun with the cold.

"Swimmin', is it?" said Terence; "sure, the divil made worse things than wather. And Hamilton's beyant."

"I reckon that'll fetch us through," Bill Cowan put in grimly.

It was a blessed thing that none of us had a bird's-eye view of that same water. No man of force will listen when his mind is made up, and perhaps it is just as well. For in that way things are accomplished. Clark would not listen to Monsieur Vigo, and hence the financier had, perforce, to listen to Clark. There were several miracles before we left. Monsieur Vigo, for instance, agreed to pay the expenses of the expedition, though in his heart he thought we should never get to Vincennes. Incidentally, he was never repaid. Then there were the French—yesterday, running hither and thither in paroxysms of fear; to-day, enlisting in whole companies, though it were easier to get to the wild geese of the swamps than to Hamilton.

Their ladies stitched colors day and night, and presented them with simple confidence to the Colonel in the church. Twenty stands of colors for 170 men, counting those who had come from Cahokia. Think of the industry of it, of the enthusiasm behind it! Twenty stands of colors! Clark took them all, and in due time it will be told how the colors took Vincennes. This was because Colonel Clark was a man of destiny.

Furthermore, Colonel Clark was off the next morning at dawn to buy a Mississippi keel-boat. He had her rigged up with two four-pounders and four swivels, filled her with provisions, and called her the *Willing*. She was the first gunboat on the Western waters. A great fear came into my heart, and at dusk I stole back to the Colonel's house alone. The snow had turned to rain, and Terence stood guard within the doorway.

"Arrah," he said, "what ails ye, darlin'?"

I gulped and the tears sprang into my eyes; whereupon Terence, in defiance of all military laws, laid his gun against the doorpost and put his arms around me, and I confided my fears. It was at this critical juncture that the door opened and Colonel Clark came out.

"What's to do here?" he demanded, gazing at us sternly.

"Savin' your Honor's prisence," said Terence, "he's afeard your Honor will be sending him on the boat. Sure, he wants to go swimmin' with the rest of us."

Colonel Clark frowned, bit his lip, and Terence seized his gun and stood to attention.

"It were right to leave you in Kaskaskia," said the Colonel; "the water will be over your head."

"The King's drum would be floatin' the likes of him," said the irrepressible Terence, "and the b'ys would be that lonesome."

The Colonel walked away without a word. In an hour's time he came back to find me cleaning his accoutrements by the fire. For a while he did not speak, but busied himself with his papers, I having lighted the candles for him. Presently he spoke my name, and I stood before him.

"I will give you a piece of advice, Davy," said he. "If you want a thing, go straight to the man that has it. McChesney has spoken to me about this wild notion of yours of going to Vincennes, and Cowan and McCann and Ray and a dozen others have dogged my footsteps."

"I only spoke to Terence because he asked me, sir," I answered. "I said nothing to any one else."

He laid down his pen and looked at me with an odd expression.

"What a weird little piece you are," he exclaimed; "you seem to have wormed your way into the hearts of these men. Do you know that you will probably never get to Vincennes alive?"

"I don't care, sir," I said. A happy thought struck me. "If they see a boy going through the water, sir—" I hesitated, abashed.

"What then?" said Clark, shortly.

"It may keep some from going back," I finished.

At that he gave a sort of gasp, and stared at me the more.

"Egad," he said, "I believe the good Lord launched you wrong end to. Perchance you will be a child when you are fifty."

He was silent a long time, and fell to musing. And I thought he had forgotten.

"May I go, sir?" I asked at length.

He started.

"Come here," said he. But when I was close to him he merely laid his hand on my shoulder. "Yes, you may go, Davy."

He sighed, and presently turned to his writing again, and I went back joyfully to my cleaning.

On a certain dark 4th of February, picture the village of Kaskaskia assembled on the river-bank in capote and hood. Ropes are cast off, the keel-boat pushes her blunt nose through the cold, muddy water, the oars churn up dirty, yellow foam, and cheers shake the sodden air. So the *Willing* left on her long journey: down the Kaskaskia, into the flood of the Mississippi, against many weary leagues of the

Ohio's current, and up the swollen Wabash until they were to come to the mouth of the White River near Vincennes. There they were to await us.

Should we ever see them again? I think that this was the unspoken question in the hearts of the many who were to go by land.

The 5th was a mild, gray day, with the melting snow lying in patches on the brown bluff, and the sun making shift to pierce here and there. We formed the regiment in the fort,—backwoodsman and Creole now to fight for their common country, Jacques and Pierre and Alphonse; and mother and father, sweetheart and wife, waiting to wave a last good-by. Bravely we marched out of the gate and into the church for Father Gibault's blessing. And then, forming once more, we filed away on the road leading northward to the ferry, our colors flying, leaving the weeping, cheering crowd behind. In front of the tall men of the column was a wizened figure, beating madly on a drum, stepping proudly with head thrown back. It was Cowan's voice that snapped the strain.

"Go it, Davy, my little gamecock!" he cried, and the men laughed and cheered. And so we came to the bleak ferry landing where we had crossed on that hot July night six months before.

We were soon on the prairies, and in the misty rain that fell and fell they seemed to melt afar into a gray and cheerless ocean. The sodden grass was matted now and unkempt. Lifeless lakes filled the depressions, and through them we waded mile after mile ankle-deep. There was a little cavalcade mounted on the tiny French ponies, and sometimes I rode with these; but oftenest Cowan or Tom would fling me, drum and all, on his shoulder. For we had reached the forest swamps where the water is the color of the Creole coffee. And day after day as we marched, the soft rain came out of the east and wet us to the skin.

It was a journey of torments, and even that first part of it was enough to discourage the most resolute spirit. Men might be led through it, but never driven. It is ever the mind which suffers through the monotonies of bodily discomfort, and none knew this better than Clark himself. Every morning as we set out with the wet hide chafing our skin, the Colonel would run the length of the regiment, crying:—

"Who gives the feast to-night, boys?"

Now it was Bowman's company, now McCarty's, now Bayley's. How the hunters vied with each other to supply the best, and spent the days stalking the deer cowering in the wet thickets. We crossed the Saline, and on the plains beyond was a great black patch, a herd of buffalo. A party of chosen men headed by Tom McChesney was sent after them, and never shall I forget the sight of the mad beasts charging through the water.

That night, when our chilled feet could bear no more, we sought out a patch of raised ground a little firmer than a quagmire, and heaped up the beginnings of a fire with such brush as could be made to burn, robbing the naked thickets. Saddle and steak sizzled, leather steamed and stiffened, hearts and bodies thawed; grievances that men had nursed over miles of water melted. Courage sits best on a full stomach, and as they ate they cared not whether the Atlantic had opened between them and Vincennes. An hour agone, and there were twenty cursing laggards, counting the leagues back to Kaskaskia. Now:—

> "C'était un vieux sauvage
> Tout noir, tour barbouilla,
> Ouich' ka!
> Avec sa vieill' couverte
> Et son sac à tabac.
> Ouich' ka!
> Ah! ah! tenaouich' tenaga,
> Tenaouich' tenaga, ouich' ka!"

So sang Antoine, *dit le Gris*, in the pulsing red light. And when, between the verses, he went through the agonies of a Huron war-dance, the assembled regiment howled with delight. Some men know cities and those who dwell in the quarters of cities. But grizzled Antoine knew the half of a continent, and the manners of trading and killing of the tribes thereof.

And after Antoine came Gabriel, a marked contrast—Gabriel, five feet six, and the glare showing but a faint dark line on his quivering lip. Gabriel was a patriot,—a tribute we must pay to all of those brave Frenchmen who went with us. Nay, Gabriel had left at home on his little farm near the village a young wife of a fortnight. And so his lip quivered as he sang:—

> "Petit Rocher de la Haute Montagne,
> Je vien finir ici cette campagne!
> Ah! doux échos, entendez mes soupirs;
> En languissant je vais bientôt mouir!"

We had need of gayety after that, and so Bill Cowan sang "Billy of the Wild Wood," and Terence McCann wailed an Irish jig, stamping the water out of the spongy ground amidst storms of mirth. As he desisted, breathless and panting, he flung me up in the firelight before the eyes of them all, crying:—

"It's Davy can bate me!"

"Ay, Davy, Davy!" they shouted, for they were in the mood for anything. There stood Colonel Clark in the dimmer light of the background. "We must keep 'em screwed up, Davy," he had said that very day.

There came to me on the instant a wild song that my father had taught me when the liquor held him in dominance. Exhilarated, I sprang from Terence's arms to the sodden, bared space, and methinks I yet hear my shrill, piping note, and see my legs kicking in the fling of it. There was an uproar, a deeper voice chimed in, and here was McAndrew flinging his legs with mine:—

> "I've faught on land, I've faught at sea,
> At hame I faught my aunty, O;
> But I met the deevil and Dundee
> On the braes o' Killiecrankie, O.
> An' ye had been where I had been,
> Ye wad na be sae cantie, O;
> An' ye had seen what I ha'e seen,
> On the braes o' Killiecrankie, O."

In the morning Clark himself would be the first off through the gray rain, laughing and shouting and waving his sword in the air, and I after him as hard as I could pelt through the mud, beating the charge on my drum until the war-cries of the regiment drowned the sound of it. For we were upon a pleasure trip—lest any man forget,—a pleasure trip amidst stark woods and brown plains flecked with ponds. So we followed him until we came to a place where, in summer, two quiet rivers flowed through green forests—the little Wabashes. And now! Now hickory and maple, oak and cottonwood, stood shivering in three feet of water on what had been a league of dry land. We stood dismayed at the crumbling edge of the hill, and one hundred and seventy pairs of eyes were turned on Clark. With a mere glance at the running stream high on the bank and the drowned forest beyond, he turned and faced them.

"I reckon you've earned a rest, boys," he said. "We'll have games to-day."

There were some dozen of the unflinching who needed not to be amused. Choosing a great poplar, these he set to hollowing out a pirogue, and himself came among the others and played leap-frog and the Indian game of ball until night fell. And these, instead of moping and quarrelling, forgot. That night, as I cooked him a buffalo steak, he drew near the fire with Bowman.

"For the love of God keep up their spirits, Bowman," said the Colonel; "keep up their spirits until we get them across. Once on the farther hills, they cannot go back."

Here was a different being from the shouting boy who had led the games and the war-dance that night in the circle of the blaze. Tired out, we went to sleep with the ring of the axes in our ears, and in the morning there were more games while the squad crossed the river to the drowned neck, built a rough scaffold there, and notched a trail across it; to the scaffold the baggage was ferried, and the next morning, bit by bit, the regiment. Even now the pains shoot through my body when I think of how man after man plunged waist-deep into the icy water toward the farther branch. The pirogue was filled with the weak, and in the end of it I was curled up with my drum.

Heroism is a many-sided thing. It is one matter to fight and finish, another to endure hell's tortures hour after hour. All day they waded with numbed feet vainly searching for a footing in the slime. Truly, the agony of a brave man is among the greatest of the world's tragedies to see. As they splashed onward through the tree-trunks, many a joke went forth, though lips were drawn and teeth pounded together. I have not the heart to recall these jokes,—it would seem a sacrilege. There were quarrels, too, the men striving to push one another from the easier paths; and deeds sublime when some straggler clutched at the bole of a tree for support, and was helped onward through excruciating ways. A dozen held tremblingly to the pirogue's gunwale, lest they fall and drown. One walked ahead with a smile, or else fell back to lend a helping shoulder to a fainting man.

And there was Tom McChesney. All day long I watched him, and thanked God that Polly Ann could not see him thus. And yet, how the pride would have leaped within her! Humor came not easily to him, but charity and courage and unselfishness he had in abundance. What he suffered none knew; but through those awful hours he was always among the stragglers, helping the weak and despairing when his strength might have taken him far ahead toward comfort and safety. "I'm all right, Davy," he would say, in answer to my look as he passed me. But on his face was written something that I did not understand.

How the Creole farmers and traders, unused even to the common ways of woodcraft, endured that fearful day and others that followed, I know not. And when a tardy justice shall arise and compel the people of this land to raise a shaft in memory of Clark and those who followed him, let not the loyalty of the French be forgotten, though it be not understood.

At eventide came to lurid and disordered brains the knowledge that the other branch was here. And, mercifully, it was shallower than the first. Holding his rifle high, with a war-whoop Bill Cowan plunged into the stream. Unable to contain myself more, I flung my drum overboard and went after it, and amid shouts and laughter I was towed across by James Ray.

Colonel Clark stood watching from the bank above, and it was he who pulled me, bedraggled, to dry land. I ran away to help gather brush for a fire. As I was heaping this in a pile I heard something that I should not have heard. Nor ought I to repeat it now, though I did not need the flames to send the blood tingling through my body.

"McChesney," said the Colonel, "we must thank our stars that we brought the boy along. He has grit, and as good a head as any of us. I reckon if it hadn't been for him some of them would have turned back long ago."

I saw Tom grinning at the Colonel as gratefully as though he himself had been praised.

The blaze started, and soon we had a bonfire. Some had not the strength to hold out the buffalo meat to the fire. Even the grumblers and mutineers were silent, owing to the ordeal they had gone through. But presently, when they began to be warmed and fed, they talked of other trials to be borne. The Embarrass and the big Wabash, for example. These must be like the sea itself.

"Take the back trail, if ye like," said Bill Cowan, with a loud laugh. "I reckon the rest of us kin float to Vincennes on Davy's drum."

But there was no taking the back trail now; and well they knew it. The games began, the unwilling being forced to play, and before they fell asleep that night they had taken Vincennes, scalped the Hair Buyer, and were far on the march to Detroit.

Mercifully, now that their stomachs were full, they had no worries. Few knew the danger we were in of being cut off by Hamilton's roving bands of Indians. There would be no retreat, no escape, but a fight to the death. And I heard this, and much more that was spoken of in low tones at the Colonel's fire far into the night, of which I never told the rank and file,—not even Tom McChesney.

On and on, through rain and water, we marched until we drew near to the river Embarrass. Drew near, did I say? "Sure, darlin'," said Terence, staring comically over the gray waste, "we've been in it since Choosd'y." There was small exaggeration in it. In vain did our feet seek the deeper water. It would go no higher than our knees, and the sound which the regiment made in marching was like that of a great flatboat going against the current. It had been a sad, lavender-colored day, and now that the gloom of the night was setting in, and not so much as a hummock showed itself above the surface, the Creoles began to murmur. And small wonder! Where was this man leading them, this Clark who had come amongst them from the skies, as it were? Did he know, himself? Night fell as though a blanket had been spread over the tree-tops, and above the dreary splashing men could be heard calling to one another in the darkness. Nor was there any supper ahead. For our food was gone, and no game was to be shot over this watery waste. A cold like that of eternal space settled in our bones. Even Terence McCann grumbled.

"Begob," said he, "'tis fine weather for fishes, and the birrds are that comfortable in the threes. 'Tis no place for a baste at all, at all."

Sometime in the night there was a cry. Ray had found the water falling from an oozy bank, and there we dozed fitfully until we were startled by a distant boom.

It was Governor Hamilton's morning gun at Fort Sackville, Vincennes.

There was no breakfast. How we made our way, benumbed with hunger and cold, to the banks of the Wabash, I know not. Captain McCarty's company was set to making canoes, and the rest of us looked on apathetically as the huge trees staggered and fell amidst a fountain of spray in the shallow water. We were but three leagues from Vincennes. A raft was bound together, and Tom McChesney and three other scouts sent on a desperate journey across the river in search of boats and provisions, lest we starve and fall and die on the wet flats. Before he left Tom came to me, and the remembrance of his gaunt face haunted me for many years after. He drew something from his bosom and held it out to me, and I saw that it was a bit of buffalo steak which he had saved. I shook my head, and the tears came into my eyes.

"Come, Davy," he said, "ye're so little, and I beant hungry."

Again I shook my head, and for the life of me I could say nothing.

"I reckon Polly Ann'd never forgive me if anything was to happen to you," said he.

At that I grew strangely angry.

"It's you who need it," I cried, "it's you that has to do the work. And she told me to take care of you."

The big fellow grinned sheepishly, as was his wont.

"'Tis only a bite," he pleaded, "'twouldn't only make me hungry, and"—he looked hard at me—"and it might be the savin' of you. Ye'll not eat it for Polly Ann's sake?" he asked coaxingly.

"'Twould not be serving her," I answered indignantly.

"Ye're an obstinate little deevil!" he cried, and, dropping the morsel on the freshly cut stump, he stalked away. I ran after him, crying out, but he leaped on the raft that was already in the stream and began to pole across. I slipped the piece into my own hunting shirt.

All day the men who were too weak to swing axes sat listless on the bank, watching in vain for some sight of the *Willing*. They saw a canoe rounding the bend instead, with a single occupant paddling madly. And who should this be but Captain Willing's own brother, escaped from the fort, where he had been a prisoner. He told us that a man named Maisonville, with a party of Indians, was in pursuit of him, and the next piece of news he had was in the way of raising our despair a little. Governor Hamilton's astonishment at seeing this force here and now would be as great as his own. Governor Hamilton had said, indeed, that only a navy could take Vincennes this year. Unfortunately, Mr. Willing brought no food. Next in order came five Frenchmen, trapped by our scouts, nor had they any provisions. But as long as I live I shall never forget how Tom McChesney returned at nightfall, the hero of the hour. He had shot a deer; and never did wolves pick an animal cleaner. They pressed on me a choice piece of it, these great-hearted men who were willing to go hungry for the sake of a child, and when I refused it they would have forced it down my throat. Swein Poulsson, he that once hid under the bed, deserves a special tablet to his memory. He was for giving me all he had, though his little eyes were unnaturally bright and the red had left his cheeks now.

"He haf no belly, only a leedle on his backbone!" he cried.

"Begob, thin, he has the backbone," said Terence.

"I have a piece," said I, and drew forth that which Tom had given me.

They brought a quarter of a saddle to Colonel Clark, but he smiled at them kindly and told them to divide it amongst the weak. He looked at me as I sat with my feet crossed on the stump.

"I will follow Davy's example," said he.

At length the canoes were finished and we crossed the river, swimming over the few miserable skeletons of the French ponies we had brought along. We came to a sugar camp, and beyond it, stretching between us and Vincennes, was a sea of water. Here we made our camp, if camp it could be called. There was no fire, no food, and the water seeped out of the ground on which we lay. Some of those even who had not yet spoken now openly said that we could go no farther. For the wind had shifted into the northwest, and, for the first time since we had left Kaskaskia we saw the stars gleaming like scattered diamonds in the sky. Bit by bit the ground hardened, and if by chance we dozed we stuck to it. Morning found the men huddled like sheep, their hunting shirts hard as boards, and long before Hamilton's gun we were up and stamping. Antoine poked the butt of his rifle through the ice of the lake in front of us.

"I think we not get to Vincennes this day," he said.

Colonel Clark, who heard him, turned to me.

"Fetch McChesney here, Davy," he said. Tom came.

"McChesney," said he, "when I give the word, take Davy and his drum on your shoulders and follow me. And Davy, do you think you can sing that song you gave us the other night?"

"Oh, yes, sir," I answered.

Without more ado the Colonel broke the skim of ice, and, taking some of the water in his hand, poured powder from his flask into it and rubbed it on his face until he was the color of an Indian. Stepping back, he raised his sword high in the air, and, shouting the Shawanee war-whoop, took a flying leap up to his thighs in the water. Tom swung me instantly to his shoulder and followed, I beating the charge with all my might, though my hands were so numb that I could scarce hold the sticks. Strangest of all, to a man they came shouting after us.

"Now, Davy!" said the Colonel.

> "I've faught on land, I've faught at sea,
> At hame I faught my aunty, O;
> But I met the deevil and Dundee
> On the braes o' Killiecrankie, O."

I piped it at the top of my voice, and sure enough the regiment took up the chorus, for it had a famous swing.

> "An' ye had been where I had been,
> Ye wad na be sae cantie, O;
> An' ye had seen what I ha'e seen'
> On the braes o' Killiecrankie, O."

When their breath was gone we heard Cowan shout that he had found a path under his feet,—a path that was on dry land in the summer-time. We followed it, feeling carefully, and at length, when we had suffered all that we could bear, we stumbled on to a dry ridge. Here we spent another night of torture, with a second backwater facing us coated with a full inch of ice.

And still there was nothing to eat.

CHAPTER XIX

The Hair Buyer Trapped

To lie the night on adamant, pierced by the needles of the frost; to awake shivering and famished, until the meaning of an inch of ice on the backwater comes to your mind,—these are not calculated to put a man into an equable mood to listen to oratory. Nevertheless there was a kind of oratory to fit the case. To picture the misery of these men is well-nigh impossible. They stood sluggishly in groups, dazed by suffering, and their faces were drawn and their eyes ringed, their beards and hair matted. And many found it in their hearts to curse Clark and that government for which he fought.

When the red fire of the sun glowed through the bare branches that morning, it seemed as if the campaign had spent itself like an arrow which drops at the foot of the mark. Could life and interest and enthusiasm be infused again in such as these? I have ceased to marvel how it was done. A man no less haggard than the rest, but with a compelling force in his eyes, pointed with a blade to the hills across the river. They must get to them, he said, and their troubles would be ended. He said more, and they cheered him. These are the bare facts. He picked a man here, and another there, and these went silently to a grim duty behind the regiment.

"If any try to go back, shoot them down!" he cried.

Then with a gun-butt he shattered the ice and was the first to leap into the water under it. They followed, some with a cheer that was most pitiful of all. They followed him blindly, as men go to torture, but they followed him, and the splashing and crushing of the ice were sounds to freeze my body. I was put in a canoe. In my day I have beheld great suffering and hardship, and none of it compared to this. Torn with pity, I saw them reeling through the water, now grasping trees and bushes to try to keep their feet, the strongest breaking the way ahead and supporting the weak between them. More than once Clark himself tottered where he beat the ice at the apex of the line. Some swooned and would have drowned had they not been dragged across the canoe and chafed back to consciousness. By inches the water shallowed. Clark reached the high ground, and then Bill Cowan, with a man on each shoulder. Then others endured to the shallows to fall heavily in the crumbled ice and be dragged out before they died. But at length, by God's grace, the whole regiment was on the land. Fires would not revive some, but Clark himself seized a fainting man by the arms and walked him up and down in the sunlight until his blood ran again.

It was a glorious day, a day when the sap ran in the maples, and the sun soared upwards in a sky of the palest blue. All this we saw through the tracery of the leafless branches,—a mirthless, shivering crowd, crept through a hell of weather into the Hair Buyer's very lair. Had he neither heard nor seen?

Down the steel-blue lane of water between the ice came a canoe. Our stunted senses perceived it, unresponsive. A man cried out (it was Tom McChesney); now some of them had leaped into the pirogue, now they were returning. In the towed canoe two fat and stolid squaws and a pappoose were huddled, and beside them—God be praised!—food. A piece of buffalo on its way to town, and in the end compartment of the boat tallow and bear's grease lay revealed by two blows of the tomahawk. The kettles—long disused—were fetched, and broth made and fed in sips to the weakest, while the strongest looked on and smiled in an agony of self-restraint. It was a fearful thing to see men whose legs had refused service struggle to their feet when they had drunk the steaming, greasy mixture. And the Colonel, standing by the river's edge, turned his face away—down-stream. And then, as often, I saw the other side of the man. Suddenly he looked at me, standing wistful at his side.

"They have cursed me," said he, by way of a question, "they have cursed me every day." And seeing me silent, he insisted, "Tell me, is it not so, Davy?"

"It is so," I said, wondering that he should pry, "but it was while they suffered. And—and some refrained."

"And you?" he asked queerly.

"I—I could not, sir. For I asked leave to come."

"If they have condemned me to a thousand hells," said he, dispassionately, "I should not blame them." Again he looked at me. "Do you understand what you have done?" he asked.

"No, sir," I said uneasily.

"And yet there are some human qualities in you, Davy. You have been worth more to me than another regiment."

I stared.

"When you grow older, if you ever do, tell your children that once upon a time you put a hundred men to shame. It is no small thing."

Seeing him relapse into silence, I did not speak. For the space of half an hour he stared down the river, and I knew that he was looking vainly for the *Willing*.

At noon we crossed, piecemeal, a deep lake in the canoes, and marching awhile came to a timber-covered rise which our French prisoners named as the Warriors' Island. And from the shelter of its trees we saw the steely lines of a score of low ponds, and over the tops of as many ridges a huddle of brown houses on the higher ground.

And this was the place we had all but sold our lives to behold! This was Vincennes at last! We were on the heights behind the town, — we were at the back door, as it were. At the far side, on the Wabash River, was the front door, or Fort Sackville, where the banner of England snapped in the February breeze.

We stood there, looking, as the afternoon light flooded the plain. Suddenly the silence was broken.

"Hooray for Clark!" cried a man at the edge of the copse.

"Hooray for Clark!" — it was the whole regiment this time. From execration to exaltation was but a step, after all. And the Creoles fell to scoffing at their sufferings and even forgot their hunger in staring at the goal. The backwoodsmen took matters more stolidly, having acquired long since the art of waiting. They lounged about, cleaning their guns, watching the myriad flocks of wild ducks and geese casting blue-black shadows on the ponds.

"Arrah, McChesney," said Terence, as he watched the circling birds, "Clark's a great man, but 'tis more riverince I'd have for him if wan av thim was sizzling on the end of me ramrod."

"I'd sooner hev the Ha'r Buyer's sculp," said Tom.

Presently there was a drama performed for our delectation. A shot came down the wind, and we perceived that several innocent Creole gentlemen, unconscious of what the timber held, were shooting the ducks and geese. Whereupon Clark chose Antoine and three of our own Creoles to sally out and shoot likewise—as decoys. We watched them working their way over the ridges, and finally saw them coming back with one of the Vincennes sportsmen. I cannot begin to depict the astonishment of this man when he reached the copse, and was led before our lean, square-shouldered commander. Yes, monsieur, he was a friend of *les Américains*. Did Governor Hamilton know that a visit was imminent? *Pardieu* (with many shrugs and outward gestures of the palms), Governor Hamilton had said if the Long Knives had wings or fins they might reach him now—he was all unprepared.

"Gentlemen," said Colonel Clark to Captains Bowman and McCarty and Williams, "we have come so far by audacity, and we must continue by audacity. It is of no use to wait for the gunboat, and every moment we run the risk of discovery. I shall write an open letter to the inhabitants of Vincennes, which the prisoner shall take into town. I shall tell them that those who are true to the oath they swore to Father Gibault shall not be molested if they remain quietly in their houses. Let those who are on the side of the Hair Buyer General and his King go to the fort and fight there."

He bade me fetch the portfolio he carried, and with numbed fingers wrote the letter while his captains stared in admiration and amazement. What a stroke was this! There were six hundred men in the town and fort,—soldiers, inhabitants, and Indians,—while we had but 170, starved and weakened by their incredible march. But Clark was not to be daunted. Whipping out his field-glasses, he took a stand on a little mound under the trees and followed the fast-galloping messenger across the plain; saw him enter the town; saw the stir in the streets, knots of men riding out and gazing, hands on foreheads, towards the place where we were. But, as the minutes rolled into hours, there was no further alarm. No gun, no beat to quarters or bugle-call from Fort Sackville. What could it mean?

Clark's next move was an enigma, for he set the men to cutting and trimming tall sapling poles. To these were tied (how reverently!) the twenty stands of colors which loving Creole hands had stitched. The boisterous day was reddening to its close as the Colonel lined his little army in front of the wood, and we covered the space of four thousand. For the men were twenty feet apart and every tenth carried a standard. Suddenly we were aghast as the full meaning of the inspiration dawned upon us. The command was given, and we started on our march toward Vincennes. But not straight,— zigzagging, always keeping the ridges between us and the town, and to the watching inhabitants it seemed as if thousands were coming to crush them. Night fell, the colors were furled and the saplings dropped, and we pressed into serried ranks and marched straight over hill and dale for the lights that were beginning to twinkle ahead of us.

We halted once more, a quarter of a mile away. Clark himself had picked fourteen men to go under Lieutenant Bayley through the town and take the fort from the other side. Here was audacity with a vengeance. You may be sure that Tom and Cowan and Ray were among these, and I trotted after them with the drum banging against my thighs.

Was ever stronghold taken thus?

They went right into the town, the fourteen of them, into the main street that led directly to the fort. The simple citizens gave back, stupefied, at sight of the tall, striding forms. Muffled Indians stood like statues as we passed, but these raised not a hand against us. Where were Hamilton, Hamilton's soldiers and savages? It was as if we had come a-trading.

The street rose and fell in waves, like the prairie over which it ran. As we climbed a ridge, here was a little log church, the rude cross on the belfry showing dark against the sky. And there, in front of us, flanked by blockhouses with conical caps, was the frowning mass of Fort Sackville.

"Take cover," said Williams, hoarsely. It seemed incredible.

The men spread hither and thither, some at the corners of the church, some behind the fences of the little gardens. Tom chose a great forest tree that had been left standing, and I went with him. He powdered his pan, and I laid down my drum beside the tree, and then, with an impulse that was rare, Tom seized me by the collar and drew me to him.

"Davy," he whispered, and I pinched him. "Davy, I reckon Polly Ann'd be kinder surprised if she knew where we was. Eh?"

I nodded. It seemed strange, indeed, to be talking thus at such a place. Life has taught me since that it was not so strange, for however a man may strive and suffer for an object, he usually sits quiet at the consummation. Here we were in the door-yard of a peaceful cabin, the ground frozen in lumps under our feet, and it seemed to me that the wind had something to do with the lightness of the night.

"Davy," whispered Tom again, "how'd ye like to see the little feller to home?"

I pinched him again, and harder this time, for I was at a loss for adequate words. The muscles of his legs were as hard as the strands of a rope, and his buckskin breeches frozen so that they cracked under my fingers.

Suddenly a flickering light arose ahead of us, and another, and we saw that they were candles beginning to twinkle through the palings of the fort. These were badly set, the width of a man's hand apart. Presently here comes a soldier with a torch, and as he walked we could see from crack to crack his bluff face all reddened by the light, and so near were we that we heard the words of his song: —

> "O, there came a lass to Sudbury Fair,
> With a hey, and a ho, nonny-nonny!
> And she had a rose in her raven hair,
> With a hey, and a ho, nonny-nonny!"

"By the etarnal!" said Tom, following the man along the palings with the muzzle of his Deckard, "by the etarnal! 'tis like shootin' beef."

A gust of laughter came from somewhere beyond. The burly soldier paused at the foot of the blockhouse.

"Hi, Jem, have ye seen the General's man? His Honor's in a 'igh temper, I warrant ye."

It was fortunate for Jem that he put his foot inside the blockhouse door.

"Now, boys!"

It was Williams's voice, and fourteen rifles sputtered out a ragged volley.

There was an instant's silence, and then a score of voices raised in consternation,—shouting, cursing, commanding. Heavy feet pounded on the platform of the blockhouse. While Tom was savagely jamming in powder and ball, the wicket gate of the fort opened, a man came out and ran to a house a biscuit's throw away, and ran back again before he was shot at, slamming the gate after him. Tom swore.

"We've got but the ten rounds," he said, dropping his rifle to his knee. "I reckon 'tis no use to waste it."

"The *Willing* may come to-night," I answered.

There was a bugle winding a strange call, and the roll of a drum, and the running continued.

"Don't fire till you're sure, boys," said Captain Williams.

Our eyes caught sight of a form in the blockhouse port, there was an instant when a candle flung its rays upon a cannon's flank, and Tom's rifle spat a rod of flame. A red blot hid the cannon's mouth, and behind it a man staggered and fell on the candle, while the shot crunched its way through the logs of the cottage in the yard where we stood. And now the battle was on in earnest, fire darting here and there from the black wall, bullets whistling and flying wide, and at intervals cannon belching, their shot grinding through trees and houses. But our men waited until the gunners lit their matches in the cannon-ports,—it was no trick for a backwoodsman.

At length there came a popping right and left, and we knew that Bowman and McCarty's men had swung into position there.

An hour passed, and a shadow came along our line, darting from cover to cover. It was Lieutenant Bayley, and he sent me back to find the Colonel and to tell him that the men had but a few rounds left. I sped through the streets on the errand, spied a Creole company waiting in reserve, and near them, behind a warehouse, a knot of backwoodsmen, French, and Indians, lighted up by a smoking torch. And here was Colonel Clark talking to a big, blanketed chief. I was hovering around the skirts of the crowd and seeking for an opening, when a hand pulled me off my feet.

"What 'll ye be afther now?" said a voice, which was Terence's.

"Let me go," I cried, "I have a message from Lieutenant Bayley."

"Sure," said Terence, "a man'd think ye had the Hair Buyer's sculp in yere pocket. The Colonel is treaty-makin' with Tobaccy's Son, the grreatest Injun in these parrts."

"I don't care."

"Hist!" said Terence.

"Let me go," I yelled, so loudly that the Colonel turned, and Terence dropped me like a live coal. I wormed my way to where Clark stood. Tobacco's Son was at that moment protesting that the Big Knives were his brothers, and declaring that before morning broke he would have one hundred warriors for the Great White Chief. Had he not made a treaty of peace with Captain Helm, who was even then a prisoner of the British general in the fort?

Colonel Clark replied that he knew well of the fidelity of Tobacco's Son to the Big Knives, that Tobacco's Son had remained stanch in the face of bribes and presents (this was true). Now all that Colonel Clark desired of Tobacco's Son besides his friendship was that he would keep his warriors from battle. The Big Knives would fight their own fight. To this sentiment Tobacco's Son grunted extreme approval. Colonel Clark turned to me.

"What is it, Davy?" he asked.

I told him.

"Tobacco's Son has dug up for us King George's ammunition," he said. "Go tell Lieutenant Bayley that I will send him enough to last him a month."

I sped away with the message. Presently I came back again, upon another message, and they were eating,—those reserves,—they were eating as I had never seen men eat but once, at Kaskaskia. The baker stood by with lifted palms, imploring the saints that he might have some compensation, until Clark sent him back to his shop to knead and bake again. The good Creoles approached the fires with the contents of their larders in their hands. Terence tossed me a loaf the size of a cannon ball, and another.

"Fetch that wan to wan av the b'ys," said he.

I seized as much as my arms could hold and scurried away to the firing line once more, and, heedless of whistling bullets, darted from man to man until the bread was exhausted. Not a one but gave me a "God bless you, Davy," ere he seized it with a great hand and began to eat in wolfish bites, his Deckard always on the watch the while.

There was no sleep in the village. All night long, while the rifles sputtered, the villagers in their capotes—men, women, and children—huddled around the fires. The young men of the militia begged Clark to allow them to fight, and to keep them well affected he sent some here and there amongst our lines. For our Colonel's strength was not counted by rifles or men alone: he fought with his brain. As Hamilton, the Hair Buyer, made his rounds, he believed the town to be in possession of a horde of Kentuckians. Shouts, war-whoops, and bursts of laughter went up from behind the town. Surely a great force was there, a small part of which had been sent to play with him and his men. On the fighting line, when there was a lull, our backwoodsmen stood up behind their trees and cursed the enemy roundly, and often by these taunts persuaded the furious gunners to open their ports and fire their cannon. Woe be to him that showed an arm or a shoulder! Though a casement be lifted ever so warily, a dozen balls would fly into it. And at length, when some of the besieged had died in their anger, the ports were opened no more. It was then our sharpshooters crept up boldly to within thirty yards of them—nay, it seemed as if they lay under the very walls of the fort. And through the night the figure of the Colonel himself was often seen amongst them, praising their markmanship, pleading with every man not to expose himself without cause. He spied me where I had wormed myself behind the foot-board of a picket fence beneath the cannon-port of a blockhouse. It was during one of the breathing spaces.

"What's this?" said he to Cowan, sharply, feeling me with his foot.

"I reckon it's Davy, sir," said my friend, somewhat sheepishly. "We can't do nothin' with him. He's been up and down the line twenty times this night."

"What doing?" says the Colonel.

"Bread and powder and bullets," answered Bill.

"But that's all over," says Clark.

"He's the very devil to pry," answered Bill. "The first we know he'll be into the fort under the logs."

"Or between them," says Clark, with a glance at the open palings. "Come here, Davy."

I followed him, dodging between the houses, and when we had got off the line he took me by the two shoulders from behind.

"You little rascal," said he, shaking me, "how am I to look out for an army and you besides? Have you had anything to eat?"

"Yes, sir," I answered.

We came to the fires, and Captain Bowman hurried up to meet him.

"We're piling up earthworks and barricades," said the Captain, "for the fight to-morrow. My God! if the *Willing* would only come, we could put our cannon into them."

Clark laughed.

"Bowman," said he, kindly, "has Davy fed you yet?"

"No," says the Captain, surprised, "I've had no time to eat."

"He seems to have fed the whole army," said the Colonel. He paused. "Have they scented Lamothe or Maisonville?"

"Devil a scent!" cried the Captain, "and we've scoured wood and quagmire. They tell me that Lamothe has a very pretty force of redskins at his heels."

"Let McChesney go," said Clark sharply, "McChesney and Ray. I'll warrant they can find 'em."

Now I knew that Maisonville had gone out a-chasing Captain Willing's brother,—he who had run into our arms. Lamothe was a noted Indian partisan and a dangerous man to be dogging our rear that night. Suddenly there came a thought that took my breath and set my heart a-hammering. When the Colonel's back was turned I slipped away beyond the range of the firelight, and I was soon on the prairie, stumbling over hummocks and floundering into ponds, yet going as quietly as I could, turning now and again to look back at the distant glow or to listen to the rifles popping around the fort. The night was cloudy and pitchy dark. Twice the whirring of startled waterfowl frightened me out of my senses, but ambition pricked me on in spite of fear. I may have gone a mile thus, perchance two or three, straining every sense, when a sound brought me to a stand. At first I could not distinguish it because of my heavy breathing, but presently I made sure that it was the low drone of human voices. Getting down on my hands and knees, I crept forward, and felt the ground rising. The voices had ceased. I gained the crest of a low ridge, and threw myself flat. A rattle of musketry set me shivering, and in an agony of fright I looked behind me to discover that I could not be more than four hundred yards from the fort. I had made a circle. I lay very still, my eyes watered with staring, and then—the droning began again. I went forward an inch, then another and another down the slope, and at last I could have sworn that I saw dark blurs against the ground. I put out my hand, my weight went after, and I had crashed through a coating of ice up to my elbow in a pool. There came a second of sheer terror, a hoarse challenge in French, and then I took to my heels and flew towards the fort at the top of my speed.

I heard them coming after me, leap and bound, and crying out to one another. Ahead of me there might have been a floor or a precipice, as the ground looks level at night. I hurt my foot cruelly on a frozen clod of earth, slid down the washed bank of a run into the Wabash, picked myself up, scrambled to the top of the far side, and had gotten away again when my pursuer shattered the ice behind me. A hundred yards more, two figures loomed up in front, and I was pulled up choking.

"Hang to him, Fletcher!" said a voice.

"Great God!" cried Fletcher, "it's Davy. What are ye up to now?"

"Let me go!" I cried, as soon as I had got my wind. As luck would have it, I had run into a pair of daredevil young Kentuckians who had more than once tasted the severity of Clark's discipline,— Fletcher Blount and Jim Willis. They fairly shook out of me what had happened, and then dropped me with a war-whoop and started for the prairie, I after them, crying out to them to beware of the run. A man must indeed be fleet of foot to have escaped these young ruffians, and so it proved. When I reached the hollow there were the two of them fighting with a man in the water, the ice jangling as they shifted their feet.

"What's yere name?" said Fletcher, cuffing and kicking his prisoner until he cried out for mercy.

"Maisonville," said the man, whereupon Fletcher gave a war-whoop and kicked him again.

"That's no way to use a prisoner," said I, hotly.

"Hold your mouth, Davy," said Fletcher, "you didn't ketch him."

"You wouldn't have had him but for me," I retorted.

Fletcher's answer was an oath. They put Maisonville between them, ran him through the town up to the firing line, and there, to my horror, they tied him to a post and used him for a shield, despite his heart-rending yells. In mortal fear that the poor man would be shot down, I was running away to find some one who might have influence over them when I met a lieutenant. He came up and ordered them angrily to unbind Maisonville and bring him before the Colonel. Fletcher laughed, whipped out his hunting knife, and cut the thongs; but he and Willis had scarce got twenty paces from the officer before they seized poor Maisonville by the hair and made shift to scalp him. This was merely backwoods play, had Maisonville but known it. Persuaded, however, that his last hour was come, he made a desperate effort to clear himself, whereupon Fletcher cut off a piece of his skin by mistake. Maisonville, making sure that he had been scalped, stood groaning and clapping his hand to his head, while the two young rascals drew back and stared at each other.

"What's to do now?" said Willis.

"Take our medicine, I reckon," answered Fletcher, grimly. And they seized the tottering man between them, and marched him straightway to the fire where Clark stood.

They had seen the Colonel angry before, but now they were fairly withered under his wrath. And he could have given them no greater punishment, for he took them from the firing line, and sent them back to wait among the reserves until the morning.

"Nom de Dieu!" said Maisonville, wrathfully, as he watched them go, "they should hang."

"The stuff that brought them here through ice and flood is apt to boil over, Captain," remarked the Colonel, dryly.

"If you please, sir," said I, "they did not mean to cut him, but he wriggled."

Clark turned sharply.

"Eh?" said he, "did you have a hand in this, too?"

"Peste!" cried the Captain, "the little ferret—you call him—he find me on the prairie. I run to catch him with some men and fall into the crick—" he pointed to his soaked leggings, "and your demons, they fall on top of me."

"I wish to heaven you had caught Lamothe instead, Davy," said the Colonel, and joined despite himself in the laugh that went up. Falling sober again, he began to question the prisoner. Where was Lamothe? *Pardieu*, Maisonville could not say. How many men did he have, etc., etc.? The circle about us deepened with eager listeners, who uttered exclamations when Maisonville, between his answers, put up his hand to his bleeding head. Suddenly the circle parted, and Captain Bowman came through.

"Ray has discovered Lamothe, sir," said he. "What shall we do?"

"Let him into the fort," said Clark, instantly.

There was a murmur of astonished protest.

"Let him into the fort!" exclaimed Bowman.

"Certainly," said the Colonel; "if he finds he cannot get in, he will be off before the dawn to assemble the tribes."

"But the fort is provisioned for a month," Bowman expostulated; "and they must find out to-morrow how weak we are."

"To-morrow will be too late," said Clark.

"And suppose he shouldn't go in?"

"He will go in," said the Colonel, quietly. "Withdraw your men, Captain, from the north side."

Captain Bowman departed. Whatever he may have thought of these orders, he was too faithful a friend of the Colonel's to delay their execution. Murmuring, swearing oaths of astonishment, man after man on the firing line dropped his rifle at the word, and sullenly retreated. The crack, crack of the Deckards on the south and east were stilled; not a barrel was thrust by the weary garrison through the logs, and the place became silent as the wilderness. It was the long hour before the dawn. And as we lay waiting on the hard ground, stiff and cold and hungry, talking in whispers, somewhere near six of the clock on that February morning the great square of Fort Sackville began to take shape. There was the long line of the stockade, the projecting blockhouses at each corner with peaked caps, and a higher capped square tower from the centre of the enclosure, the banner of England drooping there and clinging forlorn to its staff, as though with a presentiment. Then, as the light grew, the close-lipped casements were seen, scarred with our bullets. The little log houses of the town came out, the sapling palings and the bare trees,—all grim and gaunt at that cruel season. Cattle lowed here and there, and horses whinnied to be fed.

It was a dirty, gray dawn, and we waited until it had done its best. From where we lay hid behind log house and palings we strained our eyes towards the prairie to see if Lamothe would take the bait, until our view was ended at the fuzzy top of a hillock. Bill Cowan, doubled up behind a woodpile and breathing heavily, nudged me.

"Davy, Davy, what d'ye see!".

Was it a head that broke the line of the crest? Even as I stared, breathless, half a score of forms shot up and were running madly for the stockade. Twenty more broke after them, Indians and Frenchmen, dodging, swaying, crowding, looking fearfully to right and left. And from within the fort came forth a hubbub, — cries and scuffling, orders, oaths, and shouts. In plain view of our impatient Deckards soldiers manned the platform, and we saw that they were flinging down ladders. An officer in a faded scarlet coat stood out among the rest, shouting himself hoarse. Involuntarily Cowan lined his sights across the woodpile on this mark of color.

Lamothe's men, a seething mass, were fighting like wolves for the ladders, fearful yet that a volley might kill half of them where they stood. And so fast did they scramble upwards that the men before them stepped on their fingers. All at once and by acclamation the fierce war-whoops of our men rent the air, and some toppled in sheer terror and fell the twelve feet of the stockade at the sound of it. Then every man in the regiment, Creole and backwoodsman, lay back to laugh. The answer of the garrison was a defiant cheer, and those who had dropped, finding they were not shot at, picked themselves up again and gained the top, helping to pull the ladders after them. Bowman's men swung back into place, the rattle and drag were heard in the blockhouse as the cannon were run out through the ports, and the battle which had held through the night watches began again with redoubled vigor. But there was more caution on the side of the British, for they had learned dearly how the Kentuckians could measure crack and crevice.

There followed two hours and a futile waste of ammunition, the lead from the garrison flying harmless here and there, and not a patch of skin or cloth showing.

CHAPTER XX

THE CAMPAIGN ENDS

"If I am obliged to storm, you may depend upon such treatment as is justly due to a murderer. And beware of destroying stores of any kind, or any papers or letters that are in your possession; or of hurting one house in the town. For, by Heaven! if you do, there shall be no mercy shown you. "To Lieutenant-Governor Hamilton."

So read Colonel Clark, as he stood before the log fire in Monsieur Bouton's house at the back of the town, the captains grouped in front of him.

"Is that strong enough, gentlemen?" he asked.

"To raise his hair," said Captain Charleville.

Captain Bowman laughed loudly.

"I reckon the boys will see to that," said he.

Colonel Clark folded the letter, addressed it, and turned gravely to Monsieur Bouton.

"You will oblige me, sir," said he, "by taking this to Governor Hamilton. You will be provided with a flag of truce."

Monsieur Bouton was a round little man, as his name suggested, and the men cheered him as he strode soberly up the street, a piece of sheeting tied to a sapling and flung over his shoulder. Through such humble agencies are the ends of Providence accomplished. Monsieur Bouton walked up to the gate, disappeared sidewise through the postern, and we sat down to breakfast. In a very short time Monsieur Bouton was seen coming back, and his face was not so impassive that the governor's message could not be read thereon.

"'Tis not a love-letter he has, I'll warrant," said Terence, as the little man disappeared into the house. So accurately had Monsieur Bouton's face betrayed the news that the men went back to their posts without orders, some with half a breakfast in hand. And soon the rank and file had the message.

"Lieutenant-Governor Hamilton begs leave to acquaint Colonel Clark that he and his garrison are not disposed to be awed into any action unworthy of British subjects."

Our men had eaten, their enemy was within their grasp and Clark and all his officers could scarce keep them from storming. Such was the deadliness of their aim that scarce a shot came back, and time and again I saw men fling themselves in front of the breastworks with a war-whoop, wave their rifles in the air, and cry out that they would have the Ha'r Buyer's sculp before night should fall. It could not last. Not tuned to the nicer courtesies of warfare, the memory of Hamilton's war parties, of blackened homes, of families dead and missing, raged unappeased. These were not content to leave vengeance in the Lord's hands, and when a white flag peeped timorously above the gate a great yell of derision went up from river-bank to river-bank. Out of the postern stepped the officer with the faded scarlet coat, and in due time went back again, haughtily, his head high, casting contempt right and left of him. Again the postern opened, and this time there was a cheer at sight of a man in hunting shirt and leggings and coonskin cap. After him came a certain Major Hay, Indian-enticer of detested memory, the lieutenant of him who followed—the Hair Buyer himself. A murmur of hatred arose from the men stationed there, and many would have shot him where he stood but for Clark.

"The devil has the grit," said Cowan, though his eyes blazed.

It was the involuntary tribute. Lieutenant-Governor Hamilton stared indifferently at the glowering backwoodsmen as he walked the few steps to the church. Not so Major Hay. His eyes fell. There was Colonel Clark waiting at the door through which the good Creoles had been wont to go to worship, bowing somewhat ironically to the British General. It was a strange meeting they had in St. Xavier's, by the light of the candles on the altar. Hot words passed in that house of peace, the General demanding protection for all his men, and our Colonel replying that he would do with the Indian partisans as he chose.

"And whom mean you by Indian partisans?" the undaunted governor had demanded.

"I take Major Hay to be one of them," our Colonel had answered.

It was soon a matter of common report how Clark had gazed fixedly at the Major when he said this, and how the Major turned pale and trembled. With our own eyes we saw them coming out, Major Hay as near to staggering as a man could be, the governor blushing red for shame of him. So they went sorrowfully back to the gate.

Colonel Clark stood at the steps of the church, looking after them.

"What was that firing?" he demanded sharply. "I gave orders for a truce."

We who stood by the church had indeed heard firing in the direction of the hills east of the town, and had wondered thereat. Perceiving a crowd gathered at the far end of the street, we all ran thither save the Colonel, who directed to have the offenders brought to him at Monsieur Bouton's. We met the news halfway. A party of Canadians and Indians had just returned from the Falls of the Ohio with scalps they had taken. Captain Williams had gone out with his company to meet them, had lured them on, and finally had killed a number and was returning with the prisoners. Yes, here they were! Williams himself walked ahead with two dishevelled and frightened *coureurs du bois*, twoscore at least of the townspeople of Vincennes, friends and relatives of the prisoners, pressing about and crying out to Williams to have mercy on them. As for Williams, he took them in to the Colonel, the townspeople pressing into the door-yard and banking in front of it on the street. Behind all a tragedy impended, nor can I think of it now without sickening.

The frightened Creoles in the street gave back against the fence, and from behind them, issuing as a storm-cloud, came the half of Williams' company, yelling like madmen. Pushed and jostled ahead of them were four Indians, decked and feathered, the half-dried scalps dangling from their belts, impassive, true to their creed despite the indignity of jolts and jars and blows. On and on pressed the mob, gathering recruits at every corner, and when they reached St. Xavier's before the fort half the regiment was there. Others watched, too, from the stockade, and what they saw made their knees smite together with fear. Here were four bronzed statues in a row across the street, the space in front of them clear that their partisans in the fort might look and consider. What was passing in the savage mind no man might know. Not a lip trembled nor an eye faltered when a backwoodsman, his memory aflame at sight of the pitiful white scalps on their belts, thrust through the crowd to curse them. Fletcher Blount, frenzied, snatched his tomahawk from his side.

"Sink, varmint!" he cried with a great oath. "By the etarnal! we'll pay the H'ar Buyer in his own coin. Sound your drums!" he shouted at the fort. "Call the garrison fer the show."

He had raised his arm and turned to strike when the savage put up his hand, not in entreaty, but as one man demanding a right from another. The cries, the curses, the murmurs even, were hushed. Throwing back his head, arching his chest, the notes of a song rose in the heavy air. Wild, strange notes they were, that struck vibrant chords in my own quivering being, and the song was the death-song. Ay, and the life-song of a soul which had come into the world even as mine own. And somewhere there lay in the song, half revealed, the awful mystery of that Creator Whom the soul leaped forth to meet: the myriad green of the sun playing with the leaves, the fish swimming lazily in the brown pool, the doe grazing in the thicket, and a naked boy as free from care as these; and still the life grows brighter as strength comes, and stature, and power over man and beast; and then, God knows what memories of fierce love and fiercer wars and triumphs, of desires gained and enemies conquered,— God, who has made all lives akin to something which He holds in the hollow of His hand; and then—the rain beating on the forest crown, beating, beating, beating.

The song ceased. The Indian knelt in the black mud, not at the feet of Fletcher Blount, but on the threshold of the Great Spirit who ruleth all things. The axe fell, yet he uttered no cry as he went before his Master.

So the four sang, each in turn, and died in the sight of some who pitied, and some who feared, and some who hated, for the sake of land and women. So the four went beyond the power of gold and gewgaw, and were dragged in the mire around the walls and flung into the yellow waters of the river.

The Crossing, Vol. 1

Through the dreary afternoon the men lounged about and cursed the parley, and hearkened for the tattoo,—the signal agreed upon by the leaders to begin the fighting. There had been no command against taunts and jeers, and they gathered in groups under the walls to indulge themselves, and even tried to bribe me as I sat braced against a house with my drum between my knees and the sticks clutched tightly in my hands.

"Here's a Spanish dollar for a couple o' taps, Davy," shouted Jack Terrell.

"Come on, ye pack of Rebel cutthroats!" yelled a man on the wall.

He was answered by a torrent of imprecations. And so they flung it back and forth until nightfall, when out comes the same faded-scarlet officer, holding a letter in his hand, and marches down the street to Monsieur Bouton's. There would be no storming now, nor any man suffered to lay fingers on the Hair Buyer.

I remember, in particular, Hamilton the Hair Buyer. Not the fiend my imagination had depicted (I have since learned that most villains do not look the part), but a man with a great sorrow stamped upon his face. The sun rose on that 25th of February, and the mud melted, and one of our companies drew up on each side of the gate. Downward slid the lion of England, the garrison drums beat a dirge, and the Hair Buyer marched out at the head of his motley troops.

Then came my own greatest hour. All morning I had been polishing and tightening the drum, and my pride was so great as we fell into line that so much as a smile could not be got out of me. Picture it all: Vincennes in black and white by reason of the bright day; eaves and gables, stockade line and capped towers, sharply drawn, and straight above these a stark flagstaff waiting for our colors; pigs and fowls straying hither and thither, unmindful that this day is red on the calendar. Ah! here is a bit of color, too,—the villagers on the side streets to see the spectacle. Gay wools and gayer handkerchiefs there, amid the joyous, cheering crowd of thrice-changed nationality.

"*Vive les Bostonnais! Vive les Américains! Vive Monsieur le Colonel Clark! Vive le petit tambour!*"

"*Vive le petit tambour!*" That was the drummer boy, stepping proudly behind the Colonel himself, with a soul lifted high above mire and puddle into the blue above. There was laughter amongst the giants behind me, and Cowan saying softly, as when we left Kaskaskia, "Go it, Davy, my little gamecock!" And the whisper of it was repeated among the ranks drawn up by the gate.

Yes, here was the gate, and now we were in the fort, and an empire was gained, never to be lost again. The Stars and Stripes climbed the staff, and the folds were caught by an eager breeze. Thirteen cannon thundered from the blockhouses—one for each colony that had braved a king.

There, in the miry square within the Vincennes fort, thin and bronzed and travel-stained, were the men who had dared the wilderness in ugliest mood. And yet none by himself would have done it—each had come here compelled by a spirit stronger than his own, by a master mind that laughed at the body and its ailments.

Colonel George Rogers Clark stood in the centre of the square, under the flag to whose renown he had added three stars. Straight he was, and square, and self-contained. No weakening tremor of exultation softened his face as he looked upon the men by whose endurance he had been able to do this thing. He waited until the white smoke of the last gun had drifted away on the breeze, until the snapping of the flag and the distant village sounds alone broke the stillness.

"We have not suffered all things for a reward," he said, "but because a righteous cause may grow. And though our names may be forgotten, our deeds will be remembered. We have conquered a vast land that our children and our children's children may be freed from tyranny, and we have brought a just vengeance upon our enemies. I thank you, one and all, in the name of the Continental Congress and of that Commonwealth of Virginia for which you have fought. You are no longer Virginians, Kentuckians, Kaskaskians, and Cahokians—you are Americans."

He paused, and we were silent. Though his words moved us strongly, they were beyond us.

"I mention no deeds of heroism, of unselfishness, of lives saved at the peril of others. But I am the debtor of every man here for the years to come to see that he and his family have justice from the Commonwealth and the nation."

Again he stopped, and it seemed to us watching that he smiled a little.

"I shall name one," he said, "one who never lagged, who never complained, who starved that the weak might be fed and walk. David Ritchie, come here."

I trembled, my teeth chattered as the water had never made them chatter. I believe I should have fallen but for Tom, who reached out from the ranks. I stumbled forward in a daze to where the Colonel stood, and the cheering from the ranks was a thing beyond me. The Colonel's hand on my head brought me to my senses.

"David Ritchie," he said, "I give you publicly the thanks of the regiment. The parade is dismissed."

The next thing I knew I was on Cowan's shoulders, and he was tearing round and round the fort with two companies at his heels.

"The divil," said Terence McCann, "he dhrummed us over the wather, an' through the wather; and faix, he would have dhrummed the sculp from Hamilton's head and the Colonel had said the worrd."

"By gar!" cried Antoine *le Gris*, "now he drum us on to Detroit."

Out of the gate rushed Cowan, the frightened villagers scattering right and left. Antoine had a friend who lived in this street, and in ten minutes there was rum in the powder-horns, and the toast was "On to Detroit!"

Colonel Clark was sitting alone in the commanding officer's room of the garrison. And the afternoon sun, slanting through the square of the window, fell upon the maps and papers before him. He had sent for me. I halted in sheer embarrassment on the threshold, looked up at his face, and came on, troubled.

"Davy," he said, "do you want to go back to Kentucky?"

"I should like to stay to the end, Colonel," I answered.

"The end?" he said. "This is the end."

"And Detroit, sir?" I returned.

"Detroit!" he cried bitterly, "a man of sense measures his force, and does not try the impossible. I could as soon march against Philadelphia. This is the end, I say; and the general must give way to the politician. And may God have mercy on the politician who will try to keep a people's affection without money or help from Congress."

He fell back wearily in his chair, while I stood astonished, wondering. I had thought to find him elated with victory.

"Congress or Virginia," said he, "will have to pay Monsieur Vigo, and Father Gibault, and Monsieur Gratiot, and the other good people who have trusted me. Do you think they will do so?"

"The Congress are far from here," I said.

"Ay," he answered, "too far to care about you and me, and what we have suffered."

He ended abruptly, and sat for a while staring out of the window at the figures crossing and recrossing the muddy parade-ground.

"Tom McChesney goes to-night to Kentucky with letters to the county lieutenant. You are to go with him, and then I shall have no one to remind me when I am hungry, and bring me hominy. I shall have no financier, no strategist for a tight place." He smiled a little, sadly, at my sorrowful look, and then drew me to him and patted my shoulder. "It is no place for a young lad,—an idle garrison. I think," he continued presently, "I think you have a future, David, if you do not lose your head. Kentucky will grow and conquer, and in twenty years be a thriving community. And presently you will go to Virginia, and study law, and come back again. Do you hear?"

"Yes, Colonel."

"And I would tell you one thing," said he, with force; "serve the people, as all true men should in a republic. But do not rely upon their gratitude. You will remember that?"

"Yes, Colonel."

The Crossing, Vol. 1

A long time he paused, looking on me with a significance I did not then understand. And when he spoke again his voice showed no trace of emotion, save in the note of it.

"You have been a faithful friend, Davy, when I needed loyalty. Perhaps the time may come again. Promise me that you will not forget me if I am—unfortunate."

"Unfortunate, sir!" I exclaimed.

"Good-by, Davy," he said, "and God bless you. I have work to do."

Still I hesitated. He stared at me, but with kindness.

"What is it, Davy?" he asked.

"Please, sir," I said, "if I might take my drum?"

At that he laughed.

"You may," said he, "you may. Perchance we may need it again."

I went out from his presence, vaguely troubled, to find Tom. And before the early sun had set we were gliding down the Wabash in a canoe, past places forever dedicated to our agonies, towards Kentucky and Polly Ann.

"Davy," said Tom, "I reckon she'll be standin' under the 'simmon tree, waitin' fer us with the little shaver in her arms."

And so she was.

Copyright © 2023 Esprios Digital Publishing. All Rights Reserved.